T0385078

THE

PUBLICATIONS

OF THE

SURTEES SOCIETY

VOL. CLXXXIII

THE

PUBLICATIONS

OF THE

SURTEES SOCIETY

ESTABLISHED IN THE YEAR

M.DCCC.XXXIV

VOL. CLXXXIII

FOR THE YEAR M.CM.LXVIII

At a COUNCIL MEETING of the SURTEES SOCIETY, held in Durham Castle on 9 June, 1970, the Dean of Durham in the chair, it was ORDERED—

"That the first volume of Dr. D. A. Kirby's edition of Durham Parliamentary Surveys should be printed as a volume of the Society's publications."

W. A. L. Seaman
Secretary.

PARLIAMENTARY SURVEYS

OF THE

BISHOPRIC OF DURHAM

VOLUME I

EDITED BY

Dr. D. A. KIRBY

PRINTED FOR THE SOCIETY BY
NORTHUMBERLAND PRESS LIMITED
GATESHEAD
1971

PARLIAMENTARY SURVEYS
OF THE
BISHOPRIC OF DURHAM

CONTENTS

PREFACE   ix

INTRODUCTION   xi

A NOTE ON THE TEXT   xix

SURVEY OF THE MANOR OF AUCKLAND   I

SURVEY OF THE MANOR OF DARLINGTON   89

SURVEY OF THE MANOR OF EVENWOOD   121

SURVEY OF THE MANOR OF WOLSINGHAM   146

INDEX OF PLACES   177

INDEX OF PERSONS   180

PREFACE

The Editor would like to acknowledge the help freely given him by Mr. J. E. Fagg, Dr. J. M. Fewster, Mrs. Drury, and not least Mr. C. R. Hudleston, all then of the Department of Palaeography and Diplomatic in the University of Durham. In addition the text of the introduction was very kindly read by Professor M. R. G. Conzen, and Roger Stone, who made several helpful suggestions.

INTRODUCTION

In the late summer of 1646 risings in papist Ireland, and the demands of the Scottish army uncomfortably settled in Durham and Northumberland obliged Parliament to collect speedily a considerable sum of money. It was decided that the most suitable way of raising the money was by way of a loan from the City of London, secured by the sale of ecclesiastical temporalities. Accordingly on 9 October 1646, an ordinance was passed abolishing

> Archbishops and Bishops within the Kingdom of England and Dominion of Wales, and for the settling of their lands and possessions upon Trustees for the use of the Commonwealth ... that the said Trustees shall have power and are authorised to make nominate and appoint from time to time fit and able persons, such as they shall think fit to survey the premises in any County or Counties of England and Wales and to hold Court of Surveys and to demand receive and in safe custody to put all the said Charters, deeds, books, accompts, rolls, writings, and evidences.[1]

Any lease made after 1 December 1641 was to be void, unless it was a renewal of an old lease.[2] The rents and profits of the lands were to be vested in the trustees until the lands were sold,[3] saving in the special case of Durham the rights of the Jura Regalia were to remain in the hands of the Trustees and were not to be sold.[4]

Once the ordinance was passed the work was quickly put in hand. Darlington ward was surveyed within the first six months of 1647, and surveys of most of the other manors were completed within the year. Eleven surveyors worked over the Bishop's estates in County Durham, although they were not surveyors in any modern sense of the word, but rather included such sympathetic local persons as George Lilburne, of Sunderland. Each of them was to swear

> that I will faithfully and truely according to my best skill and knowledge, execute the place of a Surveyor.... I shall use my best endeavour and skill to discover the estates therein mentioned, and every part thereof which shall be given me in charge, and to

xi

finde out the true values and improvements thereof, and thereof shall make true particulars, according to my best skill and cunning; and the same from time to time deliver in writing close sealed up, unto the said Trustees or any two of them, according to the true intent and meaning of the said Ordinance; and this I shall justly and faithfully execute, without any gift or reward directly or indirectly, from any person or persons whatsoever.[5]

The method commonly employed in the county was that three or more of the surveyors would summon all the tenants of a manor to a special court at the chef lieu, at which a jury of local men would be empanelled. Freehold deeds, court rolls and leases would then be examined. For every leasehold property the true annual value of the holding would be decided upon and expressed as the sum of the annual reserved rent plus its improved annual value. The model form of the surveys can be illustrated in the survey of Auckland. The survey is headed by the surveyors' commission and the names of the jurors, followed by a general prospectus of the manor set out as the answers to the questions noted on page xxi. Then follows freehold, copyhold and leasehold rentals for each township within the manor, although not necessarily in that order. At the end of the survey comes any other information thought desirable to be set down by the surveyors.

The desire of the House to make a quick sale led however, to difficulties. Because the surveyors were not compelled to

make any admeasurement of the Lands, or in any particular survey of the number of acres, unless they in their discretion shall think fit,[6]

many of the surveys were far from accurate. It became necessary for the Trustees to

peruse all Surveys returned and to be returned ... and to amend upon due proof made before them upon Oath all mistakes in Misnomer of any person or persons, places or things, and likewise without Oath to amend all other misprisions in miscasting the total of any particular sums of money or numbers of Acres or such other like mistakes ... and also to add by way of supplement Certificates of any Estates or Interests,[7] and in 1648 Parliament was moved to set up a committee to resolve

> the many Obstructions that have and do daily happen in and about
> the sale of the Mannors, lands Tenements, and Hereditaments of
> the late Archbishops and Bishops.[8]

Thus it is plain that many of the surveys were not worth the name, and were inaccurate approximations to the truth. However, confidence is inspired in the Durham surveys by three things: the jurors and the surveyors did not always agree on the valuations of lands, suggesting that a degree of care was taken with the entries, and the two opinions were inserted into the survey; secondly supplementary surveys or certificates only accompany the surveys of Wolsingham, the collieries on the Tyne, and one entry in the manor of Chester le Street—although this does not necessarily mean that they did not once exist for other surveys—and, lastly, the fact that the surveyors make frequent reference to the rent rolls at Durham, and to tenants who did not appear before them, suggests that they took their job seriously. For the most part then, the Durham surveys are probably an accurate account of the bishopric.

It has long been a subject of controversy whether on the one hand it is possible to think of any normal rural life during the civil wars, or whether the political and military turmoils of the times made little impact on grass roots society. At a time when provincial life was still predominantly self sufficient in most things, if less so than two centuries before, the answer hangs on how deeply particular places were subject to the vicissitudes of war and the spoliation of armies. Some areas suffered less than others, but the North-East, and especially County Durham was perhaps worse off than most. The Scottish victory in the second Bishops' War, in the autumn of 1640, resulted in the quartering of the Scottish army upon Northumberland and Durham until the late summer of 1641. Cut off from supplies from Scotland, the Scots exacted supplies from the country.

> What they (the local population) supplied at their (the Scots) first
> coming abroad is spent, their horse do now daily go through all
> the Bishopric, and bring in cattle wherever they find them,
> pretending the county does not supply them with markets to
> satisfy their army which is indeed impossible.[9]

Later the Scots demanded £350 per day from Co. Durham, £300

from Northumberland and £200 from Newcastle, sums well beyond the ability of the area to provide.

After the Scottish withdrawal in 1641 barely 2½ years elapsed
before they were again settled on the county, consequent on the
withdrawal of the Earl of Newcastle's army in February 1644. This
time they remained for three long years. Before the end of the first
year Sir George Vane wrote to his father Sir Henry,

> 'The truth is the soldiers are our masters and do what they like.
> Your tenants have generally suffered very much and are likely
> to continue in a suffering condition without speedy remedy from
> above.'[10]
>
> 'If the Scots' writes Sir Lionell Maddison, 'will not be content
> with such provision as is left and eat together . . . one or both must
> starve.'[11]

In February 1647, however, the Scottish army withdrew from
the North, and from this time there is evidence of a slow but steady
recovery of the local economy. In the country as a whole the period
1620-1650 is characterised as one of poor harvests and a general
downward trend in the level of economic activity. The coal trade
had reached a peak of production in 1633, which was not surpassed
until 1658, and the trend in the '40's was generally downwards, a
trend not helped by the blockade of the Tyne in 1644, even if this did
give a boost to the Wear section of the trade.[12] Add to this frequent
local outbreaks of plague, occasionally severe, and the presence of
an occupation force, then the condition of the area at the time of the
surveys can not have been its best.

The condition of the area, however, is not simply a result of the
economic and political vicissitudes of the times, but also of the
fundamental quality of the land, and to appreciate fully the information provided by the surveyors, it is necessary to know something of
the ground they surveyed, the general economic system in which
it existed and the agrarian system by which it was cultivated.

It is essential to realise that the area covered in these surveys is
far from uniform and that the physiographical qualities of the area
vary from one manor to the next. First of all considerations is that
the County slopes down from high Carboniferous Limestone moorlands in the west, rising to over 2,000 feet, and penetrated by the
narrow valleys of the Wear, the Tees and the Derwent to a more

gentle countryside in the south and east around the open vale of the lower Tees, here floored with Triassic Sandstones. Running across this lower area is a pronounced escarpment of Magnesian Limestone, stretching from South Shields to Bishop Auckland and falling away eastwards to a line between Hartlepool and Darlington. Between the Magnesian Limestone and the Carboniferous Limestone of the moors lies the exposed coalfield itself, partially covered, like the Magnesian Limestone to the east with an uneven veneer of glacial sands, gravels and thick sticky clays.

The geological structure of the county obviously affects the local economy by providing lead and silver in the limestone moorlands of the west, coal in the lower slopes of the Pennines in the centre of the county, and lime in the Magnesian Limestone in the east, but of rather more fundamental importance in an agricultural society is the effect this structure has on relief and thus upon local climatic conditions, for altitude and aspect are major factors in determining annual precipitation and insolation. Thus in a general way conditions become drier and warmer from west to east, but the presence of the Magnesian Limestone escarpment along the coast makes the mid-Wear Lowland the driest part of the county, although even here summer sunshine is reduced by the frequent incursion of stratus cloud from the North Sea.

The farmer, however, sees his livelihood in the soil, but here again the picture is complicated by the area's history of glacial deposition, giving such diversity of soil quality that A. E. Smailes has noted that 'there can be few farms in the north of England on which soil conditions can be regarded as really homogeneous'.[13] In a period in which man and land were much more finely attuned than today, subtle differences in soil quality must have meant much in the utilisation of the land.

It is, then, difficult to generalise in a useful way but this at least can be noted. Wolsingham manor lies in the far west of the county, and occupies most of Weardale. Although the valley floor contains relatively fertile river and glacial deposits, the majority of the area consists of Carboniferous Limestone moors, with a few outcrops of Millstone Grit on the crest of the hills in the east of the manor. Described as 'moorish wastes' by Grainger in 1794[14] the soils are of very mixed quality, always acidic, and because of the high rainfall (65″–70″ on the higher slopes on the west) very wet, and in the seventeenth century fit only for extensive grazing, except for improved pasture at lower altitudes. To the south-east of the manor of Wolsingham lies the manor of Evenwood, standing almost entirely on the Coal Measures, along the upper valley of the Gaunless. Standing at a lower elevation, and with an uneven cover of glacial drift, the soils are of better quality than those of Weardale, but still acidic, and inclined to be poorly drained, characteristics shared with the northern part of the manor of Auckland, and in the north of the county, with the higher parts of the manors of Whickham, Gateshead and Chester le Street. Alongside the Tyne and the middle Wear, however, the soils become more loamy in character, while annual precipitation falls to 25″–30″, but here too the glacial history of the area has bestowed very mixed characteristics on the land, and a light sandy soil can just as easily be found as a thick and heavy clay.

The manor of Easington, the majority of the manor of Houghton le Spring, and the eastern townships of the manor of Chester le Street stand upon the Magnesian Limestone escarpment. A clayey loam characterises the area, derived from varied parent materials, but apart from a narrow coastal fringe, the soils are well drained and the area is generally regarded as being 'good quality' land.[15]

The most favoured area is the south-eastern quarter of the county in which stand the manors of Bishop Middleham, Darlington, and the southern part of the manor of Auckland. Bishop Middleham comprises a particularly fertile stretch of land characterised by a welcoming brown calcareous soil. Around Sedgefield, too, the land is of a high quality, particularly to the north and east, although to the south Morden Carrs stand out as a poor and water-logged area. The manor of Darlington stands partly on the reddish till of Triassic origin in the east and a mixture of Permian and Coal Measure till in the west, and particularly on the edge of the Tees the soils are deep and rich, noted by Grainger to be of 'unctuous quality'. With an annual precipitation of 25″, this area stands out as being particularly benevolent to the farmer.

In national terms the most striking feature of the local economy was the rise of the coal mining industry over the past century. Although this is usually associated with the city of Newcastle upon Tyne, rather than with County Durham, the great majority of the coal exported by the Newcastle merchants came from the Durham side of the river. In addition, one of the more notable aspects of the coal trade itself was the rapid increase in coal production around the head of the tidal section of the river Wear, and the export of coal to London through Sunderland.

Of the four major coal producing areas in the county that of Tyneside was by far the most important. In the episcopal manors of Gateshead and Whickham the Five Quarter and Main coal seams came close to the river side, thus allowing the easy export of good quality household coal downstream by keel boat and by coaster to the metropolitan market. Considerable attention has been paid to the importance of this trade to Newcastle, but little has been paid to the equally important effect this trade must have had on the local agricultural economy. In direct terms commons were spoiled by waste heaps, and fields crossed by trackways. More importantly the presence of many hundred non food-producing workmen, not only in the coal mining and exporting industries, but in the penumbra of associated trades, such as glass making and salt boiling must have created a not inconsiderable market for agricultural produce. Disturbance of the coal trade, besides halting the flow of ready money in the area, for which Newcastle was the principle channel, must have had a direct effect in the surrounding food-supplying zone, an effect which must have been echoed in the growing industrial area at the mouth of the Wear. In the south of the county, too, the coal industry was developing along commercial lines, sending coal down the 'coal street' to Darlington and to North Yorkshire, and here too, there must have been some impact on the local economy.

The second most striking feature of the Durham economy in the mid-seventeenth century is the rate at which agricultural practice was being changed. Since the fusion of Anglian and Celtic societies in the years before the conquest townships had joined together to inter-common their beasts during the summer months on the extensive wastes in which the townships were set. Now some of the commons were being broken up, and enclosed for grazing in severalty. Similarly common arable land, formerly laid out in two, three or more open fields about the village nucleus was also under pressure, and in many cases the ancient communal agricultural system was being abandoned in favour of cultivation in severalty. New meets and bounds, hedges and fences began to divide the country up, a feature often noted by the surveyors which gave the countryside something of a modern appearance.

Between 1550 and 1685 there were some 71 enclosures in the county, about half of which had taken place before 1647. Most of the earliest enclosures took place in the south of the county, in agriculturally benevolent Stockton Ward, but during the seventeenth century enclosure is particularly found in those areas where coal mining was expanding, along the banks of the Tyne, around Chester le Street at the head of the navigable stretch of the Wear, and around Bishop Auckland. There is little evidence of similar agricultural innovation in the upland west, but here population densities were lower, communal farming in the first place was probably less important and arable farming certainly less important than in districts to the east, so there was less opportunity for this kind of change.

In terms of crops produced, the North-East was not particularly favourable to wheat production, and although some was grown, especially in the east of the county, rye, oats, and barley predominated. Especially in the east of the county, too, peas and beans were grown as a fodder crop, but the Palatinate was better known for its grass rather than its grain production and both sheep and cattle were popularly raised. Rearing and breeding tended to be more important in the western uplands, with fattening on the lower ground and enclosed pastures of the south and east, a practice known in the mediaeval period, and although not universal, commonly applied in the seventeenth century.

From all this it will be apparent that the south and east of the county were very different from the west, and that very special conditions existed in the north along the banks of the Tyne. It is within this very varied physical, economic, and social framework that the surveys are set. They must now speak for themselves.

A NOTE ON THE TEXT

By the mid-seventeenth century the ancient groups of townships, noticed by Canon Greenwell in 1852 had come to be known as manors, and this present volume contains surveys of the manors of Auckland, Darlington, Evenwood and Wolsingham, all in Darlington Ward. A subsequent volume will contain surveys of the manors of Bishop Middleham, Easington, Houghton le Spring, Chester le Street, Gateshead, Whickham and the collieries of the Tyne. Surveys once existed of the episcopal property around the City of Durham, of the manor of Stockton,[16] Archdeacon Newton, and Spennymoor.[17] There is no surviving record of any survey of the lands at Lanchester. In the surveys a freehold entry is written—

James Coward By deede poll 4 May 9 Jac Re. Holdeth That whole little house and ptn on the North of the Quire to hold to him and his heyres for ever in free and Comon Socage By the Graunte and Surrender of Anthony Greggson. And payeth rent per ann. 4d.

This is rendered in the text as—

JAMES COWARD
4 May 9 Jac. Little house on the North of the Quire in free and comon socage. By the graunt and surrender of Anthony Gregson.
  Rent 4d.

A copyhold entry appears in the survey : —

Clement Widdifield by coppie dat 17 Maii 7 Jacobi Re holdeth one Cottage and 6 acres of land and one other Cottage and ptn in Midleham 4 acres of land pasture for 10 sheepe upon the Moore and his parcell of meadow called Grange brigg Crooke. By the surrender of Raphe Hutton et al And payeth rent p. ann. 6s. 8d. Fine 7s. 10d.

xix

This is rendered in the text as—

CLEMENT WIDDIFIELD
17 May 7 Jac. One cottage and 6 acres of land and one other Cottage and ptn in Middleham, 4 acres of land, pasture for 10 sheep upon the Moor, and his parcell of meadow called Grange Brigg Crooke.
    By surrender of Raphe Hutton et al. Rent 6s. 8d. Fine 7s. 10d.

A leasehold entry is written—

Henrie Hutchinson by Indre Dat 22 October 7. Carol Re Holdeth by graunt of John Bp. of Durham One messuage or tenement 30 acres of Chequor lands 6 acres of arable land meadow and pasture and ptn.
For 21 years from the date thereof paying per ann at the Exchr att Durham at Martinmas and Pent £2. 0. 4. The lease to be voyde for non payment of Rent within 20 days of the Freasts. Worth upon Improvement above the Rent £6. 0. 0. per ann.

This is rendered in the text—

HENRIE HUTCHINSON
22 October 7 Car. One messuage or tenement 30 acres of Chequor lands 6 acres of arable land meadow and pasture and ptn.
    For 21 years.
    Rent £2. os. 4d. Improvement £6. os. od.

In leasehold tenure rent was always to be paid at Martinmas and Pentecost, the lease to be void if the rent was not paid within 20 days. Only deviations from this formula have been specifically mentioned in this edition.

The Questions to be put by the Surveyors

No complete series of the questions or 'articles' has survived. Not all the surveys contain answers to a complete set, and not all the replies are in the same order, so it is therefore difficult to reconstruct their exact wording. However, it is likely that they took something of this form.

1. Is there a mansion, manor house or castle belonging to this manor, and what are its appurtenances?

2. Are there any demesne lands, and if they are farmed out who are the tenants?

3. Is there any park, warren or sheep walk?

4. Are there any common lands?

5. Are there any foreign or outwoods belonging to this manor, does the pannage, mastage or herbage belong to the tenants, and how far are these woods from a navigable waterway or the sea?

6. Is there any fishery or chase of game?

7. Does the lord of this manor have any wind, water or horse mills?

8. Do the tenants of this manor owe service to the mills?

9. Are there any mines or quarries of stone, lead, iron or coal, or any salt pans belonging to this manor?

10. What rents are paid by the several tenants?

11. Are there any freeholders, and do they owe suit to the lord's court?

12. Are there any customary or copyhold tenants on this manor?

13. Are fines paid to the Lord of this manor upon the death of a tenant or the alienation of his tenement, and are such fines certain?

14. Are the copyhold tenements in good repair, and if not is there wood and stone upon the several copyholds for them to be repaired?

15. What are the works, customs and services of the copyholders?

16. Are there any cottagers within this manor?

17. Have any encroachments been made upon the lord's waste?

18. Are there any markets or fairs held in this manor?

19. Does the lord of this manor have the profit of courts, waifs, and strays?

20. Does the lord of this manor have free warren within his manor?

21. Are there any benefices within this manor, and does the lord of the manor have right of presentation to them?

22. To whom belong the tithes?

23. In what state of repair is the rectory of the church, and are there any other premises or glebe lands belonging to the said rectory?

24. Are there any woods or coppices and how are they measured?

25. Are there any patents or duties granted out of the profits of this manor?

REFERENCES

1. Firth, C. H., & Rait, S. R., *Acts and Ordinances of the Inter-regnum* London, 1911, 881.

2. ibid. 882

3. ibid. 889

4. ibid 891

5. ibid. 881

6. ibid. 902-3

7. ibid. 1029

8. ibid. 1106. It is not apparent what proportion of the Durham lands were sold by this date (21 November 1648). A list entitled 'Sales of Bishopric Lands' is to be found amongst the Allen MSS in Durham Cathedral Library. The list does not contain sales of every manor, but is appended at the end of this volume.

9. Calendar of State Papers Domestic, 1640-1, 29.

10. ibid. 1644-5, 174.

11. ibid. 162-3

12. For a detailed account of the fluctuations of the coal trade over this period see Nef, J. U., *The Rise of the British Coal Industry*, London, 1932, Vols I and II.

13. Smailes, A. E., *North England*, London, 1960, 56.

14. Grainger, J., *General View of the Agriculture of the County of Durham*, London, 1794.

15. Daysh, G. H. J., *A Physical Land Classification of Northumberland and Durham*, Newcastle, 1950.

16. The first part of the survey of Stockton survived until the early nineteenth century when it was printed in Mackenzie, E., and Ross, M., *View of the County Palatine of Durham*, Newcastle, 1834, II, 16-18.

17. Of these two there is no trace.

SURVEY OF THE MANOR OF AUCKLAND

Manerium de
Auckland cum
Membris

An exact and perfect Survey of
the aforesaid Manor of Bishop
Auckland in the Co. of Durham
late Dr. Thomas Morton Bishop
of Durham and of the severall
townships belonging to and pte of
the said Manor (vizt)

Bondgate in Auckland, Borough of Auckland, Byers Green, Counden, Eastcombe, Heighington, Middridge, Newton Cap, and Redworth, had made and taken as well by us Samuel Leigh and Thomas
Saunders Esqs Edward Colston and Thomas Dale gentlemen in
the months of March and Aprill in the years of our Lord God 1646
By virtue of a Commission to us made and Directed bearings date
the Eighteenth day of January Anno Domini 1646 from the trustees
in the said Commission named Authorised by two severall Ordinances of the most high and Honourable Courte of Parliament,
trustees by the disposing of Archbishops and Bishops lands with in
the whole Kingdome of England and Wales as by the said Ordinance appeareth. As also by the presentmt and verdict of a Jury
hereafter named and Sworne by us to enquire upon the severall
Articles hereunto annexed given them in Charge The tennor and
effect of which said Survey and Presentment as well of us as of the
said Jurors are hereunto fixed and followeth in the ensuing pages.

The names of the Jurie charged
and sworne before us the Commissioners before named to enquire on the behalfe of the said
Trustees in the foresaid Court of
Survey began in the Manor Castle
or Pallace of Bishop Auckland the
two and twentie day of March
Anno domini 1647

Geo. Burne Gent
Robt. Ridlington Gent
Ambrose Johnson Gent
John Bell yeo
John Smithson yeo
George Lax Gent
Robt. Darneton yeo
Robt Adamson yeo
Wm. Shephard yeo
Christopher Dobson yeo
Robt. Baker yeo
John Dawson yeo

Robert Vincent yeo
Thomas Trotter yeo
John Woods yeo
Miles White yeo
James Dunne yeo
John Mayor Gent
Tho Hixon yeo
Richard Hobson yeo
Robt. Adamson yeo
Wm. Adamson yeo
John Slayter Gent
Robt. Laxe yeo

The which foresaid persons beings in due forme of lawe sworne to enquire upon Certaine Articles hereunto annexed did upon the Thirteenth day of Aprill Anno domini 1647 Deliver unto us under their hands and seales: the presentment or verdict following.

Heere is Likewise a Survey of the Ruines of the Castle or Pallace or Bishop Auckland taken by very able sufficient workmen the 23rd May anno domini 1647 being herein likewise Certified

Manerium de Auckland
Epi Cum Membris

The presentment and verdict of the Jurors hereafter named being Sworne upon the holy Evangelist at a Court of Survey held for the said Manor at the Castle or Pallace of Bishop Auckland in the County of Durham beginne the 22nd day of March Anno domini 1646 before Thomas Lambert Esq. Edward Colston and George Dale gent. to enquire upon severall Articles delivered us in Charge The tenor and Effect of which our said presentment hereafter followeth and was delivered by us the 13th day of Aprill Anno domini 1647 to Samuel Leigh and Thos Saunders Esqs Edward Colston and Geo Dale

Geo Burne Gent of Neusham
Robt. Ridlington Gent of auld
    Parke
Ambrose Johnson Gent of
    W.hauleston
John Bell yeo of Headlam
John Smithson yeo of
    Houghton
George Lax Gent of Westerton
Robt. Darnton yeo of Ferehill
Robt. Adamson yeo of Eldon
Wm. Shephard yeo of the same
Christopher Dobson yeo of
    Bishop Auckland
Robt. Baker yeo of the same
John Dawson yeo of the same
Robert Vincent of the same

Thomas Trotter yeo of Merring-
    ton
John woods yeo of Merrington
Miles White yeo of Merrington
James Dunne yeo of Merrington
John Mayor Gent of Helmington
    Row
Tho Hixon yeo of Middleston
Richard Hobson yeo of Denton
Robt. Adamson yeo of Whitworth
Wm. Adamson yeo of Whitworth
John Slayter Gent of Bishop Auck-
    land
Robt. Laxe yeo of Ferehill

1. Imprimis we present that there is a very stately Mannor howse called the Castle or Pallace of the late Bishop of Durham situate in Bishop Auckland with two Chappells to it one over thereof built of stone and Covered with lead and so are some other partes of the house. And also Grounds whereon the house is situated, walled about wth stone and in some placed imbattailed having thereto belonging a stately gatehouse, Stables, Brewhouse Bakehouse and other offices necessary. All which are in their severall conditions in dilapidations as appeareth by the Survey and view of Severall workmen and Articles. The severall Courtyards and Gardens within the wall containing by estimation—5 acres. That there is a Park adjoyning Conteining by estimation 500 acres That there is no timber growing thereon at all fitt for the repaire of the house or pales of the Parke. But certaine old Dotards and Rampikes fitt only for Bordwoods for the hearthes being all oake.

The parke was formerly inclosed parte with a dry stone wall wthout mortar, the rest paled but the pales now totally ruined and the walls being in decay. The deare and game vizt:—fallow deere and Wild bulles or Bisons utterly destroyed, except two or three of the said Bisons and some few conies in that part of the Parke called the Hagge under the walles of the Castle or Pallace. That the said Parke is worth per annum £120. 0. 0. That there is also belonging to the demeasnes two meadows called by the names of Tile Close and Rough Mires adjoyning to Newgate and of Bishop Auckland Conteyning by estimation—30 acres which together with the said Parke were by the Committee of the County of Durham let to Collonell Wren for one yeare ending at May Day 1647 for £120. 0. 0. The said Castle, Pallace or Manor House is situated in Bishop Auckland a Markett Towne and seaven miles from the Citty of Durham, there being two very fine streames or Rivers called Weare and Gaunless running neare the said Manor House, but no Navigable River or Sea Roads within many miles. There is also a wood called Birtley Wood belonging to the said demeasnes adjoyning to the River Weare which conteynes by estimation 160 acres And one Mr. Henry Blackston by Patent for his life is Woodreeve thereof and hath a certain standing fee about £30 per annum and the herbage for the preserving the same. That there is in the said woods good staves of Pollards fitt for Bordwoods and little else. And the same which the Barke is as they believe worth to be sould £100. That the Parke is some parte fitt for tillage.

2. Item Wee present that there belonges to the said Maner the several Townships followeth Vzt. Heighington, Middridge & Middridge Grange, Counden & Counden Grange, Escombe, Biers Green, Newton Cap, Redworth, Bondgate in Auckland and Bishop Auckland. The tenants of all which do suit and service to the Lordes Courtes And pay such rentes as will appeare by their leases and Evidences by which they hold to which We referre ourselves. That there is little or no timber in the several townships and granges before mentioned and that no sufficient to repair the houses and farms. That the said Landes lye in a hilly Country yet are for the most part enclosed with quick hedges or dry ditches and bankes.

3. Item we find that there is no park or warren in this Mannor other than what is mentioned in the first Article. That there is no particular sheep walkes but the Lord of this Mannor may put what Sheep he pleaseth upon the Commons being his own soyle.

4. Item we present that there is within the precincts of this Mannor and the Several towneshippes before mentioned these several Commons butted and bounded as followeth vizt—
  Biers Moore boundeth on the west upon Binchester and the Newfields on the North by the West Isle on the East by the town

callers Biers Greene and on the South by the ould Park and con-
tayneth by estimation 300 acres.

Hunwicke Moore Bounded upon Bichbourne on the west and
South upon Newton Capp on the East and upon Rumby Hill on
the North Conteyning by estimation 400 acres.

Etherley Moore bounded on the North by Escomb on the East
by Etherley and on the West and South by Woodhouses conteyning by estimation 100 acres.

Redworth Fell bounded on the west by a more called Wideopen
on the south by Houghton on the side on the east by Mr. Crosivers
grounds on the north by west Thickley and contained by estimation 100 acres.

Middridge Moore bounded on the east of a towne called Wood-
holme on the West on the town inclosures on the North on the
townshipp of Eldon and on the south of Aycliffe moor and con-
tayneth by estimation 200 acres.

Raley Fell is a very greate and vast moor being 12 miles in
length in some partes 5 miles in breadth and in the narrowest
place two miles. The herbage or Comon of which belongeth to
the tennants of the Severall townes aforesaid and of several towne-
ships. That the tenants of this Mannor have comon of pasture
appurtenent to their severall tenements for so many cattle as they
can winter upon their severall tenements. That the Lords of this
Manor cannot make any improvement upon the said Commons
without consent of the tenants and Freeholders. That wee do not
know of any woods upon the said Comons or of any benefitt that
the Lord made by his agistment upon the said Commons.

5. Item to this Article wee answer Negatively to all Particulars.

6. Item wee present that the Lords of this Mannor hath the Fishing of all the Rivers, Streames, waters and pooles within the said
Mannor but wee knowe of no meares within the same Mannor nor
of any proffit the Lord made of the Fishing within the said Mannor.

7. Item wee present that there are 3 water corn mills and one fulling mill belonging to this Mannor (vizt):
Burne Mill now lett for 21 yeares with a meadow containing 6
dayes work and a horse gate in the parke aforesaid to Emanuell
Grice as appeareth by his lease att the yearely rent of £6-0-0 and to

grind the lord's corne spent in the Mannor House of Auckland Moulter free. Worth upon improvement per annum besides the rent and services reserved by lease £20-0-0.

West Mill in the tenure of Brian John and Raphe Walker to which the tenants of these severall towneshippes vzt Bondgate in Auckland, Escomb, Newton Capp & Byers Greene are tied to grind such corne as they spend in their houses; lett with a horse-gate upon West Mill batts (standing upon the river Weare) for 3 lives as appeareth by the lease at the yearly rent of £4-0-0. Worth upon improvement besides the rent reserved £20-0-0.

A Fulling mill much in decay in the tenure of Thomas Walton and others as appeareth by lease for 21 yeares att the yearly rent of £4-0-0. And payeth to the tenants of West Mill for mendeing the damme yearly £1-0-0. Worth upon improvement besides the rent charges aforesaid £2-0-0.

The Fourth and last Mill is letten with Middridge Grange to one Mr. Bierly being a small mill but the certenty wee know nott being lett with other lands.

8. Item we present that the tenants of this Mannor do grind at the Lord's Mill (except regrators who as they pretent may grind at other mills if they please).

9. Item wee present that there is one Colliery in the West Moore called Bitchbourne now in the occupation of Mr. John Wilkinson gent. and others which yield to the Lords of this Mannor such rents and profitts as by the said Indenture of lease made to the said Mr. Wilkinson and others is reserved but the true yearly value thereof wee knowe nott. That there is another Colliery upon Etherley Moore in lease to the said Mr. Wilkinson and others, which is now in working but not brought to effect, as to the yielding of proffitt And therefore what it may prove we know not. That there is no Coleryes of Salt (Slate) open mynes or quarries of stone or delfes which yield profitt to the Lord, but there is a Myne of iron stone upon Hunwicke Moore yielding no profit to the Lord.

10. Item we present that it will or ought to appeare by every tenants severall deeds what rents of Assize they are to pay to which deedes we refere ourselves.

11. Item we present that the freeholders of this Manor do suite

and Service att the Court Leete and the Lords Court Baron as often as they shall be called, under the severall tenures vizt some by knights service in Capite, and others vizt those in Auckland in Burgage, but of the tenures of Socage or Gavell kind we know none in this Manor. And as to reliefs or herietts to be paid to the Lord upon the decease or alienation of the tenant within this Manor we knowe of none.

12. Item we present that there are many Copiholders and Customary tenements belonging to this Manor But how many or what their names are, or what lands or tenements they hold or by what rents or services we know not, but referre ourselves to the Severall Copies and Rentroles of the severall townshippes.

13. Item we present that the Fines upon death or Alienation of Copyhold tenements are certaine as we truly believe, and not a bit vary for that time beyond the memory of man to the Contrary, the severall Copiholders upon Death or Alienation have paid a certaine summe to the Lords of this Manor imposed upon them under the name or title of a Draft which hath been always and certaine upon every tenury. Although upon some lesse than the Annuall rent reserved, in others the full rent And on others more than the rent. Butt all these certaine as appeareth by their severall Copies of one and the same thing for many descents as by the Rentalls Terrars and ould books of entry in the hands of the Lords of this Mannor to which we refer ourselves more fully will appeare.

14. Item wee present that the Copihold tenements are for aught we know in good repare. And that there is very little Woode upon Copihold lands within this Mannor but such timber or Woode as is growing upon the same doth belong to the Lords of this Mannor. And that by the Custom of this Mannor the Lord is bound to graunte and allowe to every several copiholder upon request thereof made to the Lord or his Bailiff sufficient timber for the reparation and upholding of his copyhold tenement. And if there happen not to be sufficient timber upon the copyhold lands of every several tenant for repaire and upholding of his said tenement in such case the tenant wanting timber for improvement may demand the same of the lord to be allowed and taken off the lands of any copyholder within the said manor. And the lord by the custom of this manor is bound by

his bailiff to allow the said timber for the uses aforesaid. And in case of refusal upon such demand made the tenants may fell and take the same for the uses aforesaid.

15. Item we present that the copyholders and customary tenants belonging to this manor do upon demand of the lord's bailiff carry coals from Carter Thorne to the manor house of Bishop Auckland for which service they receive ten pound of coal or fodder and meate and drink if they carry two loads in one day, or if (as sometimes) in the lord's absence they want meat and drink then they are to have ten pence in liew of meat and drink. And likewise to carry three loads of hay on a day out of Auckland Park and the demesne meadows to the said manor house, for which they receive fourpence a load, and meat and drink or in liew thereof ten pence in money.

16. & 17. Item to the sixteenth and seventeenth articles we present that Nicholas Fleming and Thomas Fleming have lately erected two poor cottages or sheddes to shelter themselves in upon the lord's waste, but there is no land belonging to the said cottages, nor any rent reserved or benefit accruing to the lord.

18. Item we present that there is a Borough Court kept every 14 days and a Market weekly kept every Thursday in the town of Bishop Auckland. And that there are two Fayres kept in the said town yearly upon Assention and Corpus Christi days. And that the toll of the said Faires and Markets do belong the lord of this manor, and also four shops under the Toll booth. All which with the yearly fee of £5 are granted by patent to the bayliffe of the said town of Bishop Auckland for regulating the said market and fayres and are worth £23 per annum. We present that there is a dy house newly erected near the water side by John Walton for which he is to make fine to the Lord the next Court Day.

19. Item we present that there are divers profits of Courtes, waifs and strayes, felones goods and amerciaments, and other casualties belonging to the lord of the manor, but what the same are worth per annum we know not, but refer ourselves to the severall bailiffs that Received the same.

20. Item we present that the lord hath free warren within this

manor and other franchises and royalties as he hath jura regalia in the County Palatine of Durham.

21. 22. 23. Item to the 21st. 22nd. and 23rd. articles every rent that the Rectory or Parsonage, Glebelands, and tithes within this manor are impropriate, and do not belong to this manor or the lord lord thereof, as we know or have heard. But that they did formerly belong to the Dean and Prebends of St. Andrews Auckland which being dissolved by Act of Parliament in the time of Henry the Eight were granted to severall patentees from the crowne. And that the lord of this manor hath nothing to do therewith.

24. Item we present that we know not by what pearch the woods within this manor are accustomed to be measured withall.

25. Item we present that the building called Colledge adjoining to the Manor House or Castle of Bishop Auckland doth belong to the Prebends of St. Andrew Auckland, a part whereof for many years last past has been in the possession of Mr. Lindley Wrenne and his Ancestors, as appeareth to us by the oathe of John Robson and John Johnson. But the garden on the back and on each side thereof as also the tower called the Sherriffes Tower formerly used for a privie as also the hedge and warren in the parke and the herd house did belong to the late Bishop of Durham.

26. Item we present that there are severall reprisalls and pensions duties and fees granted by patent or otherwise out of this manor but to whom or what the same are we knowe not but referr ourselves to the severall patents thereof granted.

27. Item we present that the lands in Whitworth are holden of the King as of his manor of East Greenwich in free and common socage. And that they came unto the crowne upon the attainder of the late Earl of Westmorland who held the same formerly of the lords of this manor by knights service by the antient rent of the fourth part of a knights fee, vizt.—25s. od. And that Mr. Baxter owner of parte thereof payeth yearly to the lords of this manor the said yearly rent and one shilling eight pence more yearly. And that there are other freeholders owners of the rest thereof.

This presentment was delivered in the 13th day of April 1647, under our hands and seales.

George Bunney
Robt. Ridlington
George Lax
Ambrose Johnson
John Bell
Jo. Smithson
Tho. Hixon
Robt. Baker
Miles Whyte
John Mayor
Richard Hobson

Christopher Dobson
Robert Laxe
John Dawson
Robt. Adamson
John Wood
Robert Darnton
Thomas Trotter
Robert Adamson
Anthony Laxe
Robert Vincent
William Adamson
John Simpson

A Survey of the ruins of the Castle or Mannor House of Bishop Auckland taken by order of the Surveyors the 23rd March by us whose names are underwritten

The ruins of the Hall in Glasse

Inpr in the Entry and low Romes by the Hall 112 foot.

In the Great Chamber and the Rome above the Hall 94½ foot.

In the gallery and the roomes on the levill of the Northsyde to the Chappell and the south syde 389 foot.

In the dyneing room and the Greene chamber 65 foot.

Over the cellar and the panthree 146 foot.

In the Porters Lodge 52 foot.

In the two Chappells 52 foot.

The total of the glasse is 1209½ foot.

The same total at 6d. per foot is £30. 4. 9. being undervalued in shortness of measure.

Timber and Carpenters Worke

Inpr in the Greate Hall one New doore for the back syde and mending the old door 214 foot six of border 1″ thick.

In the inner panthree one doore 30 foot of borde.

In the inner seller one doore 30 foot of borde.

For the stayre foot doore 30 foot of borde going up by the South Hall doore.

For the trencher house two doores 60 foote.

For the Backhouse door 30 foot.

For the Washhouse doore and one doore to be mended 36 foot.

For Mr. Wainerleyes chambers 4 doors and one wood casement 120 foot.

For one doore in the Brewhouse 30 foot.

Item for the doore cheekes in the Brewhouse 8" square, 24 foot.

Item for a doore and the windowleaves in the Bakehouse 60 foot of Boards and 90 foot of 6" square timber for the Backehouse.

For the salthouse doore and window 30 foot of boord.

For the stablegroomes doore 30 foot of board.

For 2 doores for 2 little stables 60 foot of boards and 24 foot of 8" square timber for door cheakes.

For 2 doores for the Slaughter house and the chamber above 54 foote of boordes.

For Mr. Baddileye's chamber 4 doores 120 foot of Boordes.

In his upper chamber 2 doores 60 foot.

Above the panthree 4 doores 120 foot.

In the wine Seller 2 doores 60 foot.

The entry doore at the west end of Hall 90 foot being a double door.

For 2 doors for a little room 60 foot.

For 6 doors belonging to the kitching 240 foot.

In the west larder one door 30 foot.

By the Stewards chamber and under the Granary 10 doors 300 foot.

In the garner 3 doors 90 foot.

In the lodgeings adjoining to the Chappell 5 doors 150 foot.

In the lodgeings adjoyning to the dineing room 2 doores 60 foot and one board for sealeing 12 foot.

For one door in the Bishops chamber 30 foot.

For one door under the same chamber 30 foot.

For 2 doores in the Chappell chamber 60 foot.

At the end of the High Chappell 2 doores 90 foot.

For 3 wainscott doores in the Dyneing room and one in the gallery val at 24s. od.

For railes at the head of the stair going into the Upper Hall 50 feet of timber 4" square.

For 2 doores in Mr. Baddeleye's Chamber 60 foote and 52 foot of timber 10" on the square to mende the principall.

In boards 98 roods being 49 yards, 5 yards one foot for felling posting and saweing at 16d. per Rood £78. 19. 5.

And in square timber 98 foot at 5d. per foot £2. 0. 0.

In sum total £80. 19. 5. And for making the doores etc £8. 0. 0.

The Iron Worke

Inpr For the 2 out doors in the Great Hall in Iron 2½ stone, £14. to the stone.

For stanchells for 4 windows in the Great Hall 25 stone the barrs 1″ square.

For 2 doors in the Pantree for bands one stone.

For one payre of bandes for the inner Buttery door, half a stone. For stanchelles 4½ stone.

For bands for one door and stanchells in the inner seller 9 stone.

For bands in the backehouse and Trencherhouse for 3 doors 1 stone.

For bands for 3 doors in the wash house 1½ stone.

Item bands for 4 doors for Mr. Wanerleye's chamber 2 stone.

For the brewhouse one payre of bands and window stanchells 8 stone.

For the brewhouse 12 iron bars 5′ length 1½″ square cont in weight 24 stone.

For the Oat Backehouse one payre of bands cont 1 stone.

For the salthouse doore and window 1 stone of iron for bands and nayles.

For bands for 2 doores in the Slaughter house 1 stone.

For 4 doors in Mr. Baddeleye's chamber for bands 2 stone.

For 2 payre of bands for 2 doores in his upper chamber 1 stone.

For bands for 4 doors about the Panteries 1½ stone.

For bands for 3 doors in the wine seller 2 stone.

For bands for 4 doors for the Entry doore and 2 little rooms, and two little roomes at the west end of the Hall 2 stone, and for stanchells 3 stone.

For bands for 6 doors belonging to the Kitching 4 stone.

For 10 stanchells in the Kitchinge 4½ foot long cont. 10 stone.

For 2 payre of bands for the larder about one stone and for 6 stanchells 3 foot long and 1″ square, 4 stone.

By the Steward's chamber and under the Garnery bands for 10 doors 5 stone.

For bands for 3 doors in the Garnery 2½ stone.

For bands for 5 doors in the rooms adjoyning to the Chappell 2½ stone.

For bands for 2 doors adjoyning to the dineing room 1 stone.

For bands for one doore in the Bishop's chamber ½ stone.
For bands for one door under the said chamber ½ stone.
For bands for 2 doors in the Chaplen's chamber.
For bands 3 doors at the end of the chappell 1½ stone.
For bands for 3 wainscott doors in the dyneing room and the gallery 7 stone.
For 2 doors at the long stayre head 1 stone.

The total of the iron is 102 stone at 2s. 6d. per stone, and 3 payre of bands for the portall doore. £13. 2. 0.
For workmanship of the said Iron into bands and hookes stanchells and nayles £12. 15. 0.   Totall £25. 17. 0.

Lead for the Repayre of the Castle wanting
Inpr over the chappell 20 foot in length 7 in breadth.
For one part of a gutter 20 foot in length and 2 feet broad.
And the Great Chamber in breadth 68 foot in flatt measure and of filleting 206 foot long and 9 in the breadth.
Over the wardrobe and over the hall and over the Entry 33 foot in flatt measure.
For the rooms at the end of the Gallery wanting in lead 100 flatt foot.
For the filleting over the Dyneing chamber wanting in lead 20 foot in flatt measure.
Over the wine seller wanting in lead 7 foot flatt measure.
For 4 spouts wanting in the hall 64 flatt foot.
For 6 spouts wanting in the Great Chamber and the dineing room 36 foot flatt measure.
Wanting of the pipe that brought the water to the house 444 foot at 8 inches broade.
For the filletting of the Chappell 128 foote and 4 inches flatt measure.
For the filleting of the Great Chamber and pipe 430 foot flatt measure.
Sum total £55. 5. 0.
The lead conteyneth 160 yards @ 5/6 parts of a 6 part.

The Stone Work
Inpr all the flat work within the whole castle is 90 Road at 49 yards the road being 7 yards valued for poynting getting flats and lime 6s. 8d. Roads amounteth to £30. 0. 0.

For the building up of 80 yards of wall finding stones and lyme 1s. 3d. per yard amounteth to £5. 0. 0.

For the Top of the High Tower above the stare and the High Chappell wanting 576 foot of stone for embattlements val at 8d. per foot. £19. 4. 0.

For the workmanship for the Timber for the Roofe £6. 13. 4.

For the lead for the said Tower 12 yards £6. 10. 0.

Summa total £67. 7. 4.

The Breweing vessells remayning in the aforesaid house valued by workmen more £20. 0. 0.

BISHOP AUCKLAND DEMESNES

Francis Wrenn, Esq., liveth in the gatehouse belonging to that great house or castle of Bishop Auckland the drafte whereof followeth (but nobody liveth in the greate house) and says he was put there by the State but produces nothing to prove the same.

Thomas Hodgson by indenture of lease dated the Fourth May A.D. 1646 23 Car. made and granted by us in the name of the trustees by Commission to us given for the disposing of Bishop's lands, holdeth all that ground or park called by the name of Auckland Park and by the names of Somer and Winter Parks containing 926 acres more or less. And all that parcell of meadow ground called Tyle close containing 16 acres and also all that other parcell of meadow called Rough Mires containing 14 acres. To hold the said same grounds vizt the Sumer Park from the 25th day of March last past and the said Tyle Close and Rough Mires from May day last past before the date paying yearly £136. 0. 0.

Dayes of payment 24th June, 29th September, 25th December, and 25th March.

This park and closes if it might be granted for 21 years would be let for £180 p.ann.

Wood in the said park being only fit for bordwood worth £350. Hereafter followeth draughts of the Parkes and closes let to Hodgshon.

Bondgate in Auckland Freeholds

These persons hereafter named do hold the severall parcells of lands under the rents mentioned in sergiance the former haveing formerly been given by some of the Bishops to one Pollard for killing a wild Boar. The service is that the owners of this land are to doe at every Bishop's first coming to be Bishop here to present him with the Falchon with which the Bore was slayne.

Mr. Richard Smith for Etherley ground		7.	8.
John Allenson per annum		3.	0.
Richard Rowser per annum		3.	0.
John Robinson per annum		2.	3.
Robert Baker and John Thompson per annum		7.	8.
Elizabeth Warde per annum			5.
Richard Pinkney per annum			5.
Thomas Brasse per annum			6.
Widow Porters per annum			6.
Thomas Longstaffe per annum			9.
Raiph Downe per annum			7.
George Nelson per annum			7.
Eleanor Rudderforth per annum			7.
Widow Farrow per annum		1.	0.
Henry Hodgshon			1.

Sum Total   £2. 9. 0.

Free Rents also payed to the Coroner of Darlington

Baxter Whitworth per annum	2.	6.	8.
Wrenne Francis for Henknowle		8.	0.
Courtpenny George for Newfield	1.	15.	2.
The denary of Auckland		10.	8.
The parsonage of Branspeth		13.	4.

Lindley Wren, Esq., payeth for his house and land called Binchester a Fee farm rent to the late Bishops of £8. o. o. p.a.

This rent is payd at the Exchequor at Durham.

JOHN TALLANTIRE

7 June 18 Jac. made and granted from Oswald Oliver all that close or meadow called Bowbagg lying in the fields of North Auckland sometime parcell of four acres of lands belonging to Martin Grimston, now in the tenure of John Tallantine, with all woods, wayes, easements and profits.

Rent 2d.

THOMAS MOORE

12 January 10 Car. made and granted from John Dawson all that his

acre and a half of arable land lying within the territories of Bond-gate in Bishop Auckland, also North Auckland.
Rent 6d.

RICHARD BOWSER son and heir of Mathew Bowser.
In capite of the Bishops of Durham two closes called Brackes Closes lying and being within the parish of St. Andrew Auckland as appear-eth by the livery sued out by the said Mathew Bowser under the great seal of the County Palatine of Durham 13 March 14 Jac.
Rent 13s. 4d.

FRANCIS WREN, COLLONELL
31 January 2 Car. from Sir Thomas Bellasis and Henry Bellasis his son inter al one close called Penny Batts.
Rent 7d.

Bondgate in Auckland Township Copyholds

RICHARD RICHARDSON son and heir of John Richardson.
30 April 16 Jac. One cottage.
Fine 12d.
Dat ut supra. One parcell of land late the lords waste called Barrat Green conteyning in length 16 yards and in breadth 8 yards.
Fine 2d. Both as copies as heir to his father. Rent for both 11d.

JANE LANGSTAFFE, wife of Thomas Langstaffe, relict of Anthony Stevenson.
21 September 22 Jac. Three sellions or ridges of land lying at Cross-towne gate containing one acre of land, two roods of land lying in the hoope, one rood of land lying in Hooke meadow side and one rood of land lying on both sides of the way leading to the windmill.
As widow of the said Anthony. Rent 2s. od. Fine 3d.

NICHOLAS GILPIN
15 October 22 Jac. One cottage with a garden (one house with a little garden belonging to the same containing in length 10 yards and a half, and in breadth eight yards and a foot, late in the tenure of widdow Robinson.
By surrender of Simon Jackson. Rent 1s. 4d. Fine 1s. 6d.

RICHARD HEVYSIDE

4 May 12 Car. 4 acres, 1 rood, 4 perches of pasture parcell of a close called Moore Close lying on the north of the land of Bryan Wright, on the east of John Curry and others, on the west the moore called Etherley Moore and on the south the way called Long Lanning.

By surrender of Richard Richardson, John Craddock, John Adamson, and John Thompson. Rent 1s. 3d. Fine 1s. 3d.

JOHN COLESON and Janett his wife.

23 April 15 Car. One messuage with a garden.

By surrender of Henry Downes, gent., Rent 4d. Fine 6d.

ROBERT CARRE, son and heir of James Carr.

10 October 15 Car. The half of one acre of land lying on the east of a parcell of land late the lord's waste containing 5 roods of land as it is now enclosed, late in the tenure of Wm. Middleton.

Fine 2d.

Dat ut supra. One parcell of land with a house built thereon containing 5 roods of land lying at the East end of Moore Close late in the tenure of William Middleton.

Fine 6d. Both copies as heir to his father the said James. Rent for both 10s. 10d.

Mem The 10s. 10d. is a Free Rent.

JOHN BELL

5 May 7 Car. One parcell of lands lying at the West End of the town of Bondgate nigh the Canongate there containing 80 yards in length, in breadth 14 yards.

By surrender of Lindley Wrenne, Esq., Rent 1s. 8d. Fine 1s. 8d.

JANE COXON

23 October 21 Jac. One cottage.

By surrender of Edward Bigland to Wm. Coxon her husband deceased.

Rent 1s. 0d. Fine 3s. 4d.

CHRISTOPHER HEARNE and Frances his wife.

6 November 14 Car. 16 acres of pasture parcell of a close called Moore Close as it is now divided with a hedge extending from the north of the said close to the south of the said pasture lying on the

west part of a tenement of the said Christopher called the Greenefield on the east and north part of Raley Fell and the west part of
the lands of John Adamson, parcell of the said close.

By surrender of William Williamson Jun. Rent 3s. 2d. Fine 5s. 8d.

EDWARD MIDDLETON

19 July 17 Car. One messuage and one croft late in the tenure of
Nicholas Craweshaw.

By surrender of Thomas Coleman. Rent 2s. od. Fine 6d.

ANTHONY ADAMSON and Jane his daughter.

24 April 13 Car. One cottage now in the tenure of Robert Winrent
on the east of Cuthbert Whitfield and on the North of the Common
Street and west of Thomas Moore and on the south of the highway.

By surrender of Thomas More. Fine 4d.

14 October 6 Car. Two acres of lands in the Church Lees parcell of
three acres of lands and a half.

By surrender of John Adamson. Fine £1. 8s. od.

10 October 15 Car. One acre and a half of land lyeing in Church lees
joyning on the west parte to the lands of John Curry on the north of
the lands of Anthony Adamson on the south of the lands of William
Rey and lyeing on the west of the highway called church lanning.

By surrender of John Adamson. Fine 6d.

Rent for these three copies 4s. 4d.

SIMON WHEATLEY

9 May 1 Car. One cottage with a croft late Wm. Starkies.

By surrender of Agnes Shortridge. Fine 1s. 8d.

10 October 14 Jac. One cottage.

As son and heir of Anthony Wheatley. Fine 1s. 6d.

Rent for these two copies 4s. od.

THOMAS WILD

12 April 3 Car. One house lately built lying on the Batts nigh the
Park wall and a garden adjoyning to the same containing in length
20 yards and a half and in breadth 11 yards.

As heir to Simon Wild his father. Rent 2d. Fine 1d.

RICHARD WRIGHTE

3 April 22 Car. The north end of one cottage late Nicholas Inglewoods.

As son and heir to Elizabeth Wrighte. Rent: no entry. Fine 1d.

MARGARET ROBSON
15 October 22 Jac. One cottage.
   By surrender of Wm. Robson. Rent 6d. Fine 1s. 8d.

THOMAS LAXE
21 September 22 Car. One cottage and one garden in Auckland.
   By surrender of John Walker. Rent 2s. od. Fine 2s. od.

THOMAS MORE
25 April 13 Car. One cottage late Christopher Bell's and one cottage late Carill Bell's.
   By surrender of Anthony Adamson and Thomas Allanson. Fine 4d.
9 May 15 Car. One rood of land lying at Johnson's garth end one rood of land at the tenters and half an acre of lands at Nabhill half an acre of lands at Hall Meadow head one rood of land in the hope half an acre of land in Henknowle field and three roods of lands in the middle field.
   By surrender of Richard Pinbury. Fine 6d.
   Rent for these two copies 5s. 6d.

MARGERY CRADDOCKE alias Maughen relict of Henry Maughen.
23 April 2 Jac. One messuage and 18 acres of land parcell of one husband's land containing 20 acres late Robert Smithe's.
   By surrender of John Swarmeston who holdeth the same in trust for John and Margery. Fine 6d.
29 October 16 Jac. One close containing four acres of lands called Robson's close under Nabhill lying on the south part of Dunston Green on the north of the Town Field late in the tenure of Henry Maughan and one rood and a half of lands in Snaylecroft then in the tenure of George Downes, Gent. to Henry Maughen and now descended to the said Margery.
   In widdowright. Fine 1s. 2d.
29 October 16 Jac. One close called Dunston Green Close containing one acre of land abutting upon a close of the said Maughen on the north part the close of Elianor Damport on the west part and the comon or waste of the Lords called Dunston green on the north and

the close of the said Henry Maughen on the east (parcell of 17 acres of land late Agnes White).

By surrender of Anthony Somer and Marian his wife, now the said Margery in widdowright. Fine 6d.

11 September 1 Jac. Two partes of one oxgang of land late Robert Manners two partes of six of one messuage and one of twenty acres of lands called oxehouse and of one parcell of lands lyeing between the tenement late of Thomas Eslington on the east and the tenement of Roger Juslipp on the west containing nineteen rods in length and four rods in breadth and pasture for two beasts in Moore close at Whyton Walls to be divided into six partes (the said messuage and pasture for two beastes in More Close excepted).

By surrender of Wm. Brabint. Fine 3s. 10d.

Rent for these four copies £2. 4s. 2½d.

EMANUEL GRICE

14 May 10 Car. Two closes of arable land called Dell bank now in tenure of the said Emanuell lyeing between the closes now in occupacion of William Damporte clark on the south and a parcell of lands called Delbank on the north of the River of Gaunless on the east and a close now in the occupacion of John Robinson on the west late Agnes Whites.

By surrender of Anthony Somer. Fine 1s. 0d.

11 May 10 Jac. One close of meadow called Sunny Croft lyeing on the east of a close late Mathew Somers.

By surrender of John Walby. Fine 1s. 0d.

OSWALD GRICE son of Emanuell Grice.

7 May 22 Jac. One close abutting upon the head of Panmire containing four acres of lands.

By surrender of John Grice. Fine 3s. 4d.

Rent for these three copies of £1. 12s. 1d.

JOHN ADAMSON son and heir of Susannah Adamson one of the sisters and coheirs of Henry Grice defunct.

5 April 13 Car. The half of one close of meadow called Lamelands The half of one close of meadow called Mill Hill the half of a close of pasture called Cow Close thirteen perches in a close called Caper Close.

As co-heir to his uncle Henry Grice. Rent 4s. 7d. Fine 2s. 6d.

ANN WHITFIELD late the wife of William Hutchinson one of the sisters and coheirs of Henry Grice defunct.
23 April 14 Car. One close of meadow called Nabhill with one close of pasture lying in a close called Caper Close.
As co-heir of Henry Grice. Rent 4s. 7d. Fine 2s. 6d.

ELIZABETH SOMER
One cottage with a little garden late in the occupation of Richard Somer (parcell of a messuage which was the said Richard's while he lived).
In widdow right of Richard Somer defunct. Rent 2s. od. Fine 3s. 4d.

ANTHONY BELL
5 May 7 Car. One cottage with a croft in Bondgate.
By surrender of John Robinson. Rent 2s. od. Fine 3s. 4d.

BRYAN WALKER Jun.
12 October 18 Car. The third part of one messuage and 21 acres of land called the Oxehouse and the third of one close of land lying between the tenement late Thomas Ellingtons on the east and a tenement late Roger Juslip's on the west containing 29 rods in length and 4 rods in breadth And also the third part of a third part of one oxgang of land late Robert Mayne's And also a third part of 10 acres of Arable lands with the townefields of North Auckland at Bishop Auckland And a third part of a third part of ten acres and a half of lands and meadowes at Church Lees abutting on the highway and Church lees and the King's Highway containing 5 acres abutting on a close of Robert Phillippe's on the south and the land called Bicotts land on the north and a close called Gaunless on the east and the King's highway on the west. Also the third part of a third part of one acre of land lyeing betweene the close of Robert Dirkett and the Church Lees and the third part of a third part of two acres and a half of lands lying in the delved bankes And the third part of the third parte of one close called the Mires Chase containing 4 acres of land lyeing on the south of Gibbs House in the town and fields of Bishop Auckland.
By surrender of Margery Craddock widdow. Rent: no entry Fine 6s. 8d.

MARY GRIMDON relict of Anthony Grimdon.
27 April 11 Car. One acre and a half lyeing in a certain place called
the New Pasture in Auckland.
   In widdowright. Rent 8d. Fine 6d.

JOHN CALVERLEY, Gent.
6 May 4 Car. 25 acres of land called Tindall Morehouses also three
roods of lands late the lord's waste late lying in woodhouse loaning.
By surrender of Raphe Pollards, as son and heir of Leonard Pollards, and George Bradley. Fine 10s. 3d.
4 May 12 Car. Eighteen acres of pasture more or less, parcell of a
close called Moore close at Whiton Wall lyeing on the East parte of
the lands in the tenure of George Moore parcell of the said close and
the King's highway on the south And a close belonging to the Lord
Bishop parcell of a certain close on the North as it is now inclosed
with hedges.
   By surrender of John Adamson and John Thompson. Fine 3s. 8d.
   Rent for these two copies 11s. 3d.

GEORGE MOORE and Jane his wife.
4 May 2 Car. One close called Richmond Close and one house there-
upon built.
   By surrender of Richard Todd. Rent 6s. od. Fine 6d.
   Idem and George Moore, son and heir of said George. 4 May 12
Car. 25 acres of lands or pastures, parcell of a pasture called Wigton
Walle also Moore Close lying on the west part of a way called Tindall
Laneing on the south of a tenement called Bayly Dubbs and the
South parcell of the said close belonging to Jane Middleton and on
the east of a parcell of the said close belonging to John Calverley.
   By surrender of Lindley Wrenne Esq. Rent 5s. od. Fine 2s. 6d.

ANN BAYLES
28 September 16 Jac. One cottage in Bondgate.
   In widdowright of Raphe Bayles. Fine 2d.
   dat ut supra. One crofte with a Tofte adjoyning at Auckland And
all buildings burgages orchards gardens etc.
   In widdowright. Fine 6s. 8d.
   dat ut supra. One tenement in Bondgate containing twenty acres
of arable land and meadow and half an acre lying in a close called
Snaylecrofte and three roodes of lands lying in a pasture called West

Field neare Shearley And one and twenty acres of land in Auckland.

In widdowright. Fine 10s. 10d.

dat ut supra. One cottage late in the tenure of Robert Thompson and three acres of land and a halfe late in the tenure of Robert Whitworth.

In widdowright. Fine 2s. 11d.

dat ut supra. The half of one tenement and the half of one gardein parcell of a tenement late in the tenure of Gregory Bucke and one close abutting upon the head of Panmire containing four acres of land.

In widdowright. Fine 11d.

dat ut supra. The east part of one tenement and half of one garden late in the tenure of Gregory Bucke as it is now divided by metes and boundes and now in the tenure of John Waiscell.

In widdowright. Fine 1s. 0d.

Rent for these six copies £2. 0s. 0d.

ISABELL HODGSON

20 October 7 Car. Pasture for one beast in Moore close also Wigton Walls.

In widdowright of Thomas Hodgshon. Fine 8d.

dat ut supra. Three acres of lands and one rood of Arable lands.

In widdowright. Fine 1s. 0d.

dat ut supra. One close of meadow containing five roods of lands lying between a close late of the said Thomas called Oxe close and a pasture close called Snaylecrofte parcell of a messuage and twenty acres of land.

In widdowright. Fine 1s. 0d.

dat ut supra. Two leas of land by estimation three roods of land in Snaylecrofte, parcell of 17 acres of land heretofore belonging to Anne Wrighte and of one messuage and 20 acres of lands.

In widdowright. Fine 6d.

dat ut supra. Five acres one rood and half of arable land in the townefield there.

In widdowright. Fine 1s. 0d.

dat ut supra. Half one acre of land late in the tenure of William Stockdale lying in Snaylecrofte and also two acres and a half of land lying in the said close late in the tenure of Gregory Dirkett parcell of 21 acres in Bondgate.

In widdowright. Fine 1s. 0d.

dat ut supra. Five acres and a half of Arable lands, one close called oxeclose, one parcell of land called the Deane head three roods of land lying on the west of Snaylecroft, one close called the tenter garth lying upon Pollards on the north the third parte of one house in Gibchare with the pitts called Lynne Pitts.

In widdowright. Fine 6s. 8d.

dat ut supra. Pasture for two beasts in Moore Close also Wigton Walls and pasture for one beast in the same.

In widdowright. Fine 2s. 4d.

Rent for these eight copies £1. 2s. od.

JANE WILSON

1 September 22 Car. One acre of lands lying betweene the kirk Lees within the territories of North Auckland.

In widdowright of Lancelott Wilson. Rent 8d. Fine 2d.

FRANCES RICHARDSON wife of William Richardson daughter and heir of Thomas Askew.

29 April 18 Car. The half of one cottage late Thomas Nertie's.

As heir to Thomas Askew. Fine 6d.

dat ut supra. One acre of land parcell of Eight acres of land called Cronny Croft in the south parte of Gaunless.

In widdowright. Fine 6d.

Rent for these two copies 1s. 2d.

WILLIAM ADAMSON son of Raphe.

20 May 15 Car. One close in North auckland called Poppie field.

As heir to Raphe. Rent 15s. 4d. Fine 10s. od.

WILLIAM DAMES

4 May 12 Car. Six acres and ten perches of pasture, parcell of a close called Moore close lying on the East part of a close of Lancellot Ettis, on the west of the land of John Craddock on the north parte of the King's highway And on the south of the lands of Walker's.

By surrender of Richard Richardson, John Damson and John Thomson.

Rent 1s. 3d. Fine 11d.

ISABELL HODGSON daughter of John Hodgson.

31 October 19 Car. One close called great thorny close.

By surrender of Henry Blakeston yeo. Rent 7s. od. Fine 4d.

JOHN HODGSON and Katherine his wife.

30 April 16 Jac. One close containing two acres of lands more or less lying on the North of Kirk lees now in the occupation of Raphe Currie.

By surrender of Henry Dames. Fine 1s. od.

27 October 17 Jac. One close of meadow called Law Crooke containing Four acres of land lying at the head of Snaylecrofte in the Westfield of Auckland parcell of a tenement containing 20 acres of arable lands and meadow.

By surrender of Raphe Bayles. Fine 2s. od.

11 October 3 Car. Two sellions or ridges of Arable lands containing Five roods of lands lying on the west parte of the lands called Fare hories lands on the North of Snaylecroft on the Easte parte of a parcell of lands in the tenure of Richard Pinkney and on the southe parte of the highway from Etherley to the towne of Auckland.

By surrender of Joseph Craddock and Margery his wife. Fine 4d.

5 May 7 Car. Three acres of meadow lying in the west pasture lying between a parcell of lands in the tenure of John Hodgson in the west, the lands of Anne Hodgson on the East, Snaylecroft in the north and the king's way on the south, and half an acre of lands in the middle of the Fields called Greenecrofte gate between a sellion of Joseph Craddock on the east and the lands of Anthony Stevenson on the west And also two Sellions in the long hinelands nigh Henknowle containing both one Acre and a half whereof one joyneth to the King's way and the land of Henry Bayle on the east and the lands of John Walker on the west.

By surrender of Richard Pinkney. Fine 6s. od.

Rent for these four copies 12s. 1d.

THOMAS SMURTHWAITE

12 April 3 Car. One cottage adjoyning to the house of John Robson on the east of the barne of Joseph Craddocke on the south of the Comon of the towns of Bondgate on the west of a parcell of land called Weare batts.

By surrender of Richard Richardson and Johanna his wife. Rent 2s. od. Fine 1s. od.

CHRISTOPHER CURRY son of John Curry.

7 May 9 Car. One cottage with one acre of land lying in church lees of Antient use with and belonging to the same cottage.

By surrender of John Curry. Rent 2s. od. Fine 1s. od.

JOHN CURRY

4 May 12 Car. Four acres and three roodes of pasture parcell of a close called Moore Close.

By surrender of Richard Richardson, John Adamson, John Craddock and John Thompson. Rent 1od. Fine 1od.

RAPHE WALKER senior and RAPHE WALKER junior son of the said Raphe.

14 May 10 Jac. One close called the Strait close containing two acres of lands lying betweene a close of John Adamson on the north and a close called Barker lands on the south the king's highway on the East and the close Anthony Walby on the west in the territories of Bondgate parcell of 20 acres of land late Hugh Beswicke's.

By surrender of Anthony Somer. Rent 2s. od. Fine 8d.

RAPHE WALKER senior by assignment from Richard Parkin and Mary his wife.

18 September 21 Car. Eight acres of land called West Mill Batts
Rent 4s. od.

JOHN WALKER

11 April 9 Car. One parcell of lands containing from the stepp of his house to the west end of the said house with a garden lying between the said house and the shore of the water of Weare And half a garden called the garths with all the meadow belonging to the said house.

By surrender of William Hutton and Margarett his wife. Fine 3s. 4d.

4 May 12 Car. 39 acres of pasture, parcell of a close called Moore close lying on the south part of the said close belonging to the bishop and on the north part of a close belonging to John Craddock on the east of the king's highway leading to Carterthorne And the west of a close of Richard and John Simpson.

By surrender of Richard Richardson, John Craddock, John Adamson and John Thompson. Fine 13s. 4d.

11 June 8 Car. Two partes of six partes of one oxegang of lands late

Robert Maine's divided into 6 partes and two partes of 6 partes of a parcell of lands lying betweene the tenement late Thomas Eslington's on the East and a tenement late Roger Juslippes on the west containing 19 yds in length and 4 in breadth divided into 6 partes And two partes of six partes of Pasture for two beastes in Moore Close also Wigton Walles divided into 6 partes of the said messuage and two pasture gates in Mooreclose aforesaid.

Fine 3s. 10d.

10 October 14 Jac. One sellion or ridge of Arable land lying betweene the land of Leonard Pinkney on the south the king's highway on the west the garden of George Dame on the east one other sellion of arable lands lying betweene the lands of Raphe Pollard Esq. the king's highway on the west and the tenement of the King on the east containing in all and betweene them six roodes of lands (parcell of 20 acres of lands).

By surrender of Anthony Somer. Fine 3d.

27 October 12 Jac. The third parte of two acres and a halfe of lands and meadow lying in Churchlees divided into three partes and the third parte of one close at the overside of Church lees abutting upon the Marleway and Church lees and the kingsway containing four acres of land divided into three partes And the third parte of a close lying upon the way called the Church Way containing four acres of lands abutting upon a close late Robert Phillipe's on the south and the land called Barker's Land on the north. And a river called Gaunless on the East and the King's way on the west to be divided into three partes Also the third parte of one half acre of land lying between the close of Thomas Dirkett and the Church lees divided into three partes and also the third part of two acres and a half of land in the Delves Bank to be divided into three partes And four acres lying on the south of Gibischaire in the town and fields of Bishop Auckland called Myreclose And the third parte of a parcell of land lying in Snaylecrofte containing nine acres of land

By surrender of Anthony Allenson. Fine 4d.

29 April 18 Car. One cottage with a garden.

By surrender of George Morley. Fine 1s. 8d.

Rent for these six copies £1. 8s. 8d.

PETER WILSON

26 May 6 Jac. The office of pindar of N. Auckland.

By surrender of Roger Willson. Rent 2s. 0d. Fine 6s. 8d.

ANNE ALLENSON

16 October 5 Car. One close containing 3 acres of lands, parcell of a close called the hakeforth.

In widdowright of Anthonie Allenson. Fine 10d.

dat ut supra. The fourth parte of a close called Holdsworth lying on the east of Gaunless containing two acres of lands And three acres of lands and one rood of arable lands and one acre of meadow lying upon kirklees And pasture for two beasts in Moore close.

In widdowright of Anthonie Allenson. Fine 8d.

dat ut supra. Half a close called Holfoote lying in the east of Gaunless containing four acres.

In widdowright of Anthonie Allenson. Fine 5s. od.

dat ut supra. One close called Howlefoote lying within Bondgate containing three acres and a half (parcell of six acres of lands nigh Sharpe Thorne).

In widdowright of Anthonie Allenson. Fine 1s. od.

dat ut supra. Two partes of six partes of eighteen acres of Arable lands lying within Bishop Auckland divided into six partes.

In widdowright of Anthonie Allenson. Fine 5s. od.

dat ut supra. Six partes of one messuage and 21 acres of lands late Robt. Maynes divided into 6 partes Also two partes of six of a messuage and one and twenty acres of lands called the oxehouse And one peece of lands lying betweene the lands or tenement late Thomas Eslingtons on the East and the tenement late Roger Juslipp west containing 19 yds in length and four in breadth And pasture for two beastes in the Moore Close late Whyton Walls and divided into six partes of the said Messuage and pasture gates in the Moore close aforesaid.

In widdowright of Anthonie Allenson. Fine 3s. 4d.

dat ut supra. The third parte of a third part of a messuage and 21 acres of land called the Oxehouse and the third parte of one peece of land lying betweene a tenement late Thomas Eslington's on the east and a tenement late Roger Juslipp's in the west containing twentynine yards in length and four in breadth And also the third parte of one oxegang of land late Robert Mayne's And also the third parte of a third parte of Eighteen acres of Arable land in the town-field of Bishop Auckland.

In widdowright of Anthonie Allenson. Fine 3s. 6d.

Rent for these seven copies £1. 3s. 11d.

ROBERT BRIGGS and Anne his wife.
27 April 16 Car. Three partes of one tenement or cottage nigh the Mannor of Auckland to be divided into four lying on the west of the tenement or cottage late of Hugh Foster descending to Gaunless.

By surrender of Moses Skepper Gent. Rent 4s. 3d. Fine 8d.

MARIOLA COLSON
8 August 17 Car. One house with a garden on the backside in Bishop Auckland late Susan Middleton's.

By surrender of Thomas Colson. Rent 2s. od. Fine 1s. 4d.

CECILLIA CARRINGTON wife of Cuthbert Carrington, coson and heir of Oswald Clover the daughter and one of the heirs of Mary Rea one of the sisters of Oswald.
12 October 18 Car. The fourth parte of a cottage to be divided into four partes in Bondgate lying in the east parte of a tenement of William Colson and also the fourth parte of two acres of land to be divided into four, (parcell of 23 acres of land called oxehouse).

As heir to Oswald Clover. Fine 10d.

Elizabeth Hodgson wife of George Hodgson, cosen and heir of Oswald Clover

dat ut supra. The fourth parte of a cottage to be divided into four partes in Bondgate lying in the east parte of a tenement of William Colson And also the fourth parte of two acres of land to be divided into four, (parcell of 23 acres of land called Oxehouse).

As heir to Oswald Clover. Fine 10d.

Dorothy Dobson wife of James Dobson sister and coheir of Oswald Clover.

dat ut supra. The half of one cottage.

As heir to Oswald Clover. Fine 1s. 8d.

Rent for these three copies 2s. od.

BRYAN WALKER son and heir of Raphe Walker.
No date. The third parte of the third parte of one messuage and 21 acres of land called the Oxehouse and the ⅓ parte of one peece of land lying between the tenement late Thomas Eslington's on the East the tenement late Robt. Juslipp's on the west containing 29 yds. in length and 4 in breadth. Also ⅓ parte of ⅓ parte of one oxegang of lands late Roger Maines also ⅓ parte of 18 acres of land arable within the townefield of North Auckland also Bishop Auckland

And the ⅓ parte of the ⅓ parte of 10½ acres of lands and meadows lying in the Church Lees abutting upon the Marleway and the Church Lees And the King's highway containing 4 acres of land. And the ⅓ parte of ⅓ parte of another close lying under the Church way containing 4 acres abutting upon a close of Robert Phillippe's on the South And the land called Barkers land on the north and one close called Gaunless on the Gaunless on the East And the Highway on the west Also the ⅓ parte of the ⅓ of one acre of land lying between the close of Thomas Duckett and the Church Lees and ⅓ of ⅓ parte of 2½ acres of lands lying in the Delves Bankes and ⅓ of ⅓ parte of a close called Moore Close containing 4 acres lying on the south of Gibschaire in the towne and fields of Bishop Auckland.

As heir to Raphe Walker his father. Rent 6s. 4d. Fine 6s. 8½d.

RICHARD PINKNEY

3 September 13 Jac. One cottage with a garden in Bondgate as it lyeth in length and breadth from the King's Highway And the water called Weare on the North Also 17 acres late Robt. Juslipp's.

By surrender of Leonard Pinkney his father. Rent 4s. 8d. Fine 19s. 4d.

Mem. 15 acres of the 17 are sould to Anne Harperley.

NATHAN LAXE

9 May 1 Car. One cottage in Bondgate (except one house on the west and 20 yds of land and 4 in breadth and a garden to the same cottage belonging).

By surrender of William Coxen. Rent 3s. od. Fine 1s. od.

THOMAS WATSON and Mary his wife.

23 October 15 Car. One cottage in Bondgate.

Rent 2s. od. Fine 2s. od.

ANNE HARPLEY and Margarett her daughter.

5 June 5 Car. 3 acres of land in the New Pasture abutting upon the highway in the south a close of Thomas Hodgson on the north ½ acre and 2 roods in Coundon Fields 2 Sellions containing 3 roods abutting upon the king's highway.

By surrender of Richard Pinkney. Rent 5s. od. Fine 1s. 8d.

ELIZABETH STOCKTON now wife of Thomas Packton.
4 May 12 Car. One close called Little Thorne Close on the south of Tyle Close.
By surrender of John Robinson and Elizabeth his wife. Fine 2s. od.

THOMAS PACKTON and Elizabeth his wife.
3 March 22 Car. One acre of meadow in Kirkless in Auckland.
By surrender of John Robinson and Elizabeth his wife. Fine 4d.
Rent for these two copies 5s. od.

ROBERT WILSON
19 July 17 Car. One messuage and one garden in Bondgate.
By surrender of John Adamson. Rent 2s. od. Fine 6d.

CUTHBERT WHITFIELD
28 September 13 Car. One house and one garden in Bondgate late Edward Stobb's and Raphe Sheetly.
By surrender of Simon Sheatley. Fine 4d.
10 October 4 Car. One close of Meadow bounded by a close called Whinny Close on the east pt. and a close called Coundon Oxe Close on the south and a close late in the tenure of Richard Thompson on the north parcell of 6 acres of land next Sheapethorne.
By surrender of Richard Hawside. Fine 2s. 6d.
Rent for these two copies 5s. od.

JOHN WARDE
25 April 13 Car. One parcell of lands called Long Lands Riding lying on the south parte of the king's highway at the end of Newgate.
By surrender of Richard Badley.
Rent 7s. od. Fine 6s. 8d.

RICHARD LANGHORNE and NICHOLAS HARPERLEY
11 October 12 Car. One cottage on the east of a tenement of William Colson alias Colmore.
By surrender of Anthony Moorman. Rent 2s. od. Fine 2s. od.

JOHN ADAMSON
15 November 5 Car. One close containing 4 acres of land lying between a close called school bankes on the east and the Church way on the west, a close called Thorney Close on the north and a close called

Small Thorney Close on the south (parcell of 7½ acres of land).

By surrender of John Adamson his father. Fine 3s. 4d.

4 May 12 Car. 2 acres of meadow lying in the church lees within the territories of Bondgate between the lands of John Trotter on the west and the Church way on the east, the lands of Elizabeth Robinson on the south and the lands of the said John on the North.

By surrender of John Adamson his father. Fine 8d.

Rent for these two copies 1s. 4d.

KATHERINE WILSON

10 October 15 Car. One parcell of land lying at the west end of the towne of Bondgate containing in length 20 yards and in breadth 6 yards of land with a little house built thereupon.

In widdowright of Edward Wilson. Rent 2d. Fine 2d.

PEETER DIXON

14 October 6 Car. One parcell of land lying at the west end of Bondgate nigh the Comon Park there containing in length 80 yds. and in breadth 14.

By surrender of Lindley Wrenne Esq. Rent 5s. od. Fine 1s. 8d.

WILLIAM DARCY, Knt.

19 June 17 Car. 12 acres of land in Moore Close also Wigton Walls.

By surrender of John Adamson. Rent 2s. 1d. Fine 3s. 4d.

ROBERT THOMPSON Clerk.

17 October 20 Jac. One messuage and two croftes in Bondgate.

By surrender of Edward Byland. Rent 2s. od. Fine 1s. od.

25 April 13 Car. One cottage by the demise of Margarett Jackson for 100 years.

By surrender of Edward Byland. Rent 1s. od. Fine 5d.

ISABELL WRIGHTE relict of Bryan Wrighte.

4 May 12 Car. 12 acres of pasture and one Rood and 8 perches parcell of a close called Moore Close lying on the North syde of the lands of Lindley Wrenne and of William Middleton on the east, the lands of Henry Boyle on the south, parcell of the said close.

By surrender of Richard Richardson, John Craddock, John Adamson and John Thompson. Fine 3s. 4d.

dat ut supra. Six acres of land in Moore Close also Whyton Walls lying on the North of Mr. Lindley Wrenne and the west of Tindall Lanning.

By surrender of Jane Middleton. Fine 6d.

Rent for these two copies 4s. 2d.

11 October 3 Car. 17 acres of land late Agnes Whykes, one messuage and 20 acres of land late Hugh Beswicke.

By surrender of William Lawe. Rent £1. 7s. 2d. Fine 3d.

THOMAS LANGSTAFFE and Margery his wife.

12 October 19 Jac. One tenement (one house with a garden parcell of the premises late in the occupation of widdow Braine).

By surrender of Bryan Wrighte. Fine 3s. 6d.

25 April 13 Car. 4 acres and (blank) of pasture parcell of a close called Moore Close.

By surrender of Emanuell Grice. Fine 4d.

Rent for these two copies 3s. 6d.

1 October 11 Car. 4 acres of pasture being parcell of a close called Moore Close also Whyton Walls lying on the south of the way called Long Lanning.

By surrender of Richard Richardson, John Craddock, John Adamson and John Thomson. Rent 1s. 0d. Fine 4d.

Mem. here wants an entry to make this rent of Thomas Langstaffe 9s. 2d.

AUCKLAND TOWNSHIP LEASEHOLDS

JOHN HODGSON

25 April 18 Car. One close called the Haver Close adjoyning upon the South side of North Auckland Park late in the tenure of William Slater. And 2 parcells of meadow in Coundon called Ettle Meadow and Bishops Meadow. And also one parcell of meadow in West Auckland Field called Hulberke or Bishops Meadow late in the tenure of John Baines.

For the lives of William Brasse son of Cuthbert Brasse of Flashe in Co. Durham. John Strangewich sone of John Strangewich of Newcastle upon Tyne gent. and Anne Smith the daughter of Edward Smith of Bishop Auckland saddler.

Rent £3. 0. 8. Improvement £16. 19. 4.

BRYAN WALKER son and heir of Raphe Walker.
19 December 1 Jac. Water corne mill called the West Mill.
   For the lives of Brian Walker now 60 yrs. John Walker now 50
and Raphe Walker now 47.
next folio (ff32) missing

Sir GEORGE TONGE, Sir PAULE NEALE, JOHN WILKIN-
SON, Gent.
19 September 15 Car. All the coales and mynes of coal on Hunwicke
Moore, Etherley Moore, Moore Close, Escombe hirst, the town
fields of Escomb, Newton and Newton Cap And also on or in the
following vizt. From that side of Newton Bridge towards Auckland
up the River Wear to the West Milne from thence to the head of
Etherley Dene boundering, on a hedge that parteth certain closes
vizt. Snaylescroft and the West Mill Batts And so from thence to
Moore Close House boundering of a hedge that parteth certein
closes belonging to Etherley and Etherley Moore and from Moore
Close house up a loaning to Tindall Houses which loaning or highway leadeth to Fielden Bridge and from Tindall House up the loaning to the Green Field which highway leadeth to Raley Fell and from
Greenefield to Bolts Burne at the south of Bolts Fyne boundering
on a hedge that parteth the severall groundes of Moore Close, Escombe hirst Bolts Fyne, and Raley Fell. And from Bolts Burn
along to Witton Parke boundering on a hedge that parteth Escombe
Carr and Reyley Fell aforesaid and downwards from Raley Fell to
the river of Weare running along Whitton Pale and then over the said
river of Weare downwards to a hedge that parteth Escombe Haugh
and the grounds of Lord Eure belonging to Bitchburne and far along
that hedge to a little Beck called Bitchburne Beck and up the said
Beck to a house called the Smiddy and from the said house to the
upper ends of Wrightes Fine Boundering on a hedge that parteth
certaine Fynes or coppyhold lands belonging to the Lord Bishop
now in the occupation of Raiphe Greene and the groundes of the
said Lord Eure belonging to Bitchburne aforesaid late in the tenure
William Greene and from Wrightes Fine, up the Beck called
Bitchburne Beck to a place called Grayes bank and from thence to a
gate called Ridding gate boundering on a hedge which parteth the
said Hunwicke Moore and the several grounds of Rumby Loaning,

Akes Rawe and Holmden and then to Hunwick Town end boundering on a hedge that parteth the said Hunwicke Moore and certain
closes called Tomb Close the Whinnes and Blakeley Hill and so
along from Hunwick Town ende to the south ende of Parke Close
boundering on a hedge that parteth Pkes Close crowes field and the
Coppyhold lands called Picksley Hills and then from the south end
of Parke Close downe to the River Weare boundering on the South
ende of Birtley Woods and so up along the said river of Wear on the
north and west to Newton Bridge aforesaid. And also all the coales
etc. from Thickley Moore alias Brisleton Moore, Redworth Moor
and the Coppihold grounds of West Thickley thereunto adjoyning.

For the Lives of Sir Paule Neale—living, John Wilkinson and of
William—living, Tonge, son of Sir George Tonge—the third life
doubtful.

Rents. For Thickley Moore, Redworth Moore and the coppyhold
ground Rent £3. os. od.

For Hunwicke Moore, Etherley Moore, etc. Rent £3. os. od.

And also deliverying yearly betwixt the feasts of the Annuncia-
tion and St. Peter ad Vincula, One hundred fother of coales at such
of the said Mynes and pitts as shall be wrought

The confirmation of the Dean and Chapter 27 February 1639.

The New working upon Hunwick Moore improvement
£30. os. od.

The New working upon Etherley Moore improvement £10. os. od

ARTHURE PHILLIPS
10 February 17 Car. The office of Bailiff of the Manor and Borough
of Bishop Auckland receiving yearly £5. Confirmed by the Dean
and Chapter of Durham 21 July 18 Car Anno 1642.

RICHARD BOWSER
10 October 19 Car. The office of Steward of the Borough Court o
North Auckland receiving yearly 26s. 8d.

HENRY BLACKESTON
6 October 10 Car. The office of Keeper of Birtley Wood with a fe
of 1 penny. Confirmed by the Dean and Chapter 7 October 10 Car

HENRY HODSHON
10 September 10 Car. Pallicer of Auckland Park and to receive th

usual fees. Confirmed by the Dean and Chapter 10 October 10 Car.

dat ut supra. The office of Keeper of Auckland Park and to receive three pence per diem (£4. 11. 3. per annum). Confirmed by the Dean and Chapter 10 October 10 Car.

HENRY BAYLES

7 May 9 Car. who assigned the lease to William Richardson 19 March 11 Car. Eight pasture gates in the moore close also Whyton Walls belonging to the town of Bishop Auckland. And four acres of waste ground lying within the township of Escomb.

For 21 years.

Rent £12. 0. 3. Improvement £3. 8. 0.

Mem That 4s. of this rent is returned by the Collector of Escomb.

JOHN WATSON, THOMAS WALTON and JOHN ROBERTS

10 June 5 Car. One parcell of waste groundes in or near Bishop Auckland situate and being about 40 yards above one of the ould walk mill steads and about 20 yards below the ould walk millstead with free liberty to erect one walk mill or fulling mill thereupon or near the water of Wear upon the northwest side of Bishop Auckland. For 21 years. The consideration given for the said lease that the tenants should build a new in liew of the ould walk mill. The lord is to provide timber and the tenants to find workmanship and all other materials.

Rent £4. 0. 0. Improvement £40. 0. 0.

JANETT WILSON widow of Lancellot Wilson.

5 November 7 Car. One close of pasture lying neer unto the west end of North Auckland one close of meadow lying on the eastside of the highway leading to the parish church of Auckland and 8½ acres of meadow in the Kirk Lees all which are formerly called Escheator lands and Booker Land late in the tenure of Gregory Butler and Henry Bayle and then in the tenure of Lancellot Willson.

For 21 years.

Rent £2. 9. 7. Improvement £7. 10. 8.

JOHN ROBINSON

7 March 17 Car. who assigned the lease to John Allenson 28 July 14 Car. One close called Whinny alias Robsons Close lying and being near Coundon Moore on the north and king's street on the east on

the west a parcell of ground now in the tenure or occupation of Thomas Parkin and on the south Coundon.

For 21 years.

Rent 10s. od. Improvement £2. o. o.

JOHN and EMANUELL GRICE sons of Emanuell Grice.

6 October 11 Car. Water corne milne called Burne Mill nigh unto Auckland set upon the Gaunless. Together with one close of meadow called Hall Meadow adjoyning upon the south west end of Newgate within the fields of Bondgate. Together with grass yearly both winter and summer time in Auckland Park for one carriage horse for the said mill so that the said horse do not depasture or feed within the hedges or rayles of the hagge of or near Auckland Park.

For 21 years. The tenants are to fetch and carry all the corn and grayn which the lord of the manor shall require within the Mannor house of Bishop Auckland and to grind the same moulture free.

Rest £6. o. o. Improvement £30. o. o.

KING JAMES

14 January 1 Jac. who assigned the lease to Sir Dudley Carleton, who assigned to Edward Easton of Greys Inn 22 June 5 Jac., who asigned to Sir William Bellasis 22 February 5 Jac., who assigned to William Greene of Saxton Co. Ebor., who assigned to Francis Wrenn the elder of Henknowle co. Durham 20 December 6 Jac., who assigned to Thomas Robson and John Martindell 19 September 1 Car., who assigned to Lindley Wrenne, Esq., 28 June 2 Car.

All those messuages called Woodhouse Close and Brakes nigh Bishop Auckland.

To King James for 80 years.

Rent £8. o. o. Improvement £33. o. o.

Sir GEORGE TONGE, Sir PAUL NEALE, and JOHN WILKINSON

19 September 15 Car. All the coals and mynes of coals within the copyhold grounds of Bondgate in Auckland.

For 21 years.

Rent 10s. od. Confirmed by the Dean and Chapter 17 February 1639. There is yet no coals wrought.

These persons hereafter named are occupiers of houses and lands within the aforesaid township and are charged with the insewing rents and have produced no evidence for us.

Brass Tomas		9	Pecton Thomas		10
Craddock John	7	6	Richardson Richard	8	4
Craddock Margery		10	Rainshaw George		6
Hodgshon Raiphe		8	Robson Mergery		3
Hodgshon Thomas	1	8	Wharton James	1	0
Key William	14	5	Wright Stephen	1	0
Painter John		6	Walton William	2	0
Parkinge Thomas	3	0	Walker Raiphe	2	11
			Walker Bryan	1	8

Borough di Auckland

These severall persons hereafter named held by coppie of court roll do pay the severall and particular rents and fines hereafter mentioned for and in consideration of their possessing of their several and respective Burgages within the said Borough *vizt*

Fine		Rent	Fine		Rent
2.	Atkinson John	2	1.0.	Middleton Margery	3
2.	Atkinson William	3	1.0.	Nelson George	8½
2.0.	Apedale Cuthbert	3		Noble Dorothie	3
2.0.	Addamson Anthony	½		Nelson Henry	3
2.0.	Addamson John	4½		Parkin Raphe	3
2.0.	Auckland Joseph	4½	1.0.	Pemberton Michael	3
1.6.	Allinson John	4½	4.0.	Pearson Ellinor	1
1.0.	Addamson Thomas	½	2.0.	Parker Isabell	½
1.0.	Addamson Jannett	½	2.0.	Portis George	3
1.0.	Addamson Elizabeth	½	2.0.	Richardson William	6
2.0.	Addamson Ann	½	1.0.	Richardson Hugh	3
2.0.	Addamson Anthony	½	4.0.	Richardson Dorothie	6
2.0.	Bamforth Richard	3	2.0.	Robinson John	1
1.0.	Bowcer Richard	3	1.0.	Robert John	½
	Baker Robert	½	2.0.	Robson Anthonie	1
2.0.	Bradford Robert	½		Robinson Frances	9
	Burlinson George	½	2.0.	Rainforth Thomas	½
2.0.	Bayles Symond	3	1.0.	Robson John	3

Fine		Rent	Fine		Rent
2. o.	Bitton William	½	4. o.	Sparke Anne	3
2. o.	Brasse William &		1. o.	Spencely William	3
	Amos	4½	1. o.	Stainabank Francis	3
	Comine Andrew	3		Simpson William	3
1. o.	Crofte James	3		Smith Edward	3
2. o.	Curry William	3	1.	Sober Christopher	½
	Clarke widdow	½	1. o.	Stobbs Anthony	1
3. o.	Curry Anthonie	9	1. o.	Stephenson Jane	3
	Clarke Thomas	3	2. o.	Simpson William	3
	Coxshawe Richard	1		Stoddart Christopher	3
2. o.	Clerke Thomas	3	2. o.	Smithson Dorothie	3
	Chantury the ladies	2. 10.	2. o.	Todd Elizabeth	3
2. o.	Clerke Edwards	½		Taylor Francis	6
2. o.	Dawson Richard	3	2. o.	Thomson John	3
	Dennison Isabell	½	2. o.	Thomson John	3
	Darvis Richard	3	4. o.	Todd Richard	6
2. o.	Eastgate Anthony	3	2. o.	Thomson Robert	6
1. o.	Eastgate John	3	1. o.	Tallentire John	3
2. o.	Ferin Magdalen	½	2. o.	Vincent Robert	½
2. o.	Garry John	3		Wren Lindley	6
	Gills John	3	1. o.	Wren Francis	½
2. o.	Grice Emanuell	4½	2. o.	Whitfield Cuthbert	2
1. o.	Grindon Mary	3		Idem	3
	Garney John	3	3. o.	Walker Raphe	7½
6. o.	Grice Susan	1½		Wright Stephen	3
1. o.	Garry John	3	2. o.	Walton William	3
2. o.	Heavieside Richard	3		Wordie	4½
2. o.	Headon John	3	2. o.	Warde William	6
2. o.	Hodgson Isabell	½		Wright Stephen	3
2. o.	Hedley John	½	1. o.	Walton Thomas	3
	Hoddison	½	1. o.	Willoughby George	½
2. o.	Headon Thomas	½	1. o.	Willoughby George	½
	Harrison George	½	2. o.	Wilson Anne	½
8. o.	Heaviside Richard	3	2. o.	Wharton James	½
4. o.	Johnson Robert	½	2. o.	Wigon Tymothie	½
	Lawson Peeter	3	1. o.	Watson John	½
	Langstaffe Thomas	3	1. o.	Wetherell John	½
2. o.	Locke John	3	1. o.	Idem	½
	Laxe John	1	2. o.	Wright John	3

Fine		Rent	Fine		Rent
4. 0.	Lawe George	3		Wetherell Richard	½
	Longhome Richard	3	2. 0.	Wright Robert	3
	Langstaffe Richard	3		Walker John	½
	Liddell William	½	2. 0.	Wharton James	½
	Longstaffe sen. John	½		Walton Thomas	3
	Longstaffe jun. John	½	1. 0.	Whitfield John	3
	Longstaffe Thomas	3	4. 0.	Ward John	2
	Middleton William	3	2. 0.	Whitfield Cuthbert	3

These persons hereafter named pay the several rents following the name of Brewing Rent.*

Arundell wid.	Eastgate Anthony	Shorte wid.
Atkinson John	Gibbon Robert	Stobbs wid.
Apedale Cuthbert	Grindell wid.	Stainbank
Adamson John	Heddon John	Thomson Henry
Bullmer William	Hutchinson wid.	Thomson John
Bainbridge Anthony	Heaviside wid.	Todd Richard
Bankes	Johnson Robert	Whitfield William
Bayles Symon	Langthorne Richard	Wright wid.
Curry Anthony	Larkey wid.	Walton William
Clayton John	Nelson Christopher	Walby Thomas
Downes wid.	Perton Thomas	Whorton James
Dawson Sam.	Robinson wid.	Ward wid.
Dawson John	Sparke wid.	Wren John

* (2d. each)

Richard Heaviside by indenture dated 18 July 15 Car. holds the common bakehouse and common oven in Bishop Auckland for 21 years, paying £1. 6. 8. rent.

Byers Green Township Copyholds

JANE ROBINSON
10 October 9 Jac. One messuage and 12½ acres of land.
   As widow relict of John Robinson. Rent 9s. 6d. Fine 3s. 4d.

MARGERY WALKER, daughter of John Walker now wife of Francis Taylor.

1 October 12 Car. One close called Charwell rice late John Walker's Rent 4s. 2d. Fine 3s. 4d.

HENRIE HALL
9 October 12 Car. One acre of meadow lying in Haysett parcell of a cottage and 7 acres of land and one other acre of land in the said close and 2 butts or rigg ends of lands.
   By surrender of Raphe Wrighte. Rent 1s. 8d. Fine 8d.

JOHN CALVERLIE
15 April 5 Car. One messuage with a crofte and 15 acres of lands the same belonging.
   By surrender of Stephen Hedge. Rent 14s. od. Fine 14s. 3d.

ANN, MARGARETT, ELIZABETH, JANE and ADALENA, JACKSON, daughters and co-heirs of Margarett Jackson defunct.
10 October 4 Car. The fourth part of one messuage and the fourth part of 29 acres of land called Parke Land which was late the land of Margarett Jackson their mother.
   Rent 5s. 8d. Fine 5s. od.

MARIE TAYLOR married now to ——— Emerson, relict of Thomas Trotter.
8 September 21 Car. One parcell of land called Grayes House.
   Late her husband's. Rent 5s. 6d. Fine 1s. 8d.

THOMAS EMERSON
7 May 9 Car. One cottage lyeing between the tenement of Thomas Walker on the one part and a tenement of John Wright on the other.
   By surrender of John Ettringham. Rent 1s. 8d. Fine 1s. od.

ROWLAND WHITE
11 October 14 Car. One messuage and 6 acres of land in the said town as heir to his father Robert Whyte. Fine 2s. od.
   dat ut supra. 1½ acres of land in High Side parcell of 15 acres as heir to his father Robert Whyte. Fine 2s. 6d.
   dat ut supra. One cottage called Lockies House with a gardein cont 3 acres and also a garden called Stockgarth and also with a house called Clarkhouse also 2½ acres of lands called Highside one parcell of land called the walles cont 2 acres in the town aforesaid.

By surrender of John Ettringham and Margarett his wife. Fine 4s. 8d.

Rent for all three copies 9s. 3d.

ELIZABETH WHITE

15 October 22 Jac. One close called Gate Close and Gateclose Green cont 4 acres parcell of the whole tenure (vizt) of 2 cottages and 12 acres of lands with houses thereupon now built which were late belonging to Laurence White defunct.

Fine 8d.

dat ut supra. One messuage and the halfe of a garden to the same belonging and 2 acres (vizt) one acre lying in the Spont haugh and another acre lying in the Highside neer South Dike one parcell of land called the Burnes cont 1 rood seed.

Fine 1d.

dat ut supra. One acre of lands lying in the side which was her late husbands. Fine 1s. od. These three copies in widdowright of Laurence White, and paying rent 5s. 10d.

BRIAN CAIRESLEY

2 coppies and 5 acres of lands

As heir to his father Robert Cairsely. Rent 3s. 0½d. Fine 3s. 4d.

RICHARD HOPPER

28 September 13 Car. The 4th part of 29 acres, one rood of land.

As heir of Richard Hopper and Anne, Richard's wife. Rent 5s. 8½d. Fine 3s. 4d.

WILLIAM HOPPER

11 May 18 Jac. The 4th part of one messuage and the 4th part of one rood of land and the 4th part of 29 acres of land called the Parkes land.

By surrender of Wm. Pearson and Jane his wife. Rent 5s. 8½d. Fine 4s. od.

JOHN WALKER

1 October 11 Car. One messuage and 24 acres of land.

As son and heir of Bryan Walker. Fine 6s. 8d.

BRYAN WALKER, son of Raphe Walker relict.

6 May 4 Car. One messuage and 14 acres of land.
   Fine 6s. 8d. Rent for both these copies £1. 17. 4.

WILLIAM SHAWE

15 October 10 Jac. One cottage and 6 acres of land late Wm. Graye's, one cottage and 6 acres of land called Parks land, one peece of land cont 14 rodds in length and 6 in breadth and one acre of land called Langarth
   As son and heir of Seith Shawe. Fine 12s. od.
   dat ut supra. One cottage and 5½ acres of land.
   As son and heir of Seith Shawe. Fine 2s. od.
   dat ut supra. One cottage and a certein parcell of land called Nuttinghagge, 1 acre of lands in Highside with one rood of land and 2 butts or selions lying together in Todhills, ½ acre of meadow in Eastcrofte, 7 buttes or selions in Sponthaugh and ½ acre and 3 selions in Grumwellside as they lie together on the north part.
   As son and heir of Seith Shawe. Fine 10s. od.

IDEM, with Janett his wife.

15 October 10 Jac. Fifthe part of one messuage, the fifth part of a rood of land and the fifth part of 29 acres of land called Parkeland.
   By surrender of William Corneforth. Fine 2s. od. Rent for all these coppies £1. 12. 10.

ELIZABETH TROTTER, late wife of Roger Taylor.

1 June 40 Eliz. One messuage and one husbandland which were late John Trotter's, surrendered to Thomas Hull, who surrendered to John Trotter and Elizabeth his wife, for their lives and paid 5s. od fine, and after their decease to the use of Roger Taylor deceased and Elizabeth daughter of the said John Trotter for their lives.
   Rent 19s. od. Fine 10s. od.

MARIE JOHNSON and ANN JOHNSON

20 January 22 Car. One messuage and one husbandland
   By surrender of Tho. Johnson. Rent 10s. 6d. Fine 6s. 8d.

CHARLES MARTINDALE

23 April 10 Car. 1 cottage and 7 acres of land and 1 acre of land lying at Highside before granted excepted.
   By surrender of George Martindale his father. Fine 6s. 8d.

IDEM and Elizabeth his wife.

9 May 14 Car. 1½ acres of lands called Cornehill (parcell of the 4th part of one messuage and the 4th part of one rood of land and of the 4th part part of 9 acres of a husbandland called Parkeland)

>By surrender of William Shawe and Jane his wife. Fine 6s. 4d.
>
>Rent for both these coppies 8s. 4d.

GEORGE TROTTER

1 October 12 Car. 1 acre of land on the south end of Byersgreene.

>By surrender of John Ettringham and Margarett his wife. Fine 2d.
>
>Rent 8d.

JOHN WALKER

22 October 44 Eliz. One close of meadow called Sponthaugh containing 2 acres of land parcell of the whole tenement and of 12 acres of land.

>By surrender of William Brasse. Rent 2s. od. Fine 1s. 4d.

GEORGE MARKINDALE

10 October 14 Jac. One parcell of land late belonging to a parcell of land called Park place (one little house and a close called the burne a close containing 1 acre parcell of the premises excepted).

>Fine 4s. 4d.

MARIE WHITE

One house and one close called the burne containing 1 acre parcell of the land late belonging to a parcell of land called Park (excepted in the former coppie).

>Fine 8d. Both these copies by surrender of Michael Farrer and Anne his wife, and paying rent 13s. 10d.

Byers Green Township Leaseholds

QUEEN ELIZABETH

15 October 23 Eliz. who assigned the lease to Geo. Frevile Esq. 1 June 28 Eliz., who bequeathed it to his wife Dame Elizabeth, who bequeathed it to Thomas Jennyson her brother, who assigned to Gilbert Frevile 6 December 6 Car.

A parcell of land called by the name of Bishops Closes.

To Queen Elizabeth for 80 years.

Rent £8. 0. 0. Improvement £38. 0. 0.

Mem There is a parcell of land in the said town called Newfield or Hermeth Hugh lying upon Byers Moore containing 40 acres being late the estate of the Earle of Westmoreland currently held of the Bishop. It is now held by George Courtpenny from his Majesty, but payeth rent to the Bishop 12s. 0d.

Robert Ridlington holdeth in free and common socage the Copihold messuage called Ould Hall alias Ould Park, with all houses and buildings thereto belonging, also somer close containing 44 acres, oxe close containing 15 acres, a close called Wheatefield containing 14 acres and one close called Ivefield or Knightfield containing 90 acres of land, also two closes called Two Loughs and wawmires field containing 50 acres, one close called Freelees containing 6 acres by a graunt from Henry Richardson and Christopher Biers as by a fine and corobery dat 27 July 6 Car. for which he payeth per annum £4. 0. 0.

Lindley Wrenne payes a fine rent of 6s. 0d. per annum but he sayes he knows not for what he payes it nor can we learn for what he paies it.

Coundon Township Freehold

ROBERT HASTLEY

15 February 6 Car. In fee farm from John Parkin who held the same by deed from George Warde dated 27 October 17 Jac., who held the same by letters patent from his majesty dated 25 July 5 Jac. (vizt) All that tenement or cottage with a garth late in the tenure of Robert Walles and then in the tenure of John Parkin with 3 acres of arable lands meadow or pasture vizt 1 acre lying in a place called Tepper Myres, and 2 acres lying at High Flawlyes within the towne of Coundon adjoyning neer unto west Merrington grounds, paying yearly to his Majesty 5s. 0d., and to the Bishop 1s. 0d.

Coundon Township Customary Tenants

William Pearson holdeth a farme or parcell of lands for which he payeth rent £2. 1. 10. worth upon improvement £15. 0. 0.

Richard Hopper holdeth certein lands for which he payeth £1. 12. 4½., worth upon improvement £13. 0. 0.

Cuthbert Hopper holdeth certeine lands for which he payeth £1. 17. 0., worth upon improvement £14. 0. 0.

Thomas Parkin holdeth certein lands and pays £1. 13. 11., worth upon improvement £12. 0. 0.

William Parkin holdeth certein lands and payeth £1. 13. 10., worth upon improvement £12. 0. 0.

James Sheraton holdeth certein lands and payeth 10s. od., worth upon improvement £4. 0. 0.

We have not seen any deeds or writings concerning these particulars nor have the tenants any as they pretend nor ever had.

Mem We find no entry on the Hallemot Court Roll nor any Memorandum in the Chancery or other writings whatsoever to convince or persuade as the verity of this challenge of the said tenants for customary estates in the abovesaid lands heretofore we rated the same after the improvement above writed and do opiniate that the pretended tenancies be meerely arbitrary and at the Lord's will.

Coundon Township Copyholds

CHARLES MARTINDALE

9 May 15 Car. The east part of the mansion house late in the tenure of George Cooke and 6 acres called the Whelad and 4 acres of land in the north part of Auckland and the land of John Lang on the east and the land of Thomas Parkin on the south and the lands called Haver Closes on the west and the lands called the west close cont 6 acres of land and one stackgarth parcell of a messuage and one husband land.

By surrender of George Martindale and Mary his wife. Rent 12s. od. Fine 5s. od.

THOMAS PARKIN son and heir of Thomas Parkin.

19 November 22 Car. One messuage and one husband land in which Elizabeth Parkin has widdowright.

By surrender of Elizabeth Parkin. Rent 3s. 1d. Fine 5s. od.

JANE PARKIN wife of Wm. Parkin, relict of Thomas Lang.
3 November 16 Car. One messuage and garden, one acre of meadow
lying at the end of the garden, ½ acre of land in the Free Noke,
and acre on the Toft, ½ acre in the Lease, ½ acre upon Ettle, ½
acre upon Drydon, ½ acre upon Fryer's Flatt and 2 closes containing 6 acres and ½ acre of land enclosed called the East Close in the
North Field. 2 acres upon Martin Peece, 2 acres upon Smith side
in the Middle Field, 1½ acres in Howletch, one acre upon the
Towne, pasture for two beasts in the West field and comon of pasture for all cattle and forage for 15 beasts in the Foggage, and all
other lands and tenements.

In widdowright. Fine 6d.

dat ut supra. 2 acres of land within the territory of Coundon lying
on the east of the land of Richard Baddely, on the west and south
of the land of William Parkin, on the north of the land of Anthony
Pearson. And also one rood of land lyeing on the east of the meadows
of Coundon and on the west of the free tenement of Thomas Pearson,
and on the north of the land of Richard Baddeley.

In widdowright. Fine 4d.

21 September 22 Car. One cottage with the garth belonging to it, and
6 acres of land arable lying in the several fields of Coundon, and
one acre of meadow more or less.

In widdowright. Fine 6d. Rent for all these coppies, £1. 1. 6.

KATHERINE BROWNE

2 February 22 Car. The south end of a barne adjoining to the mansion house of John Hopper and now in the tenure of John Coaforth
with one parcell of land at the south end of the same barne containing 6 rodds in length and 6 in breadth. And also 3 acres of arable land
in 3 several fields of Coundon parcell of 4 acres of land arable, vizt.
5 selions or riggs of land lying in the Eastfield, in a certein place
called Easell, 2 selions in Smithside in the Middlefield of Coundon
and 4 selions of land in Howlidge in the south field, and pasture for
2 beaste upon the common moor, and pasture for one beast in the
former foggage, and one other beast in the Latter Fogage of the
town there and pasture for one hogg.

As widdow of Thomas Browne defunct. Fine 6d.

23 April 13 Car. One barne with a little garden called the Killgarthes
end and 3 acres of land arable of which one acre lyes at the Toft in
the North Field, one acre lyeth at the wheale laire in the west field,

one acre lyeth at the Smitheside in the Middle Field and also one acre of meadow called the towne end close with pasture for one horse two kine and a halfe and 5 sheep.

As widdow of Thomas Browne defunct. Fine 3s. od.

WILLIAM BROWNE
7 May 22 Jac. The halfe of one Cottage late Martin Richardson's
    By surrender of Wm. Browne. Fine 2d.
    Rent for these three copies 13s. 6d.

THOMAS PARKIN
13 October 42 Eliz. One acre of land meadow lying in Coundon.
    As heir to his father Thomas Parkin. Rent 1s. od. Fine 1s. od.
24 March 17 Jac. 3 Barnes with a garden thereto belonging. 3 acres of arable land lying in the 3 severall fields of Coundon one acre of lands lying in Low Drithop in the North field betweene the lands of Agnes Parker on the East John Long on the west another acre of land lying at Smithsyde in the Middle Field betweene the land of Henry Sharp on the east and Thomas Parkin junior on the west. Pasture for 4 beast in Coundon oxe pasture for two beasts in Coundon Moore 2 beast gates in the Foggage of the Towne parcell of the whole tenure.
    By surrender of Nicholas Forrest. Fine 12s. od.
    Rent for these two copies 10s. od.

THOMAS PARKIN junior.
11 May 18 Jac. One close called Wheate land containing one acre of land, one acre of meadow adjoyning the Easte parte of the same close and halfe of one rodd of arable land adjoyning to the end of the same meadow.
    By surrender of Richard Parkin. Rent 11d. Fine 6d.

THOMAS ROBINSON
One little house and one parcell of a garden containing in breadth 8 rodds of land being parcell of a messuage with appurtenances.
    As heir to Nicholas Robinson. Rent 6d. Fine 6d.

JOHN GARVIE
9 June 21 Car. Two acres of land, one at Pearebank the other in Holridge parcell of 6 acres of land and 2 acres of meadow lying in Coundon.

By surrender of Thomas Colson. Fine 8½d.

2 May 11 Car. One close called Crossehope Carr adjoyning to a close called Crossopp on the West parte late in the occupation of Thomas Browne containing 7 acres of land also 1 acre of land lying in Free Flatt.

By surrender of James Parker. Fine 10d.

12 April 17 Jac. One house called Topleggs with a garden

By surrender of Robert Parking. Fine 6d.

dat ut supra. 3 roods of lands lying in 3 several fields and pasture for 1 house.

By surrender of Robert Parking. Fine 4d.

Rent for these four copies 5s. 8d.

RICHARD HOPPER

27 October 17 Jac. One acre of land in a field of Coundon lying at Crawley Bank and one close called Wardoesend Close and pasture for 1 horse in the faugh and averidge and pasture for two beasts in the Foggage.

By surrender of Thomas Colson. Rent 3s. 4½d. Fine 2s. od.

SAMUELL HOPPER

12 October 18 Car. One garden called Londonston garthes late devided into 2 closes.

By surrender of Thomas Hopper. Rent 3s. 4d. Fine 4d.

WILLIAM PARKIN

19 November 22 Car. One close of meadow lying between the Comon Moore called Coundon Moore on the north and a close called Pollard Brack on the west and a close called Whinny Close on the south and east and a parcell of 6 acres of land.

As son and heir of Thomas Parkin. Rent 3s. od. Fine 5d.

FRANCES HEIGHINGTON

23 April 14 Car. One house with 2 gardens.

By surrender of John Colson and Jane his wife. Rent 1d. Fine 6d.

THOMAS COLSON

29 October 16 Jac. One house or chamber with a garden and 6 acres of arable land and 2 acres of meadow lying in the severall fields of Coundon vzt. 1 acre of lands lyeing at Crawley Banck, another

acre of land at Parsons Peece, another at Jackley peece, another at Holridge another at Smithside another at Wellestofte another at Laymes well head and pasture for two beasts in Warlehead Close, pasture for 4 beaste upon the Comon Moore and pasture for a horse in the Faugh at Tothaugh and pasture for one calfe in Crossehop Carr And pasture for 10 sheep in the Moore and Faugh and pasture for one hogg late the lands of Henry Harper attained for felling.

Rent 3s. 2d. Fine 4s. 6d.

Mem Colson confessed he gave the Bishop £60 for a fine.

MARGARET KNAGGS
One house late in the occupation of Elizebeth Coultman wife of Cuthbert Coultman who held the same by surrender of Robert Laing.
Rent 2d. Fine 2d.

THOMAS PARKIN
11 May 18 Jac. Pasture for 2 beasts in the Westfield.
By surrender of Richard Parkin. Rent 10d. Fine 1s. 1d.

ROBERT HASTLEY
9 May 15 Car. Pasture for 2 beasts and half of one pasture for one beast upon the Moore.
By surrender of Anthony Pearson. Rent 4d. Fine 4d.

RAPHE SHORTE
30 April 16 Jac. One messuage or tenement with one oxehouse and garden joyning to the backside with free ingress and egress to go to a close called Rawe Crofte and one parcell of meadow lying neere the west pasture dike in the meadow of the said Towne of Coundon on the North of the Towne and also 3 acres of arrable lands in 3 severall fields and pasture for 1 horse the Averridge and Foggage for 10 sheepe feeding with the sheep of the towne And also pasture for 2 other kine in the new pasture there feeding with the Averidge, and pasture for 1 sowe and 2 sellions of land lying at the end of the lees in the Eastfield of the Town, parcell of one messuage and one husband land.
By surrender of Thomas Parkin son of William Parkin. Rent 2d. Fine 4d.

RICHARD LANGE
12 October 18 Car. 10 acres of arable lands lyeing within the Towne

fields of Coundon (vizt) 2 acres of land upon Ettle and 2 acres in Tree Flatt in the North Field. Also 2 acres of land in Smithsyde in the Middlefield and 2 acres upon Long Flatt and one acre upon Cranley in the south field parcell of his tenure in Coundon.

By surrender of John Lange his father. Fine 6s. od.

dat ut supra. 1 acre of Meadow called Marleridge dale late in the occupation of the said John, pasture for 2 cows in the East field with Foggage for the same in the towne fields for two hoggs and 3 acres of arable land lying in the 3 several fields of Coundon (vizt) in every field one acre wch were late John Lang's the father.

By surrender of John Lange his father. Fine 6d.

dat ut supra. 3 cottages, one close call hilner roods and one garden and another garden called Backhouse Garth and another garden called the waste garth and 3 acres of land in 3 severall fields of Coundon (vizt) in every field one acre, also pasture for 2 beast in the new pasture, and pasture for 2 beasts in the out Moore, parcell of his whole tenure in Coundon.

By surrender of John Lange his father. Fine 4d.

Rent for these three copies 12s. 8d.

Allanson Raphe	Rent 6d.
Coatesworth John	Rent 3d.
Hodgshon John with other lands grannted by lease	Rent 6s. 8d.
Head Isabell	Rent 2d.
Lanze Thomas	Rent £1. 1s. 6d.
Parkin Thomas	Rent £3. 1s. od.
Pearson Richard	Rent 12s. od.
Pearson Thomas	Rent 11s. 9½d.

We have not seene any of these deedes (save only Hodgshon) or coppie or any writing whatsoever to manifest what these tenants hold by what tenure or wherefore they pay there rent.

Coundon Grange Township Leaseholds

GERRARD SALVIN

16 October 17 Car. Grainge, farme or tenement comonly called Coundon Grange late in the several tenures of Samson Eure of Gray's Inn and William Eure of Rachard Hill in Co. Durham.

For 21 years.

Rent £24. os. od. Improvement £106. os. od.

There is in the said lease a covenant that the said Gerrard shall repaire all hedges, sewers, watercourses, houses, buildings thereunto belonging. And to find one able horse and one horseman with sufficient Arms and apparell etc. to serve the Bishop upon the borders of England against Scotland for the said tenure.

Mem. This lease was taken in trust for the use of Mr. Thomas Bullock for two parts of three of the foresaid grainge, and of Mr. John Markindale for a third parte by assignment from the said Gerrard Salvin.

East Combe Township Copyholds

RICHARD TODD

2 May 14 Jac. 2 messuages with 2 gardens one close called the Hirst containing 19½ acres adjoyning to a close in the tenure of William Grice on the east of the Long Lanning on the south and by closes of William Trotter and George Moore on the west and west Lanning on the North parte also one other close called uper Crooke containing 5 acres butting upon the field on the east and the close of Christopher Pearson on the South and a house and a garden of George Downes on the west and the Weare butts on the North. Also one close called East field containing 27 acres butting upon a close of Christopher Pearson called Lambeside and Morebrow waste on the east and North the close of William Grice on the south and the close of William Trotter on the west, also one parcell of pasture called West haughe and Comon of pasture containing 19½ acres And 14 acres of land late William Grice now not to be divided.

By surrender of George Robinson and William Cooke. Fine £1. 3s. 4d.

19 June 21 Jac. One little close fenced with hedges in the occupacon of Rich Todd and Wm. Cooke containing 5 acres parcell of a close called West Field containing 22 acres.

By surrender of John Todd and Anne his wife. Fine 2s. od.

One messuage and garden in the occupation of Robert Nicholl one close called the Hirst containing 7 acres butting upon the East field and a close of Richard Hodgshon on the south and a close of William Grice west and Long Lanning on the north another close called the Middle Field Close containing 12 acres butting upon a garden and Long Lanning on the east and a close of Christian Colt gent on the south the close of Elizabeth Thomson on the west and the close of William Grice on the north And also one parcell of pasture called Westhaugh and comon of pasture containing 7 acres with Moores and Comons of pasture in Eastcombe.

Fine 6s. 8d.

THOMAS TODD son and heir of Richard Todd.

14 October 6 Car. One close called the Hirst containing 14 acres of land abutting on the several closes of Cuthbert Vasey, Richard Hodgson and Robert Nichols on the east, the Long Lanning on the south and north and the close of Richard Todd on the west. And one close called East field containing 26 acres of land butting on the East Moore on the east and south the closes of Robert Trotter and Richard Todd on the north.

By surrender of Richard Todd. Fine 2s. 10d.

Rent for these four copies £3. 5s. 7d.

MARGARET BROWNE

9 May 15 Car. One close of meadow containing 2 acres.

As heir of Gilbert Robinson. Rent 9d. Fine 3s. 4d.

MARTIN HARPER

10 October 5 Car. One messuage wth a garden adjoyning to the land of Richard Hodgson on the north and west and the Lanning lyeing to the towne fields and the lands of William Crooke on the south and the towne greene on the east with comon of pasture.

By surrender of John Colman. Rent 8d. Fine 6d.

ELIZABETH COOKE

22 April 16 Car. The north part of one close called West field containing 6 acres as it is now fenced and divided from the other parte of the same west field.

As widdow relict of Bryan Cooke. Fine 1s. 0d.

dat ut supra. 5 acres of arable lands in the Comon pasture called the Lawme Laine haugh and 2 acres of land lying in Westhaugh, parcell of half a husband land.

As widdow relict of Bryan Cooke. Fine 2s. 4d.

Rent for these two copies 5s. 4d.

BRIAN ATKINSON

2 May 15 Jac. One close containing 21½ acres called the Hirst lying between a close of Elizabeth Thomson's on the east and Lang Horne on the south, a close of John Todd's on the west and the comon on the north One other close called the west field containing 21 acres as lies between the close of the said Elizabeth Thompson on the east and the Comon Moore called West Free on the south and the comon pasture called the Carr on the west and north as it is now fenced and devided wth hedges And also one parcell lyeing in West haugh, and Comon of pasture containing 19 acres with moores and comons of pasture.

By surrender of George Robinson. Rent £1. 3s. 8d. Fine 3s. 4d.

Sir WILLIAM DARCIE Knt.

11 October 12 Car. 90 acres of land antiently enclosed now parcell of the east Parke of Witton.

By surrender of William Lord Eure and Raphe Eure his son and heir.

Fine £1. 10s. od.

dat ut supra. ½ acre of lands late the lord's waste nigh the park of Witton now enclosed.

By surrender of William Lord Eure and Raphe Eure his son and heir.

Fine 2d.

Rent for these two copies £1. 12s. 11d.

MARIE SUDDICK

3 April 22 Car. 2 messuages or tenements lying in Escomb with orchards and gardens and one close called Haughwell Close containing 12 acres lyeing between a close of Richard Hodgson on the east and a close of Elizabeth Thomson and Brian Bolt gent. on the south and west a close of Robert Nichols and Comon pasture called the Lawned on the north and west And also one parcell of pasture in Westhaugh and Comon of pasture containing 9 acres with moores and comon of pasture.

In widdowright relict of John Suddick. Rent 10s. 5d. Fine 2s. 6d.

GEORGE MOORE and Jane his wife.

2 May 13 Jac. One messuage with a garden adjoyning to the backside in the tenure of the said George and one backhouse built upon the

same One close lying in the East field of Estcomb called huds burne containing 9 acres 3 roods lying on the east of the comon lanning on the south of the close of Brian Bell gent called Divil Riding and on the west and south of the Close of William Trotter called East Close And also one other close called the Hirst cont. 5 acres 1 rodd lyeing on the west and south partes of the close of Richard Todd and on the east parte of a close of Christopher Pearson and 5 acres 1 rood lying in West haugh and Comon of pasture yett not fenced and divided wth moores and comons of pasture.

By surrender of George Robinson. Rent 8s. 1od. Fine 3s. 4d.

RAPHE ADDISON

5 June 5 Car. One messuage with a garden late in the occupation of John Thomson and one close called the Hirst containing 14 acres abutting upon a close of William Trotter east and upon Long Lanning south and a close of William Thomson west and on western lanning north And one other close called Middle field close containing 25 acres abutting on the closes of Cuthbert Vasey and Brian Bell south and west and the closes of John Suthwick, Richard Hodgson and William Grice north And also one parcell of pasture called west haugh and comon pasture containing 14 acres Moores and comon of pasture in Estcombe.

Rent £1. 4s. 4d. Fine 8s. 0d.

MARY TROTTER

1 May 10 Car. One messuage and garden late John Dalton and 7 acres and one rood of land parcell of a close called the Hirst containing 12 acres and 1 rood of land abutting on 2 severall closes of Richard Todd and Christopher Pearson lyeing on the East upon the west the lanning on the south. Also 12 acres of land and 3 rodds of land parcell of one other close called East field adjoyning to the house and garden containing 21 acres and 3 rodds of land abutting upon a close of Richard Todd on the east and a close of William Grice and the East field on the south 2 severall closes of Bryan West and George Moore on the west parke and the Mansian House and garden of the said William on the North parte. Also 7½ acres of land parcell of one parcell of pasture called West Haugh and Comon of pasture containing 12½ acres wth moore and comon of pasture.

As widdow relict of William Trotter. Fine 6s. 8d.

dat ut supra. One messuage and half of one husband land late of John Dalton.

As widdow relict of William Trotter. Fine 6s. 8d.

Rent for these two copies £1. 2s. 7d.

HENRIE HODGSON

27 April 11 Car. One close called the Hirst containing 12 acres abutting upon a close of Elizabeth Thomson's wife of John Thomson junior on the east the Long Loane on the south on a close of Brian Atkinson on the west and the west Lanninge north. One close called Middle field containing 12 acres abutting on a close of Brian Bolt on the east and north and the west loaning on the south And one other close called West Field close containing 24 acres and 3 roddes abutting on a close of John Todd on the east and the common moore on the south and a close of Brian Bolt on the west. And also one parcell of a certain pasture called west haugh and comon of pasture containing 14 acres of land with moores and comon of pasture.

Fine 8s. od.

WILLIAM THOMSON

8 September 13 Car. One parcell of land late the lord's waste containing one rood lyeing at the west end of Escomb Hirst neere the Moorehouse.

As son and heir of William Thomson. Fine 1d.

dat ut supra. ½ acre of land lyeing near the Oxefeild.

As son and heir of William Thomson. Fine 2d.

dat ut supra. The halfe of one messuage and garden and the half of 6½ acres of land called toward side late in the tenure of Anthonie Maddison.

As sone and heir of William Thomson. Fine 2s. od.

Rent for these three copies £1. 1s. 11d.

These persons hereafter named are coppieholders but brought not their coppies.

Atkinson Thomas	Fine 2d.
Hodgson Robert	Fine 11s. 10½d.
Shafto Mark	Fine £1. 6s. 5d.
Sayer Laurence	Fine 1s. 4d.
Shirfoote Robert	Fine 2s. 4d.
Todd William	Fine £1. 5s. 11½d.

ELIZABETH COOKE

3 April 22 Car. One messuage wth a garden adjoyning to the back-side containing by estimation 2 acres now in the tenure of Anthony Deanes gent. abutting upon the Mansion House of Robert Nichols on the east and the Comon Fields of Eastcombe on the south and west with one housestead (now decayed) and one parcell of land adjoyning to the same containing in length 29 rodds and in breadth at the east and 9 rodds and at the west and 9 rodds being on the south parte of the garden of Raphe Bayles in Estcombe.

By surrender of William Cookes. Rent 1s. 0d. Fine 6d.

THOMAS TODD and Cuthbert Todd his son.

28 October 11 Jac. The half of one messuage and of one garden and the half of 6½ acres of land called Woodside late in the tenure of Anthony Maddison.

By surrender of John Todd. Fine 1s. 6d.

dat ut supra. One parcell of land late the lord's waste lying on the west parte of the woodside containing 1 rood with a house built thereupon.

By surrender of John Todd. Fine 1d.

Rent for these two copies 1s. 7d.

ROBERT NICHOL and Margarett his wife.

[*no date*] One cottage and one barne and half the west end of a garden as it is now divided late in the occupation of William Nowe, Robert Nicholl and his wife and one close called Clubhill close containing 10 acres and 28 perches abutting upon the comon pasture east and the close of John Suddick south west on the close of John Todd and north on the pasture called Haugh.

Rent 2s. 5½d. Fine 3s. 4d.

ANTHONY TODD

10 October 5 Jac. The half of a messuage wth a garden adjoyning parcell of half of one messuage and halfe of one husband land.

By surrender of John Todd. Rent 9d. Fine 9d.

RAPHE TROTTER

19 June 21 Jac. One parcell of pasture called pasture haugh and common of pasture cont. 7 acres of land wth moore and comon of pasture.

By surrender of Robert Nicholls and Margery his wife. Fine 8d.
7 May 22 Jac. One tenement or messuage lying in Escombe wth
orchards and gardens betweene the land of Richard Hodgshon on
the west and the lands of Symon Birbeck on the east and the lands
called the Lawne on the north and the lands of Richard Hodgson.
By surrender of John Suddick. Fine 6d.
Rent for these two copies 2s. 2d.

ANN BAYLES late widdow now Anne Brasse.
[*no date*] One close called Estcomb haugh, one other close called
Coleswell containing 26 acres lying on the east and south upon the
water called Weare and upon the west banded with the lands of
John Suddick and upon the north upon the lands of Newton Cap.
In widdowright relict of Raphe Bailes. Rent 11s. 2d. Fine 6s. 2d.

CHRISTOPHER PEARSON and Margarett his wife.
2 May 14 Jac. One messuage and 2 gardens now in the occupation of
the said Christopher, and one close called the Hirst containing 5
acres and one rodd of land lyeing betweene the close of George
Moore on the east and the loaning on the south and the close of
William Trotter on the west and north, one other close called the
east field cont 9 acres and one rodd of land butting upon Lambside
and the close of Richard Todd on the south and west and also one
close of Brian Bolts on the north and also one parcell of pasture called
west haugh and comon of pasture containing 5 acres and one parcell
of land wth moores and comon of pasture in Escomb.
By surrender of George Robinson and William Cooke. Rent
8s. 10d. Fine 3s. 4d.

GEORGE WHITE
21 September 22 Car. One close called the Hirst containing 6 acres
of land butting upon the East Moore on est parte and the loaning
on the south and a close late William Grice on the west and a close
of Richard Hodgson on the north.
As son and heir of William White. Rent 3s. 0d. Fine 1s. 2d.

AGNES COOKE
15 April 6 Car. One close containing 2 acres of meadow called towne
land, more or less, with free ingrees egress and regresse to the close
parcell of a close called Naphill.

By surrender of Robert Nicholls and Margery his wife. Rent 1s. 0d.
Fine 8d.

RAIPHE EDEN gent and Elienor his wife.
27 November 21 Car. The third parte of one messuage and one garth
and one close called the Heilde containing 6 acres of land, the third
parte of one acre of land in the west haugh sometimes in the tenure of
Thomas Binchester and Cuthbert Harrison, the third parte of one
parcell of land containing 4 roods of lands formerly in the tenure of
Christopher Wrenne, the third parte of one messuage and one
croft called Edmonds Close containing one acre and one half rood of
land late in the tenure of Bryan Bolt and the third parte of one acre
of land lying over against the tenement at the Moore House.
   By surrender of Christopher Stoddart. Fine 11d.
   dat ut supra. The third parte of 2 messuages and one close called
Rydeing and the third pte of 24½ acres of land and the halfe of one
rood of land at Petmyers on the west of the hirst.
   By surrender of Christopher Stoddart. Fine 1s. 4d.
   dat ut supra. The third parte of one close called west hirst containing 3 acres of land lyinge between the Close now or late in the
occupation of John Todd on the east and on the south of the west end
of the long loaning the waste or moore called Raley Fell on the west
and Moore Close late in the occupation of Bryan Wall on the north
and the third parte of one other close called Middle field containing
46½ acres of land adjoyning upon a close now or sometimes Elizebeth Sympson, widdow on the east West Loaning on the south and
the close now or sometimes William Thompson on the north and
the close now or sometyme John Todd and John Studdick on the
north containing 46½ acres of land and an half rood of land, together with the ⅓ parte of one other close called the Rydeing containing 19 acres of land lyeing betweene the close now or late
William Trotter's on the east, east moore on the south, the loaning
on the west and a close now or late George Moore's on the north
together with the third parte of one parcell of pasture called west
haugh and comon of pasture containing 28 acres of land with moore
and common of pasture now not devided.
   By surrender of Christopher Stoddart. Fine 1s. 1d.
   Rent for these three copies £1. 6s. 5½d.

JOHN EDEN

3 November 22 Car. The half and third parte of the half of 2 messuages and one close called Rydeing Hill.

As heir to Barbara late wife of Raiphe Eden defunct. Fine 2s. 8d.

dat ut supra. The half and the third pte of the half of 24 acres of land, and the half of one rood of land at pit myers on the west of the hirst.

As heir to Barbara late wife of Raiphe Eden defunct. Fine 10s. 10d.

dat ut supra. The half and the third part of the half of one acre of land lying over against the tenement called the Moore House as heir to Barbara late wife of Raiphe Eden defunct. Fine 5d.

dat ut supra. The half and third parte of the halfe of one close called West Hirste containing 30 acres lying between the close late in the occupation of John Todd on the east and in the south of the West end of the long lanning, the waste or moor called Raley Fell on the west and the Moore House Close late in the occupation of Bryan Wall on the south. And the half and third parte of the halfe of one close called Middlefield containing 46½ acres of land adjoyning upon the close of Elizabeth Thompson widdow on the east and the west loaninge on the south and the close of William Thompson on the west and the close of John Todd's and John Suddick on the north containing 46 acres and a halfe rood of land together with the half and the third parte of the halfe of a close called the Rydeing containing 19 acres between the close of William Trotter on the east, east moore on the south long lanning on the west, a close of George Moore's on the north together with the half and the third parte of one halfe of one parcell of pasture called West Haugh and comon of pasture, now not divided.

As heir to Barbara late wife of Raiphe Eden defunct. Fine 4s. 0d.

dat ut supra. The half and the third parte of the halfe of one Messuage and one garden and one close called the Heilde containing 6½ acres of land and third parte of the half of one acre of land in the west haugh late in the tenure of Thomas Binchester and Cuthbert Harrison the half and third parte of the halfe of one parcell of land containing 5 roodds late in the tenure of Christopher Wrenn, the half and third parte of the halfe of one messuage one crofte called Edmond Close containing 1 acre and ½ rood of land late in the tenure of Bryan Bolt.

As heir to Barbara late wife of Raiphe Eden defunct. Fine 3s. 4d.

Rent for these five copies £1. 6s. 5½d.

These persons hereafter named are charged in this towne in the Coronor's Rentall wth these rents following: but wee have seene noe deeds or writings in whch it appeares for what the said rents are paid.

Sir William Darcy, knt. for Witton Hall	Rent £11. 1s. 2d.
John Appleby for Boote hill	Rent 6s. 8d.
Anthony Todd Thomas Taylor	Rent £1. 9s. 8d.
Christopher Hodshon for East macknale	Rent 5s. 0d.
Harply	Rent £1. 0s. 0d.
Thomas Taylor of Bitchburne	Rent £1. 0s. 0d.
Nicholas Hutchinson	Rent 7s. 6d.
Mr. Hutton for Hunwick	Rent 8s. 6d.
Mr. Trotter for Helmedan	Rent 19s. 3d.
Mr. Downes for Wadley	Rent 5s. 0d.

Wee shall make a more exact retaine of these particulars when wee retorne the Coronor's Rentall in Darlington ward of wh. Division this survey is but a parte.

Heighington Township Freeholds

LAMERICK TEWER son and heir of William Tewer son and heir of Nicholas Tewer.
7 May 25 Elz. By deed poll from Henry Tewer to the foresaid Nicholas Tewer all that third parte of one messuage or tenement in Heighington aforesaid then or late in the tenure of John Robinson of Heighington and also one Oxgang of Land two closes, of which one called braxes close and the other called Toopehome close lying in the Territories of Heighington wth all singular lands arrable, meadow pasture Comons of pasture to the said belonging.
Rent 2s. 9d.

PERCIVAL TEALE
4 December 6 Elz. Made from Edward Parkinson Esq. to the said Percivall all that messuage and 2 barnes in Heighington in the tenure of the said Percivall. And also his rents reversions and services Moores Meadowes and pastures and hereditaments whatsoever.
Rent 2s. 6d.

Heighington Townships Copyholds

ISABELL HALL wife of Thomas Hall brother of George Foster.
11 October 18 Car. The half of one cottage with the half of Four
acres of lands as it is now devided.
  By surrender of George Foster defunct. Rent 2s. 8d. Fine 8d.

EDWARD FOWLER
16 May 20 Jac. The eighth part of one cottage and the eighth parte
of 4 acres of lands devided into 8 parts.
  By surrender of Leonard Fowler and Margery his wife. Rent 8d.
Fine 8½ d.

LANCELLOT MARTIN and Anne his wife.
1 May 10 Car. One messuage with a garden.
  By surrender of William Tower. Rent 1s. 0d. Fine 6d.

ELIZABETH DOBSON widdow.
25 April 13 Car. One cottage with a garden which was the land of
Thomas Dobson her husband.
  As relict of Thomas Dobson. Fine 1s. 0d.
  dat ut supra. One cottage with a garden late William Taylor's and
one cottage and 4 acres of land late John Heighington's.
  As relict of Thomas Dobson. Fine 5s. 0d.
  Rent for these two copies 11s. 3d.

WILLIAM THIRSBIE
27 April 11 Car. One messuage and one oxgang of land in the towne
and territory of Heighington.
  By surrender of Symon Thirsbie. Rent 10s. 0d. Fine 10s. 0d.

MARIE DOBSON
29 April 18 Car. One messuage and one oxgang of land.
  By surrender of Mathew Dobson her husband defunct. Fine 2s. 6d.
  dat ut supra. One messuage and 4 acres of land.
  By surrender of Mathew Dobson her husband defunct. Fine 1s. 4d.
  dat ut supra. One messuage and one husbandland late Margery
Jowell's.
  By surrender of Mathew Dobson her husband defunct. Fine 8d.

Rent for these three copies 12s. 9d.

WILLIAM WILKINSON

28 September 19 Car. 2 acres of land lying on the Comon Moore the one parcell called the rigg on the south of a close of Martin Richmond.

By surrender of Mathew Dobson. Rent 4d. Fine 2d.

MARY PRIERMAN

15 October 10 Jac. One cottage in Heighington lying between the tenement of William Venham on the one part and the lands of (*blank*) on the other part.

As relict of Michael Prierman her husband. Rent 1s. 6d. Fine 2s. 0d.

LAMERICK TOWER

26 September 22 Car. 4 acres of land in Heighington whch were the lands of William Tower his father while he lived.

By surrender of Anne Tower widdow of William Tower. Fine 5s. 0d.

dat ut supra. The half of the south half of one cottage as it is now devided late in the occupation of Isabell Harrison and the half of the half of 4 acres of land in Heighington late the land of Wm. Tower while he lived.

By surrender of Anne Tower widdow of William Tower. Fine 1s. 3d.

Rent for these two copies 5s. 4d.

ANNE SOMER and CIRILL wife of Frances Stokell, sisters.

1 May 10 Car. One cottage with a garden and 4 acres of land.

As co-heirs of Mathew Somer. Rent 5s. 0d. Fine 5s. 0d.

ANTHONY ATKINSON

15 April 13 Car. The 4th part of one messuage and the 4th part of 2 oxgangs of land being the 4th part of the whole tenure of John Atkinson.

By surrender of John Atkinson. Fine 11s. 0d.

dat ut supra. The half of the whole tenement or tenure (vzt) the half of one messuage and 2 oxgangs of land.

By surrender of John Atkinson. Fine 5s. 0d.

Rent for these two copies £1. 0s. 1½d.

ANTHONY ARIAM and Anne his wife.

11 October 14 Car. One cottage wth a garden belonging to it.
    By surrender of Roger Hixon and Jane his wife. Rent 1s. 6d. Fine 6d.

WILLIAM COOKE

13 October 6 Car. One cottage with a garden.
    By surrender of Thomas Bigott. Rent 2s. 6d. Fine 1s. 4d.

JOHN NORTH

19 July 18 Car. One cottage with a garden.
    By surrender of Anthony Ariam and Anne his wife. Rent 1s. od. Fine 1s. od.

EDWARD MEASON

20 April 16 Car. The eighth parte of a cottage.
    By surrender of John North. Rent 8d. Fine 4d.

JOHN PARNABIE

2 May 14 Jac. One cottage.
    By surrender of George Howell. Rent 1s. od. Fine 1s. od.

AGNES HOLBECK

11 December 18 Jac. One cottage with a garden.
    As widdow relict of Thomas Holbeck. Rent 1s. 6d. Fine 4s. od.

FRANCIS CRESSET gent.

[*no date*]
    Mem. we have not seen this coppie Mr. Cresset lyveing at London. Rent 1d.

Heighington Township Leaseholds

EDWARD FOWLER

8 October 17 Car. All that tenement and one oxgang of land lying in the town and territories of Heighington late in the tenure of Leonard Fowler now in Edward's tenure. The particulars: One dwelling house, 2 closes, one called Eastfield the other called Oremoore containing 29 acres.

For the natural lives of Elizabeth wife of the said Edward, and John Fowler and Wm. Fowler both sons of Edward, all in being.

Rent 13s. 4d. Improvement £3. 10s. 0d.

THOMAS GARTHWAITE

16 October 14 Car. The moietie or half of a messuage or tenement and one oxgang of land in the towne and fields of Heighington late in the tenure of Barnard Wake and Robert Crawforth, one acre of arable land late in the tenure of Francis Young. The particulars: One dwelling house: a stable. 3 closes lying together called Doddrige containing 27 acres. One close called Cow Moore containing 5½ acre.

For the natural lives of Joseph Garthwaite, Thomas Garthwaite, sons of the said Thomas and Marth Garthwaite daughter of the said Thomas. All in being.

Rent 14s. 0d. Improvement £3. 6s. 0d.

MATHEW DOBSON

7 January 12 Car. An oxgang of townland and 2 oxgang of demesnes late in the occupation of Mathew Dobson and now in the tenure of John Richmond. Particular: Divers closes in all containing 20 acres or thereabouts.

For the naturall lives of Thomas Dobson aged 28, Anne Dobson 15 years and for his own life. All the lives in being.

Rent 13s. 4d. Improvement £3. 10s. 0d.

MARTIN RICHMOND

7 October 18 Jac. One messuage or tenement in Heighington. Particular: One house and one barn standing in a moore 60 acre of land lying in severall parcells.

For the naturall lives of Christopher Richmond then aged 1 year John Richmond aged 3 and himself.

Rent £2. 14s. 6d. Improvement: not mentioned.

HENRIE ATKINSON

22 January 11 Car. All that messuage or tenement and one oxgang of demeasne land lying and being wthin the territories and precincts of the Township.

For the naturall lives of his the said Henry Atkinson, John Atkinson his son aged 6 years and of Anne his wife. Anne his wife is dead.

Rent £1. 14s. 6d. Improvement £5. 15. 6d.

CHRISTOPHER WRAINE

8 November 17 Car. The moytie or one half of a messuage or tenement and one oxgang of towne land in Heighington late in the
tenure of William Edmondson and now in the tenure of the said
Christopher. Particular: A dwelling house and half a barne. Two
closes containing 24 acres, another small parcell of land called
Cathedrall Free.

For the lives of John Raine brother of the said Christopher then
aged 7 Christopher Trotter then 9, and Thomas Trotter then aged 6.
All in being.

Rent 13s. 8d. Improvement £3. 10s. 0d.

GEORGE BRABANT

10 October 3 Car. 2 oxgang of demeasnes land in the fields of
Heighington late in the tenure of Hercules Brabant.

For the lives of Adelyne Cholmley then aged 33 wife of James
Cholmeley of Cramlington Co. Northumberland, George Brabant
then 5 and Raphe Brabant then aged 4. All in being.

Rent 9s. 8d. Improvement £3. 6s. 8d.

FRANCIS CRESSITT

[no date] 3 messuages or tenements and 6 oxganges of land and a
half of towneland and also one messuage or tenement and 13 oxgang
of demeasne land and one house and a garth thereto belonging in
Heighington and 6 acres of land betweene the lands late Thomas
Laytons on the east, Christopher Raines on the north Thomas Dobson on the west and the Oxemoor, Christopher Raines on the south.

For the naturall lives of Francis Cressett, Mary his wife and
Henry Robinson of Cramesley in Co. Northampton. All in being.

Rent £8. 0s. 0d. Improvement £32. 0s. 0d.

Sir WILLIAM DARCIE knt. JOHN SKELTON and JAMES CLAXTON Esq.

[no date] All that capitall house or messuage called Ricknell
Grainge together with Little Ricknell Brough closes and Coplawe.

For the naturall lives of John Lord Bellasis John Skelton aforesaid
and John Trawman of Thirkesby in Co. Ebor. All in being.

Rent £30. 0s. 0d. (£26. 10s. 0d. to the Exchequer at Durham and

£3. 10s. 0d. to the Coll of Heighington for a mill). Improvement
£160. 0s. 0d.

Mem. The deed we have not seen there is belonging to the foresaid Grange 6 small dwelling houses A water corne mill.

JOHN TEWART

10 October 18 Jac. All that his messuage or tenement in Heighington
agoresaid 2 oxgang of towne land, 2 oxgang of demeasne land lying
wthin the fields and precincts of the Heighington then in the tenure
of Robert Tewart and William Tewart.

For the naturall lives of John Tewart then 4 years, Mary Tewart
then 2 years and Elianor Tewart then aged 3 months.

Rent £1. 16s. 4d. 6s. 8d. for a veal at Martinmas. Improvement
£8. 6s. 8d.

GEORGE SHAUTER

7 November 17 Car. All that his tenement wherein the said George
now dwelleth belonging to the Towne and one oxgang of demeasne
lands Particular: One dwelling house and a barne 2 closes, one
called Greene's Close, the other Banckton cont. in all 9 acres.

For the naturall lives of George Shawter the younger, Thomas
Shawter, Ann Shawter. All alive.

Rent 5s. 0d. Improvement £2. 0s. 0d.

JOHN DOBSON and THOMAS DOBSON

23 September 17 Car. All that tenement and one burgage of townlands in Heighington late in the occupation of John Thomson and
Nicholas Thomson. Particular: One dwelling house and a garth
adjoyning to it. One close called the Eastfield containing 23 acres.

For the naturall lives of John Dobson, Thomas Dobson, and
William Dobson all sons of the said Thomas Dobson. All the lives in
being.

Rent 13s. 4d. Improvement £3. 6s. 8d.

WILLIAM MORLEY

7 June 17 Car. All that messuage or tenement with 3 oxgangs of
townland in the Towne fields with all pasture lands arrable and not
arrable.

For the lives of William Morley aforesaid Margarett Morley and
Diones Morley. All alive.

Rent £2. os. od. Improvement £4. 8s. 4d.

GEORGE MORLEY

7 June 17 Car. One messuage or tenement and 2 oxegangs of townland lying within the town fields of Heighington now in his own
possession.

For the lives of George Morley aforesaid Isabell his wife and John
Morley son of the said George then aged one year. Isabell dead.

Rent £1. 6s. 8d. Improvement £6. 13s. 4d.

WILLIAM RUNTHWAITE and Anne his wife.

9 December 17 Elz. One messuage or tenement with 2 oxgangs of
land town land and 4 oxgangs of demeasne land within Heighington
town field.

For the lives of William and Anne his wife, and William their son.
Anne dead.

Rent £1. 6s. 8d. Improvement £6. 13s. 4d.

MARTIN RICHMOND

1 May 10 Car. Tenement and 2 oxgangs in Heighington of townland now in the tenure of the said Martin. 3 closes cont. 30 acre.

For the lives of John, William and James Richmond.

Rent £1. 6s. 8d. Improvement: no entry.

Mem. Martin Richmond has been sent for by us severall times to
produce his writings that wee might see what he held (being informed he hoults one oxegang of land belonging to the late Bishop
in which hee hath noo right) to the end wee might have Surveyed the
same and sett a full value thereof but he hath nott repaired to us.
However upon information of honest men and in our own judgement we think fitt to value all such lands as he hoults at £30 p.an.
above the rent.

RICHARD ROBINSON

14 January 11 Car. One mansion house or tenement in Heighington
and 2 oxgangs of demeasne lands there in the town fields, also 2
oxgangs right of hay in the 5 acres in Heighington late in the
tenure of Richard his father. And also all that his tenement and one
oxgang of demeasne land in the townfield of Heighington sometymes conveyed by Nicholas Thompson to the said Richard the

elder but now Richard the younger's. Particular: One dwelling house, one barn, one Oxehouse, Two closes, one called 5 acres, the other called Crofts, One other parcell of lands called Bauckton cont. 19 acres.

For 21 years.

Rent 17s. 4d. Improvement £6. os. od.

HENRY ATKINSON

22 January 11 Car. One oxegang of demeasne land in the townfield of Heighington late in the tenure of William Pickeringe and now in the tenure of the said Henrie. Particular: One close called High-side bank. The other Garrends Close cont. 4 acres.

Rent 4s. 1od. Improvement £5. 15s. 2d.

Heighington Township

These persons hereafter named pay the yearly rents hereafter expressed but have produced no evidence or writings how they hold the same.

	£	s	d
Brabant George		1	8
Dobson Thomas		2	6
Dobson vid		9	8
Earyholme Anthony		1	6
Pickering Hartley		3	2
Raine vid		6	6
Robinson Richard		3	0
Robinson Thomas		1	6
Runthwaite William		19	4
Richmond Martin	3	19	8½
Tewart Robert		1	8
Bakehouse rent		1	0
Smiths rent			6

Middridge Township Copyholds

WILLIAM JACKSON

19 June 17 Jac. One cottage with one toft and croft.

By surrender of William Jackson his father. Rent 1s. 0d. Fine 1s. 0d.

dat ut supra. One tenement and 2 oxgangs in Middridge.

By surrender of William Jackson his father. Rent 5s. 0d. Fine 6s. 0d.

ROBERT HUNTER

12 October 18 Car. One messuage and one cottage and 3 oxgangs of land.

By surrender of George Marreson. Rent £1. 16s. 0d. Fine 6s. 8d.

RICHARD BOWSER

12 May 19 Car. One cottage and 20 acres of lands lalled Old Towne.

By surrender of Christopher Byerly esq. Rent £1. 0s. 8d. Fine 6s. 8d.

RAPHE BAMBRIDGE

16 October 5 Car. One cottage and 5 acres of lands late in the tenure of Robert Hunter.

By surrender of Henry Bambridge his father. Rent 5s. 2d. Fine 3s. 0d.

JOHN BAINBRIDGE

21 September 22 Car. One cottage and 5 acres of land late in the tenure of Robert Hunter.

By surrender of Henry Bainbridge. Rent 5s. 2d. Fine 3s. 4d.

dat ut supra. One cottage with a garden and one oxgang to the same belonging.

By surrender of Henry Bainbridge. Rent 13s. 4d. Fine 2s. 6d.

Middridge Township Leaseholds

ROBERT WALKER son and heir of John Walker.

2 November 5 Car. All that messuage, two cottages and two oxgang of lands late in the tenure of the said John. Particular: 2 dwelling-houses in Middridge. One close adjoyning to the Common Moor called Middridge Moore.

For the lives of the said John, Robert Walker aforenamed and son of the said John now 30, and John Walker younger son of the aforesaid John now 20. John Walker the father is dead.

Rent £1. 6s. 8d. Improvement £5. 0s. 0d.

RICHARD PALLACER son of Robert Pallacer.

2 November 5 Car. One messuage and one oxgang of land lyeing in Middridge township and fields. These lands now lye with other lands demised to him for terme of years in 2 closes called Garre ends and North close.

For the lives of Robert Pallacer then 50, Richard Pallacer then 35, Richard Pallacer son of the said Richard Pallacer then 3. Robert Pallacer is dead.

Rent 13s. 4d. Improvement £2. 8s. od.

WILLIAM JACKSON

7 April 14 Car. All that his messuage or tenement in Middridge, sometime in the tenure of Robert Walker and now in his own occupation, and all that his other messuage or tenement wth one oxgang of land in Middridge. Particular: 2 dwelling houses, 4 oxgangs of land in all. Comon without stint.

For the lives of John, George and Christopher Jackson. All alive.

Rent £2. 16s. od., for 2 capons 4s. od. Improvement £10. 4s. od.

RICHARD CRAGGE

2 November 5 Car. All that messuage in Middridge now in his possession Particular: One dwelling house and barne. One plott of ground called Flaver.

For the lives of the said Richard, James his eldest son and William Cragg. James Cragge is dead.

Rent £1. 6s. 8d. Improvement £4. 10s. od.

ROBERT CLEATON, Jane his wife and MARY WHITFIELD

30 September 6 Car. One messuage or tenement in Middridge and also 30 oxgangs of land lyeing in the fields of Middridge late in the tenure of James Whitfield. Particular: 2 dwelling houses one Barne and Oxehouse. Two parcells of land called the Flaver.

For the lives of Thomas, Roger and John Megson. All in being.

Rent £2. os. od. Improvement £7. 12s. od.

CHRISTOPHER BYERLIE

1 May 17 Car. All that Manor or Grainge of Middridge and one water corne milne to the same belonging 21 oxgangs and 5 acres of arrable lands lyeing betweene Kimbleburne and Middridgeburne and the house or Grange on the east 240 acres of land lying on the

west of the said mannor 85½ acres of meadowe 158 acres of pasture
60 days worke in Corne or hay of divers the Bishop's tenants as
others in the towne of Middridge, Killerby, and Redworth as also
all singular messuages etc. as they were sometime in the occupation
of Richard Franklyn Esq.

For the lives of Anthony Byerley and Robert Byerly sons of the
said Christopher and Stephen Hall sone of Thomas Halle of
Horneby in Cleveland.

Rent £26. 9s. 8d. Improvement £250. os. od.

ELIZABETH LIDDELL late Butler.
7 November 7 Car. All that messuage, tenement or farme hould
situate in the town and fields of Middridge togeather wth one Coate-
house and a garthe.

For 21 years.
Rent £2. os. od. Improvement £7. 10s. od.

RICHARD PALLACER sone of Robert Pallacer deceased.
29 September 6 Car. All that messuage or tenement and 4 oxgang
of land lyeing in the town and fields of Middridge late in the tenure
of Jannett Simpson widdow then in the tenure of the said Robert
Particular: 3 dwelling houses, 1 barne, 1 Oxehouse, 1 stable and
small outhouse. One close called the Garr ends. One other close called
the North close together wth the 4 oxgangs.

For 21 years.
Rent £2. 13s. 4d. Improvement £9. 10s. od.

RICHARD PALLACER
16 December 9 Car. One parcell of lands called Newlands acre lyeing
in the Northfield of Middridge in the tenure of the said Richard.

For 21 years.
Rent 1s. od. Improvement 4s. od.

GEORGE DUNNE son of John Dunne deceased.
27 January 9 Car. All that messuage or tenement and 4 oxgang of
land lyeing in the township and fields of Middridge sometimes in
the tenure of the said John. Particular: 4 small dwelling houses wth
2 barns. 2 closes one called the Oxeclose the other called Carre ends.

For 21 years.
Rent £2. 12. od. Improvement £9. 15s. od.

RICHARD CRAGGE junior by assignment from John Simpson who holds from the Bishop.

22 August 14 Car. One messuage or tenement and cottage in Middridge and 3 oxgangs of Townelands lyeing in Middridge Fields. Particular: One dwelling house and an old barn and cottage house 2 closes one called Thickley Dike the other Thomes.

For 21 years.

Rent £1. 18s. 4d. Improvement £7. os. od.

ROWLAND BUTLER

16 July 16 Car. All that messuage tenement or farmhold in Middridge with one coate house and a garth.

For 21 years.

Rent £2. os. od. The smythy shopp standing upon the Lord's waste payeth 1s. od. Improvement £7. 10s. od.

Newton Cap Township Copyholds

JAMES BAYLES

1 October 11 Jac. By special command of the Lord of the Manor holds one parcell of lands lyeing betweene the Pasture called Greenefield and the water called the Wear containing ½ acre. Excepted to Lord and his successors liberty at all times to digg coales and all other minerals.

Paying rent with the lands of Mr. Richardson. Fine 2s. od.

THOMAS RICHARDSON

28 September 18 Jac. 2 acres of land in Newton Cap by the demise of Ann Bayles for 60 years from the feast of St. Michael next.

Fine 1s. 8d.

dat ut supra. One parcell of land parcell of a close called Toms Close containing 4 acres of land lying at the south end of a parcell of land then in the tenure of William Aude and a parcell called Toms Close lyeing between the lands late George Butler's gent on the east and the land of Emanuell Grice on the west, also the west part of one close called Toms Close containing 5 acres of land parcell of a messuage called Pickesley Hill lying neare Birtley by the demise of Anne Bayles for 60 years ut supra.

Fine 11d.

dat ut supra. 2 partes of a tenement late Richard Morlands by a demise from Anne Bayles.

Fine 10s. 0d.

Rent for these three copies £7. 10s. 3d.

Mem. That Joane Bayles widdow administratrix of James Bayles her husband deceased holdeth the lands mentioned in the 3 last fines by copie dates 10 September 21 Car. which were her late husband's by the grant of William Brasse and Anne his wife for the term of 20 yeares yet to come mentioned in the former demise.

HUGH STOBART

20 October 7 Car. By special command of the lord one house built upon the lord's waste at Low Bitchburne near the pitts called Bitchburne cole pitts And one parcell of land in the Backeside containing 80 yds in length and breadth.

Rent 8d. Fine 6s. 8d.

23 October 15 Jac. One acre of land adjoyning to the river called Roddingburne now inclosed wth hedges late in the tenure of Christopher Hey and late the lord's waste.

By surrender of Christopher Hey. Rent 4d. Fine 4d.

RICHARD WALL son and heir of James Wall.

16 October 5 Car. One messuage and 4 acres of lands or meadow parcell of one close called Toms close.

By surrender of James Wall. Rent 1s. 0d. Fine 1s. 0d.

JOHN GARRY

1 May 10 Car. One close called Lowsery side parcell of a messuage called Picksley hill lying neare Birtley.

By surrender of Thomas Smethwayte. Rent 1s. 8d. Fine 1s. 6d.

LINDLEY WRENNE Esq. son and heir of Sir Charles Wrenne knt. and Barbary Blakeston one of the daughters of Sir William Blakestone of Gibside knt.

18 Jac. The third parte of the whole tenement of John Staniforth.

By surrender of Sir Charles Wrenne. Rent £3. 1s. 0d. Fine 13s. 4d.

ELIZABETH HODGSON now wife of John Hodgson daughter and heir of Anthony Todd.

One close called Over Serviside containing 12 acrese of land late parcell of the land called Picksley Hill abutting upon a parcell of lands called Nether Serviside late in the tenure of Anthony Allenson on the south and a certaine close called Parkes close on the east the Common moore on the west and the lands of Robert White and a close called Birkes close on the north.

As heir to Anthonie Todd. Rent 4s. od. Fine 1s. od.

JOHN ATKINSON
20 October 17 Car. One parcell of land called Bracken Hill containing 4 acres of land.

As heir to John Atkinson his father. Fine 3s. 4d.

dat ut supra. The 4th parte of 2½ acres of lands lying nigh Holmeden And also 3 partes of 2½ acres of land nigh Holmeden.

As heir to John Atkinson his father. Fine 8d.

Rent for these two copies 2s. 6d.

CUTHBERT JACKSON
11 October 3 Car. ½ acre of land lying at Aikesraw.

By surrender of George Downes, gent. Rent 2d. Fine 2d.

MARGARETT ATKINSON
9 October 19 Car. One rood of land late in the lord's waste upon the end of Wardsworth, one other rood lying at the west end of a close of William Lord Eure also a parcell of land late the lord's waste containing 2 acres lying neer small lees of the opposite tenure and another parcell of land containing 2 acres of land lying near small lees.

By surrender of Richard Corneforth and Anne his wife, and William Phillips and Jane his wife. Fine 2s. 8d.

dat ut supra. One rood of land of the opposite tenuret.

By surrender of Richard Corneforth and Anne his wife, and William Phillips and Jane his wife. Fine 6d.

Rent for these two copies 1s. 8d.

ANNE CORNEFORTH now the wife of Richard Corneforth.
9 October 19 Car. One messuage and one place of Chequor land called Smallees (except the half of one barn and the half of a garden) and one close of meadow called Broad Meadow at West Close wth a house built thereon 2 other closes of meadow called Savoy Close

and Four Acre Close lying at the north of Broad meadow parcell of the said messuage and the said place of land.

By surrender of Margarett Atkinson widdow and William Philip and Jane his wife. Fine 1s. 8d.

dat ut supra. 3 acres of lands at the Nether head of Whin close of Hunwick Moore.

By surrender of Margarett Atkinson widdow and William Philip and Jane his wife. Fine 1s. 0d.

Rent for these two copies 3s. 0d.

RAPHE TROTTER son and heir of John Trotter.
2 May 14 Jac. One messuage and 14 acres of land called Over Small Lees.

By surrender of John Trotter. Rent 10s. 0d. Fine 6s. 0d.

FRANCIS TAYLOR
28 October 17 Car. One tenement called Rombaldy House containing 6 acre of land and one parcell of lands called the Intack.

By surrender of Henry Trotter. Rent 7s. 0d. Fine 6s. 8d.
15 April 6 Car. The north half of one parcell of lands lying nigh Wardsworth containing 15 acres of land (one parcell of land lying on the south parte of the oulde hedge extending itself from the Close late Anthonie Allenson's on the west and the Common Moore on the east as it is now inclosed with hedges excepted).

By surrender of John Atkinson. Rent 2s. 0d. Fine 2s. 0d.

JOHN ALLINSON
10 October 4 Car. One parcell of land called Wardsworth Close lying betweene Rathingburne and one small close.

By surrender of Raphe Allenson his brother. Rent 15s. 3d. Fine 2s. 6d.

MARY GREENE now Bateman and ELIZABETH GREENE.
15-6 Car. One water mill on a certein river called Bitchburne joyning to the south end and east of a close called Smithy close extending itself towards the moore called Hunwicke Moore between the river called Bitchburne on the west and the said close called Smithy close and a way leading from Wolsingham to Bishop Auckland on the east.

By surrender of Raphe Greene. Rent 5s. 8d. Fine 5s. 0d.

JOHN BENNETT

10 September 21 Car. 2 partes of 6 of a parcell of land lying upon Roughside containing 4 acres.

By surrender of Wm. Bennett his father. Fine 1s. od.

dat ut supra. One parcell of land lying upon Langlee cont. 4 acres.

By surrender of Wm. Bennett his father. Fine 1s. od.

dat ut supra. One parcell of land containing 12 acres butting upon the south angle of a parcell of land called Toms Close Ashletts and Trotters riding side late in the occupation of Lancelott Holby gent. on the North parte. And the said Trotters riding and a certein parcell of land called Coniers riding and the water of Weare on the east and a parcell of land called the Fencings late in the tenure of Christopher Wright on the south and the said parcell of lands called Toms Close on the west.

By surrender of William Bennett. Fine 4s. od.

Rent for these three copies 12s. 6d.

ELIZABETH NATTERES

20 October 1 Car. One messuage called Pickesley Hill lying near Birtley and the west part of a close called Long Close lying betweene a backhouse of Robert White on the east and the way leading to Auckland on the south and one close called the Crossehouse Field on the west and a close called the Brakes on the north parcell of a messuage called Pickesley Hill lying neare Birtley and a parcell of pasture lands to the same messuage belonging.

By surrender of John Suddick. Rent 5s. 3d. Fine 1s. od.

WILLIAM WHITE

9 October 19 Car. One house called a bakehouse and the south parte of a close called long close from the said house and an ould hedge there towards the south lying on the west of the land late in the tenure of Thomas Hutchinson parcel of a tenement called Piskley Hill.

As heir of Thomas White his father. Rent 4s. od. Fine 4s. od.

JOHN ALLENSON the younger, son of Anthony Allenson.

13 May 21 Jac. One close of pasture lands containing 17 acres of land called High close with a house built thereupon also one close called Lingie Close also one close of meadow containing 5 acres of land lying between the Vicar's hedge on the west and the pasture of

Roger Smurthwayte on the east and the Parke Close on the north and the comon moore on the south parcell of the land called Pickesley Hill neare Birtley.

By surrender of the said Anthony Allenson. Rent 9s. 2d. Fine 5s. 3d.

AGNES WRIGHT daughter of Anthony Wright.

30 April 16 Jac. The half of one messuage and one place of Chequer lands called Smallees.

By surrender of Jane Wright her mother. Rent £2. 12s. 11d. Fine 2s. 2d

dat ut supra. One rood of land lying on the opposite side of a bakehouse.

By surrender if Jane Wright her mother. Rent 1s. 7d. Fine 3d.

RICHARD CORNEFORTH

7 May 12 Car. One tenement called Akehouse with 2 acres of land and one close called Toppcliffe close one acre of land called Bracken Hill lying in Newton Cap.

By surrender of Lindley Wrenne Esq. Fine 3s. 4d.

7 May 9 Car. One parcell of lands lying on the west side of bracken hill containing 2 acre of lands and other 2 acres of lands within a certeine close of land newly inclosed one tofte of Chequor land called Glendhirst one acre of land lying at the head of Swinherd Field and one parcell of land called Varringer.

As heir to William Corneforth defunct. Fine 10s. 0d.

dat ut supra. One parcell of land lying in the south of the ould hedge there extending itself from the close of Allinson on the west and the Comon moore on the east as it is now inclosed parcell of a close called Newfield lying nigh Wordsworth.

As heir to William Corneforth defunct. Fine 6d.

dat ut supra. The south half of one parcell of lands called Newfield lying nigh Wardsworth cont. 15 acres of land.

As heir to William Corneforth defunct. Fine 1s. 3d.

Rent for these four copies £1. 1s. 4d.

GERTRUDE TROTTER wife of Anthony Trotter.

1 October 11 Car. One close called Toms Close lying upon Roughlee parcell of a messuage called Picksley Hill lying neare Birtley.

By surrender of Leonard Pilkington. Rent 1s. 0d. Fine 1s. 0d.

Sir WILLIAM DARCY Knt.

11 February 14 Car. One parcell of land containing 6 acres of land lying on the west of a parcell of land belonging to the Free schole of Auckland and on the east parte of Witton Parke.

By surrender of Elizabeth Jackson. Rent 2s. od. Fine 2s. od.

These persons hereafter named are Tennants in the foresaid Towne and doe pay the severall rents hereafter mentioned but for what wee knowe not they having produced no deeds or writings to us expressing the same.

Cornforth William	Rent 12s. od.
Idem	Rent 6d.
Craddock vid.	Rent 1s. od.
Dawson Thomas	Rent 2d.
Hodgeson vid	Rent 10d.
Nicholson et al	Rent 4s. od.
Suerties Christopher	Rent 2d.
Shafto Marke	Rent 3d.
Idem	Rent 4d.

Redworth Township Freeholds

HERCULES PICKERING son of Cuthbert Pickering.

5 May 8 Jac. In free and comon socage from Giles Gawthwaite to Cuthbert the father deceased and to the said Hercules All that messuage, tenement with a garden and 7 acres of land late in the tenure of Giles Gawthwaite in Redworth and now in the tenure of the said Hercules.

MARGARETT SEAMOR widdow relict of John Seamor son of William Semor deceased.

26 April 13 Hen. VIII. In free and common socage from Alice Smerthwaugh to the said William Semer all those lands feedings and pasture then in the possession of the said William containing 4 acres wth one messuage and a garth.

Rent 7½d.

Redworth Township Copyholds

RICHARD ROBINSON
4 May 12 Car. Half of 4 acres of Chequor lands.
   By surrender of John Robinson. Fine 6d.
11 October 12 Car. Half of 4 acres of Chequor lands.
   By surrender of Elizabeth Hornesby.
   Rent for these two copies 6s. 8d.

WILLIAM ANDWOOD
7 May 9 Car. One house wth a garden.
   As heir to Francis Andwood his father. Rent 1s. 2d. Fine 1s. 1d.

CHRISTOPHER WRAINE, CHRISTOPHER TODD son of
Richard Todd and WILLIAM DOBSON son of Thomas Dobson.
11 May 13 Jac. One parcell of land called Kempe milne dam and
another parcell of land called Galgarth Crofte in the name of all
the tenants of Redworth township and by the special command of the
Bishop to them and their sequells to the use and behoof of all the
tenants of Redworth.
   Rent 3s. 10d. Fine 2s. 0d.

MARTIN RICHMOND
29 October 16 Jac. The whole tenement late of Peeter Willis lying
in the towne of Redworth.
   By surrender of Christopher Richmond. Rent 12s. 2d. Fine 3s. 4d.

The persons hereafter named are Tennants within the foresaid
towne and are charged with and doe pay the severall rents hereafter
expressed but wee have not seene any deedes or writing expressing
for what the said rents are paid or whether freeholders coppieholders
leaseholders.

Brabant John	Rent 3s. 10d.
Dobson Thomas	Rent 8s 0d.
Gibson George	Rent 6d.
Rivington School	Rent 1s. 4d.
Simpson John	Rent 7d.
Swinbanke Rayphe	Rent 1s. 2d.
West and East Moore	Rent 4s. 6d.
Trotter James	Rent 16s. 4d.
Todd Christopher	Rent 5s. 10d.

William Church of the City of Durham gent. holdeth by patent bearing date 11 March 14 Car. graunted from Thomas late Bishop of Durham the office of Clarke of all the Halmott Courts within the Bishopricke of and County of Durham Bedlington and Bedlington-shire within the diocese of Durham wheresoever to be held within the counties and dioceses aforesaid before the Bishop or his successors or Stewardes of the said Courtes. To have hold exercise and enjoy the said office of Clarke of all the halmott courtes aforesaid within the Bishoprick County of Durham Bedlington and Bedling-tonshire and diocese aforesaid by himself or his sufficient deputy or deputies for whom he will answer during his naturall life wth the yearly fee of £3. 6. 8d. to be paid to him by the receiver general for the time being at the Feasts of Pentecost and St. Martin in equal portions with all and singular Vales, Fees, Profitts comodities rights emoluments in as ample manner as Moses Skepper, Hugh Wright, Christopher Skepper, Christopher Browne or Christopher Mayne or any who held or enjoyed the said office before him.

Confirmed by the Dean and Chapter 15 April 10 Car.

By the Honourable Sir Henry Vane Lord Leiuetenent of the County of Durham etc. the Standing Orders for the same.

Whereas the coronorship within the Ward of Darlington in the foresaid County sometimes holden by patent from the late Bishop of Durham is now vacant and voyde by the death and descease of Thomas Barnes of Darlington gent late coronor of the foresaid ward Whereby the service due and accustomed to be performed by the said Coroner is now neglected to the great prejudice of the state. These are therefore to authorise and depute George Daile gent of the City of Durham, to doe execute and perform the dutys or office of coronor within the Ward of Darlington aforesaid and to collect gather and receive the rents and revenue late belonging to the Bishops of Durham by himself or his lawful deputy usually collected and received by the coronor of the said ward his deputy or deputies as parte of his office and charge and pay the same over into the Clarke of the great Receipt at the Bishop's Exchequor upon the Pallace Greene at Durham as usually hath been accustomed for the use and benefitt of the Comon Wealth as by Ordinance of Parliament is appointed And the said George Daile or his deputy is further hereby authorised to collect gather and receive all such some or somes of monay Coroner's rents, coronor's corne, fees stipents profitts and

other emoluments usually accustomed to be payed to the Coroner
of the said Warde With all arrearages thereof behind and unpaid
And such person or persons soe arreared as well for the said Rents
late belonging to the said Bishops of Durham as for all other duties
due and accustomed to the said Coronor or his deputy are hereby
required to pay the same unto George Daile or his deputy aforesaid
And the late Coroner or Deputy Coroner of the said Ward are likewise hereby required to deliver over perfect Rentalls and Accounts
of all forms of money rents or other profitts by them received together
with all arrears behind and unpaid And if any person or persons shall
refuse to make a payment of the Rent or other the dutyes aforesaid
That then it shall and may be Lawful for the said George Daile or
his deputy to Leaf the same by distress or sale of the goods of such
persons for refusing returning unto the Coronor the overplus thereof And to give acquittance and discharge under his or his said
Deputy's hand for all such summes of money or other profitts or his
said Deputy soe received as aforesaid. And furthermore to doe
execute and performe All other matters and things which Right and
by Law may or ought to be had done executed and performed by the
said George Daile or his lawful Deputy in that behalfe authorised
or deputed. In witness thereof wee have hereto sett or hand the 2nd
December Anno Domini 1645. Vera Copie.

Henry Vane	Clem Fulthorp
Lionel Maddison	Richard Lilburne
Richard Bellasis	Geo. Lilburn
Geo Vane	Tho. Shadforth
Chr. Fulthrop	Geo. Grey
Francis Wren	Nicholas Heath

To all Christian people to whom this present Writing shall come
Edward Wrighte of Grayes Inn in the Co. of Middlesex sendeth
greetings in the Lord God Everlasting Whereas the honourable the
Trustees nominated and appointed in and by lawful ordinance of
Parliament made by both houses of Parliament made for and concerning the lands and possessions of all the late ArchBishops and
Bishops within the Kingdom of England and dominion of Wales
by their commission in writing dated 17 March last past gave
nominated authorised and appointed mee Edward Wright to be
Steward and to have the office of Steward or Stewardship of all
and singular the Halmotes and copyhold courts late belonging to Dr.

Thomas Morton late Bishop of Durham in the County of Durham in the right of his said Bishoprick To have hold exercise receive and enjoy the office aforesaid together with all and singular Fees Rewards Profitts advantages whatsoever to the said Office of Steward of Right belonging or appertaining by myself or any sufficient deputies for and during the pleasure of the said Trustees as by the said Commission more at large appeareth. Now know ye that the said Edward Wright have made deputed, appointed and authorised and by these presents do make depute and authorise my beloved friend George Kirkby of the City of Durham gent my true and lawful deputy for me and in my place and stead to execute the said office of Steward of the said Halmotes and Coppyhold courts and to do and execute all and every such act and acts thing and things as to the said Office appertaine and to receive the dues and lawful fees thereunto belonging. In witness whereof I have hereunto set my hand and seal the 7th April 23 Car. 1647

Edward Wright

Signed sealed and delivered
in the presence of—
Henry Briggs Edwd Collingwood
Vera Copie Ex^t per
Chr. Mickleton
Edw. Colson
Tho Saunders
Geo Dailes
Sam Leigh

To all people to whom this present writing shall come Sir John Wollaston Knt John Fouke Alderman, James Prince Alderman William Gibbs Alderman, Samuell Aneric Alderman, Thomas Noel Christopher Parke John Bellamie Edward Hooker Thomas Arnold Richard Glyde, William Gobson, Francis Ashe, John Babington Lawrence Bronfield, Alexander James, Richard Vennor, Stephen Estwick, Robert Meade and James Storey, Trustees nominated and appointed in and by several ordinances of Parliament made by both houses of Parliament made for and concerning the lands and possessions of all the late Archbishops and Bishops within the kingdom of England and Dominion of Wales send Greetings. Know ye that we the said Trustees in pursuance of the said Ordinance have nominated authorised constituted and appointed And by these pre

sents nominate authorise constitute and appoint Edward Wright of
Grays Inn to be Steward and to have the office of Steward or Steward-
ships of all and singular the Halmotes and Copyhold Courts late
belonging to Dr. Thomas Morton late Bishop of Durham in the
County of Durham in the Right of his said late Bishopric. To have
hold exercise receive and enjoy the office of Steward of Right belonging or appertaining unto the said Edward Wright by himself or
his sufficient deputy for whom he will answer from henceforth during the pleasure of the said Trustees in as full and ample a manner
as John Heath Esqr late Steward of the premises heretofore held or
enjoyed or of Right aught to have held or enjoyed the same Provided always that the said Edward Wright or his Deputy shall Rate
and assess all arbitrarie Fines of Coppyholders according to such
Rates and Directions as shall from time to time be set down and
given to him by us the said Trustees or the major part of
us and not otherwise. In witness whereof we the said Trustees have
hereunto put our Hands and seales the 17 March 1646 22 Car Re.

John Woollaston, James Prince, Alex Jones, C[hristo]pher Pack,
Richard Glyd, Samuel Ardie, Edw. Hooke, James Story, Stephen
Elwick Richard Venner, Robt. Meade.
Vera Copie Tho. Saunders
        Chr. Mickleton
        Edw. Colston
        Geo. Daile
        Sam. Leigh

Here followeth the perfecte accompte of the Rents received and
charged in this Survey of the Mannor of Bishop Auckland and the
several Townships thereto belonging (vzt) Bondgate in Auckland,
Borrough in Auckland, Byersgreen, Counden, Eastcombe, Heighington, Middridge, Newton Cap and Redworth. As well of the moneyes
paid unto the Exchequer at Durham, Coronor of Darlington Warde
and to the Bayliff and Collectors of the several townships vzt.

	£	s	d
Bondgate in Auckland	208	7	10½
whereof paid at Durham	167	9	2½
to the coronor at Darlington	6	2	6
Soe there remains to be gathered			
by the collector of the said Towne	34	16	2½

Burrough in Auckland	3	7	7
Byersgreene	22	3	6
paid at Durham	4	0	0
Soe there remains to be gathered			
by the Collector	18	13	6
Counden	44	1	2½
paid at Durham	23	19	0
Soe there remains to be gathered			
by the Collector	20	2	2½
Eastcombe	35	14	0
paid at Durham	17	2	9
soe there remains to be gathered			
by the Collector	18	11	3
Heighington	66	0	7¾
paid at Durham	26	0	0
To Revington Schoole		14	4
So there remains to be gathered			
by the Collector	39	6	3¾
Middridge	51	8	4
paid at Durham	28	9	8
Soe there remains to be gathered			
by the Collector	22	18	8
Newton Cap	19	18	0
Redworth	3	7	2

These Fees hereafter expressed are payable out of the Revenues before mentioned by Pattent certified by us in this Survey (vzt)

	£	s	d
To the Steward of the Hallamot Courte	20	0	0
To the Clerke of the Hallamot Courte	3	13	4
To the Keeper of Auckland Parke	4	6	8
To the keep of Auckland Gardens	2	0	0
To the Bayliff of Bishop of Auckland	5	0	0
To the Pallacer of Auckland Parke	1	10	0
To the Coronor of Darlington Warde	6	13	4
To the Keeper of the Mannor of Auckland	2	0	0
To the Steward of the Borrough Cts of Bishop Auckland	1	6	8

The sume total of the severall Townships rents Improvements and payements to Pattentees are as followeth (vzt)

Bondgate in Auckland	208	7	10½
Burrough in Auckland	3	7	7
Byersgreene	22	13	6
Coundon	44	1	1½
Eastcombe	35	14	0
Heighington	66	0	7¾
Middridge	51	8	4
Newton Cap	19	8	8
Redworth	3	7	2
Sum Total	454	18	3¾
Improvements amount to	921	17	8
Defalcacons amount to	46	10	0
Soe there remains de clara per annum	408	8	3¾
Edw. Colston	Sam Leigh		
Geo. Dailes	Tho. Saunders		

A survey of the Mannor House or Castle of Bishop Auckland in
Com. Durham And of the materialle thereof vallewed and apprised
by us George Lilburne, Sam Leigh, Tho. Saunders, Geo. Grey, Edw.
Colson, John Horsbank, Geo Daile, Gentelmen Surveyers of the
lands belonging to Doctor Thomas Marton Late Bishop of Durham
wth the assistance of severall able and honest Artists: as Carpenters,
Masons, Glassiers Plainers, and Smiths the 13th 14th and 15th dayes
of December Anno Domini 1647 as sequit

	£	s	d
Imprimis in Floores of Tymber of woodworke 60 roodes every roode containing 7 yards square in flatt measure (vzt) 49 single yards at 40s. per rood.	120	0	0
Item the tymber of the severall roofes of the said house wee vallew and apprise to bee worth	550	0	0
Item the wainscott containing 260 yards wee valew	21	0	0
Item the glass containing 500 feete at 3d. per foote we valew	6	5	0
Item the lead on the Gatehouse, Dwelling house Sheriffe Tower and garden house or tower court 6260 Stone of lead 14 pound to the stone wee valew at 12d. per stone which comes to	313	0	0
Item the Slate containing 300 loades wee valew at	75	0	0
Item the pipe of leade containing 2,500 yards			

weighing 2,000 stone as wee gesse at 12d per stone
comes to   100 0 0
Item the Brewering vessills vizt Fatts, Coolers,
Cupp and Lead and aboute them wee valew   50 0 0
Item the Iron aboute the gatehouse, Dwelling
house and other out housing containing 352 stones
at 16d. per stone wee valewe at   23 10 0

Sum total   1259 5 0

£ s d

Wee sett noe valewe of the stoneworke there being
soe many Quaries aboute neere the said house
Indeede if soulde it will but defray the charge
of pulling down the other materialle of building
aboute the said house.

Here follows the Materialls of the Chappells as wee
valew them to be sould.
Imprimis the glass in the upper and lower Chappell
containing 1300 foote 3d. per foote wee valewe at   16 5 0
Item the roofe over the Chappell and the seates
in the upper Chappell wee valewe at   80 0 0
Item the seates wainscott and tables in the lower
Chappell wee value at   10 0 0
Item the Lead on the Chappell cont. 2160 stone
at 12d. per stone wee valewe at   108 0 0
Item the Iron aboute the Chappell wee valew   16 14 0

The materialls of the chappells come to   230 19 0

The materialls of the whole housing and chappells
as we have valewed the same all Charges deducted
for the pulling downe thereof comes to in the
whole   1490 4 0
Whereof the Chappells comes to   230 19 0
Signed
Geo. Lilburne, Sam Leigh, Tho. Saunders, Geo. Grey, Edw. Colson, John Horsbank, Geo. Daile.

SURVEY OF THE MANOR OF DARLINGTON

Darlington Township Leaseholders

MOSES SKEPPER
17 January 13 Chas. Two oxeganges of land lying and being in the Townshipp territoryes and fields of Darlington Together with one cottage or little house therupon lately built and one close called three Acres close or Dobsons Close lying in west field upon the River of Skearne neer Darlington, And also three acres of land and three acres of meadow called escheat lands situat and being in the said Township and fields of Darlington And sometime in the possession of John Darlington or Robert Darlington or one of them and of Christopher Skipper gent deceased and now in the possession of the said Moses Skipper or his Assigns.

For the lives of Moses Skipper, John Skipper and Hugh Skipper (Moses Skipper dead, John being 18 and Hugh 16 years of age).

Rent £2. 5. 4. and one fatt lamb at Pentecost or 4s. 8d. in liew. Improvement £20. 0. 0.

KING JAMES, 14 January 1604, assigned to Dudley Carleton 10 May 1604, assigned to Toby Mathew of London, Esq., 26 April 1605, Edward Easton assigned the same to Thomas Blakiston of Newton, Esq., 13 September 1607, who assigned the same to William War-mouth 30 January 1606, who assigned to Bulmer Isle 28 June 1608 for the sum of £230.

All those closes grounds lands and tenements in or near Darlington or Darnton lately leased to Francis Storey for divers years yet enduring by deed 17 March 1592 and also a certeyn parcell of ground now devided into two closes called Darlington closes sometimes allowed and set forth by petition for waste ground lying near Darlington late in the possession of Christian Plaice gent or his assigns.

To King James for 80 years.
Rent 10s. 0d. Improvement £13. 6. 8.

WILLIAM BARNES, formerly Bailiff of Darlington and now sequestered for his delinquency.
The tolls of the bakehouse of Darlington.
We know not for what period.
Rent £16. os. od. Improvement £40. os. od.

HENRY WARMOUTH and JAMES ISLE
High Park, Low Park and Fethams.
Holdeth by lease but hath not shown it.
Rent £10. 13s. 4d. Improvement £40. os. od.

JOHN STEVENSON and Frances his wife.
26 February 21 Jac. Water corn mills in Darlington and the water corn mill in Blackwell.
For the lives of the said John Stevenson now aged 40, Frances his wife now 48 or thereabouts and Ann Stephenson then aged three and now deceased.
Rent £22. os. od. and 3s. 4d. for every day the rent remains unpaid. Improvement £50. os. od.

The said John Stevenson by patent dated the 28 September 3 Chas I which we have seen and perused holdeth from the said Bishop the office of Porter and keeper of the Mannour House of Darlington for which he is to have paid him yearly from the Tenants of Blackwell within the said Mannor of Darlington 4 qtrs of Breadcorn. And also by the same patent he holdeth the Bayliff's office of Coatham Mundeville with all fees profits thereunto belonging and to have paid him yearly out of the rent there to belonging of Cottam Mundeville the sum of 53s. 4d. The values of the said corn for exercising the said office of Porter and keeper being this present year as it is now sold in the Market at 8s. bushell Winchester measure is Twelve pounds sixteen shillings or thereabouts. The said Mr. Stevenson hath been a captain against the Parliament and is still of a malignant spirit and said before some of us that he would live and die so.

And we find that there is 2 acres and a rood of land devided into 2 closes which is adjacent to the said house which he claimeth to be comprehended within the grant of his patent which is worth as we conceive £5 p.ann.

Examinat   Gulielm Ayloff
Nich Malet

Rentall

Darlington and Bondgate in Darlington	75	0	11½
Coronor's Rentall of the Free Rents within			
his collection in the Ward of Darlington	21	12	7
Blackwell Township	24	7	2
Cockerton and Whessay Rental	38	2	8
Cottam Mundavill, Morton Tinmouth,			
Brafferton and Beaumond Hill	50	8	1½
Haughton	17	3	4
Sadberge	29	18	0

Improved Rents of the Leased Lands besides the Lord's Rent:—

Darlington	183	6	8
Blackwell	8	0	0
Cottam Mundavill	79	6	8
Cockerton and Whessay	6	13	4
Haughton	36	0	0

The names of those which stand charged in the severall Rentalls with the several Sumes following and appeared not neither shewed any Writing or Evidence how they hold their said Estates.

Darlington Towne and Bondgate in Darlington

Abrey John	10	0	The poore land	5	7
Browne Christ	2	5	Priscott William		2
Browne William	14	6½	Robinson Robert		4
Idem Barnes	16	0 0	Robinson William		6
Dobson Alice		4	Smith John	3	10
Foster Richard	10	0	Thorpe Robert		6
Gilpin Anthony	3	2½	Walton Michael		4
Husband Dorothy		2	Wivel Marmaduke	1	0
Hall Christopher		4	Wood Dorothy		8
Hey Widdow	1	15 10	Wood John	3	2½
Oswald Elizabeth	11	0			

Cockerton and Whessay

Bowbanke George	1	0	Corneforth John	2	9

Blackwell

Name	£	s	d	Name	£	s	d
Blackwell Ralph		2	4	Thompson Ann		2	8
Dark John		10	0	Wan Robert		2	2
Gainforth Ellianor			10	Wastell Henry			2
Marshall wid		7	10	Welford Thomas		19	8
Robinson Ralph		13	0	Stapelton wid	2	5	0

Cottam Mundavill, Morton Tinmouth, Beaumond Hill & Brafferton

Name	£	s	d	Name	£	s	d
Bellingham James Kt.	16	0	0	Idem		9	0
Bradforth John & Marshall John		18	0	Idem			4
Mr. Brasse		4	5½	Johnson Mrs.			6
Thos Greaves of Darlington		7	6	Richardson Thomas		4	5
Jackson John		17	0	Smith Henry		3	4
Idem		3	0	Mrs. Skepp		13	0
				Mr. Henry Warmouth	10	13	4

Haughton

Name	£	s	d
Dickon Hugo		2	0

Sadberge

Name	£	s	d	Name	£	s	d
Allen William		16	8	Johnson Nicholas		3	4
Addy John		9	10	Killingworth Wm		1	2
Addy Richard		9	6	Milbanke Marke	1	0	0
Andrew William			6	Morton wid		10	0
Burbeck Thomas	1	3	0	Morly Dear		1	0
Cockerell Richard			2	Miles George			3
Parson of Dinsdale			4	Pemerton Michael	3	0	0
Foster Richard	1	0	0	Plard Rowland		3	0
Foster William		5	0	Pinkney Margery		5	4
Garmondsway Edward			6	Pemerton Ralph		6	4
Grainger John		1	6	Pudsey George		3	4
Harrison John		10	0	Sir Peter Riddell heir	1	0	0
Hurworthe Lando	1	8	8				

Hulton gen	1	0	Standforth Richard	4	0
Hutchinson William	1	0	Smith gen	2	0
Hedworth John	1	0	Scurfield William	2	3
Hodgshon Lance		3	Saurkeld Lance	16	0
Hilton gen	1	5	Tunstall Thomas		3
Haward Leonard	13	4	Whitfield Thomas	1	0
Mr. Jennison	2 1	8	Wormersley Robert		6
Jackson John	1	1½	Widdower John	10	8
Jackson Richard	1	1½	Wilkinson Robert		7
Jackson gen	1	7	Wilkinson Thomas		1
Johnson Robert	3	4	Wetherell William		9
Johnson Thomas	3	4	Waitering William	2	6
			Walker William	3	4

Bondgate in Darlington Copyholders

JOHN SOBER

26 October 13 Jac. One close called Pounder Close and one other close called Pounder Bank and one Barn called Beachinglaithe and one Thrave and six sheaves of oats parcel of the pounder office of Darlington.

By surrender of Edmond Sober. Fine 1s. 6d.

18 June 21 Jac. Two oxgangs of land.

By surrender of Robert Sober. Fine 9d.

16 October 9 Car. Moytie of one oxgang of land called Maylands in the town and territories of Bondgate.

Fine 2s. 6d.

Moytie of one oxgang of land called Halland and the moytie of one oxgang of Husbandland.

Fine 10s. 0d. Paying rent for all £1. 4. 0.

RALPH COLLING

6 June 22 Car. One cottage formerly Thomas Wrights and one parcell of land in a place called the Markett Place in Darlington.

By surrender of Robert Thorpe. Rent 6d. Fine 1s. 0d.

MERIELL FAWCETT

By severall datts 4th part of an oxgang of land within the Territories of Darlington and also one parcell of land in Clagrand containing ½ acre.

Rent 1s. 9d. Fine 1s. 0d.

PHILIP WHARTON
By severall dates One messuage one Orchard and a garden and part of a close.
Rent 2d. Fine 2s. 3d.

JANE MARSHALL widow.
24 April 10 Car. One half of one oxgang of land called Grange Field.
Rent 5s. 10d. Fine 3s. 4d.

GRACE NICHOLSON widow.
16 October 9 Car. The east part of one cottage and the half of one parcell of land in Darlington.
Rent 1d. Fine 1d.

JOHN GILL
11 April 3 Car. One oxgang of land in Grange Field And also the 4th part of an oxgang of land lying in the same field.
Rent 11s. 8d. Fine 6s. 8d.

RICHARD WODD
10 October 3 Car. One land of Grange land in Northgate lying in one close called Graingefield land and containing 13 acres of land and pasture abutting upon the King's highway on the east parcell of the lands called Grange Close on the north parcell of the lands late in the occupation of John Lisle Gent. Bailiff of the Burrough of Darlington and Widow Nicolson on the west and Beckfields on the south.
By surrender of Thomas Catterick and Margaret his wife. Fine 6s. 8d.
24 April 10 Car. One close called Grange Field as it lies on the west of the close of the said Richard and of the east of the close of John Oswald.
By surrender of Francis Oswald. Fine 1s. 8d.

THOMAS WOOD
17 November 8 Car. One close of meadow called Graunge Field containing 9 acres.
By the surrender of Thomas Bowes gentleman Fine 2d. Rent along with the two former copies £1. 1. 9.

WILLIAM WHITTON

15 April 22 Car. One messuage in Bondgate between the tenement of John Bell and William Gastory.

By surrender of John Applegarth. Rent 1s. od. Fine 6d.

CHRISTOPHER WILKINSON and his daughter ALICE WILKINSON.

3 November 17 Car. Moytie of one tenement with the moytie of one garth and one close lying neere the well.

By surrender of William Wood. Rent 10s. od. (half with John Avery, and a hen or 3s. 4d.) Fine 3s. 4d.

PETER ROBINSON

29 May 40 Eliz. One messuage and half an oxgang of land.

As heir to his father Thomas. Rent 11s. 6d. Fine 3s. 4d.

DOROTHY LAYTON, coson of Thomas Middleton deceased, daughter and heir of Mary Layton deceased, one of the coheirs of the aforesaid Thomas and Michael Willson sonne and heir of Jane Wilson wife of John Wilson deceased one of the daughters of Thomas Middleton deceased.

17 November 20 Car. One messuage in Darlington.

Rent 1s. od. Fine 1s. od.

THOMAS WARD

4 May 23 Car. Moytie of one oxgang of land Townland lying in Bondgate and also 17 acres of land parcell of one oxgang of lands of Townlands and also the moytie of one oxgang of lands of Halland lying in the town and territories of Darlington.

As heir to his father William. Rent 18s. od. Fine 9s. 6d.

LEONARD PILKINGTON

10 October 14 Car. One messuage one barne and one garth lying on the backside of a barn formerly Francis Laing's.

By surrender of Sampson Squire. Rent 4d. Fine 6d.

ELIZABETH SMITH widdow.

24 April 19 Car. One halfe of one oxgange of lands called grange fields in which John Oswald had right.

Rent 5s. 10d. Fine 1s. od.

FRANCIS SEAMER
8 October 4 Car. One cottage with one garth in Northgate.
By surrender of John Doyle. Rent 4d. Fine 1s. od.

JANE APPLEBY widdow of John Appleby.
4 March 23 Car. One house with a garth in Bondgate.
In widdowright. Rent 1s. od. Fine 6d.

JOHN BRADFORTH
15 April 22 Car. Two chambers and the moytie of one garden lying on the north of the Mansion House of one John Stanley and parcell of one messuage and garth in Skinnergate formerly in the tenure of William Burnett.
By surrender of John Stanley. Rent 4d. Fine 4d.

Dat ut supra. Moytie of one messuage and of one garth in Skinnergate between the tenement of Widdowe Dossey and the tenement of widdow Dawson.

In right of Jane his wife who holds in widdowright as relict of William Sober her husband. Rent 3d. Fine 2d.

GEORGE STANLEY
4 May 23 Car. One messuage with a garth in Skinnergate formerly in the tenure of William Burnett.
As heir to his father John. Rent 4d. Fine 4d.

ANN LODGE relict of Thomas Lodge.
15 April 22 Car. One garden and the moytie of the half of the half of one garth lying on the backside of the garden in Skinnergate.
In widdowright. Rent 3d. Fine 6d.

ELIANOR NEWTON wife of Thomas Newton.
3 November 17 Car. One parcell of lands late built upon lying on the east of Isabell Reynolds on the north of the Blackhouse containing 10 yards in length and 6½ yards in breadth with liberty to repair the same.
Fine 1s. 2d.
17 September 22 Car. One parcell of land near the forge 10yds. x 7yds.
As heir to her father. Rent 1s. 10d. in all. Fine 6d.

WILLIAM CHARLESWORTH

13 March 1 Car. One cottage with a garth with the east side adjacent in Darlington.

By surrender of George Bellamy and Roger Jewett. Fine 6d.

14 July 2 Car. One messuage with a garth in Bondgate.

By surrender of William Hilton & Elizabeth his wife. Fine 6d. Rent in all 1s. 6d.

JOHN MIDDLETON

17 November 8 Car. Two acres of arable land lying upon Oxnett Flatt being parcell of a moytie of one oxgang of land in Bondgate.

Rent 2d. Fine 8d.

FRANCIS TOWNDRYE

14 April 6 Car. The office of pinder of Darlington.

Rent £1. 12. 0. Fine 4d.

JOHN DENNIS

26 April 13 Car. 4th part of one messuage and two oxgangs of land lying in Bondgate And also the fourth part of one other oxgang and a half of land called Bondland.

Rent 5s. 7d. Fine 16s. 8d.

JOHN ROBINSON

16 May 9 Car. One parcell of lands con. 4 acres 3 roods lying under Bydale Bank.

Rent 3s. 6d. Fine 2s. od.

GILES WHITTON

20 May 12 Car. One house and a garden in Bondgate.

Rent 5s. 8d. Fine 1s. 4d.

MILES BAILES

23 December 21 Car. One cottage and a garden.

Rent 4d. Fine 2s. od.

JAMES ARMSTRONG

12 October 16 Car. 2 parts of a messuage and one garden.

Rent 4d. Fine 4d.

JOHN HODGSON

By severall dates Two oxgangs of land and one parcell of land in a close lying neare the King's Street containing 8½ acres and also one close called Darlington Site.

Rent £2. 1. 8. Fine 12s. 8d.

THOMAS EMERSON

4 August 3 Car. One close of meadow called Lowfields and one other close of meadow called Wetherell close and one close of pasture called Hamersnott field and one other close of pasture called Leyfield and one other close of pasture called Calfs close containing together an oxgang and a half of land and one messuage with a garden in Darlington.

Rent £2. 9. 8. Fine 9s. 2d.

MARY ELGYE

15 April 22 Car. 4 oxgangs of land in Bondgate.

As relict of John Elgye. Rent £2. 19. 1. Fine 12s. 6d.

JOHN MORLEY

16 April 13 Car. A fourth part of one messuage and two oxgangs of land in Bondgate and a fourth part of another messuage and other oxgang and a half called Bondland.

Rent 5s. 7d. Fine 16s. 8d.

ELIZABETH ROBINSON

18 June 14 Jac. One messuage in Bondgate.

Rent 1s. od. Fine 6d.

JOHN BELL

20 April 17 Jac. One cottage in Darlington.

Rent 1s. od. Fine 2s. od.

WILLIAM BAXTER

24 June 22 Car. One parte of a messuage and the halfe of the entrye and the two doors and one small house lying backwards of the said messuage And yard belonging thereunto.

Rent 1s. 2d. Fine 1s. 2d.

THOMAS DUNWELL

4 May 23 Car. South end of one messuage and parcell of a garden.

Rent 2s. 2d. Fine 4d.

CUTHBERT NICHOLSON
By severall dates. One messuage and one oxgang of land and a third part of an oxgang of land in four part devided and also one cottage and a gardin.
  Rent 16s. od. Fine 13s. od.

ISABELL DUNWELL
17 November 8 Car. One cottage and a garth in Northgate.
  By surrender of Isabell Dunwell. Rent 3s. 4d. paid with Thomas Dunwell. Fine 2d.

ROBERT THOMPSON
26 October 13 Jac. One messuage with a gardeine.
  Rent 1s. 8d. Fine 3s. 4d.

EDWARD HODGSON
13 May 5 Car. One messuage.
  Rent 1s. 8d. Fine 1s. 8d.

EDMUND HODGSON
23 May 6 Jac. A 4th part of a messuage and a 4th part of 2 oxgangs of land and a 4th part of one other messuage and a 4th part of one other oxgang and a half of land called Booreland.
  Rent 5s. 7d. Fine 4s. 2d.

JANE CORNIFORTH
18 June 15 Jac. One messuage and 2 oxgangs and a half parcell of 3 oxgangs of land and a half called Adamland.
  As relict of Cuthbert Corniforth. Rent 14s. 7d. 13s. 4d.

RICHARD OSWOULD
3 November 17 Car. A fourth part of one oxgang of Halland Land and 3 acres and a halfe of land being parcell of a close called Halland.
  Fine 3s. od.
  Ut supra. the moytie of one oxgang of Halland.
  Fine 10d. Rent for both 11s. od.

JOHN MARSHALL
17 October 22 Car. One oxgang of land called Granfield and a parcell

of land called Chowbanke in which Lawrence Catterick sonne and heire of Francis Catterick deceased had right.

Rent 13s. 8d. Fine 5s. od.

7 April 16 Car. One parcell of land called Ellins Close.

Rent 9s. od. (on Coatham rental) Fine 9d.

4 May 7 Car. 19 acres of land parcell of one oxgang of Towneland and half an oxgang of Hallland.

Fine 3s. 4d.

Ut supra. 6 acres of land called Mooreland.

Fine 2d. (Rent for these two copies charged on former copy for Bondgate).

MARY, ANN, and JANE OSWALD, daughters of Henry Oswald. 19 October 7 Car. 3 oxgang of land called Townefield Land in which Henry Oswald has right.

Rent £1. 10. 1. Fine 3s. od.

JOHN and THOMAS TURNER, sonnes and heires apparent of John Turner.

10 August 16 Car. One parcell of land called Blackwell Hill containing 10 acres of land lying and being on the west of the King's highway unto Croft on the south to Blackwell and from there extends to the lands of Bulmer Hey parcell of one oxgang of land formerly Robert Dossy.

By surrender of Henry Oswald and Elizabeth his wife, Mary Comin, Anne Oswald, and Jane Oswald daughters of the said Henry and Elizabeth Oswald. Fine 3s. 4d.

12 May 1 Car. One croft lying at the west end of Bondgate.

As heir to their father deceased. Fine 2d.

JOHN TURNER

3 February 17 Car. The half of a half of a half of one oxgang.

By surrender of Robert Bowes and Margaret his wife. Fine 10d.

Paying rent with the two former copies, in all £5. 1. 6.

Blackwell Township Leaseholder

JOHN CORNEFORTH

15 July 13 Car. 20 acres of arable land within Blackwell allotted unto

the Bishop for his waiste upon the division heretofore of the Townshipp.

For the lives of the said John Corneforth, Richard Corneforth and Thomas Corneforth, all in being.

Rent £1. o. o. Improvement £8. o. o.

Blackwell Township Copyholders

THOMAS SWINBURNE, immediate tenant.

23 June 18 Car. John Middleton did demise unto Thomas Swinburne all his state, term of years and demaund which he has of and in 2 oxgangs of townland and one close called Tressam also Tresham containing 24 acres parcell of two oxgangs of land in Blackwell which the foresaid John Middleton had of Leonard Emerson for the term of divers years yet to come.

Fine 3s. od.

23 June 18 Car. John Middleton did demise to Thomas Swinburne all his state term of years and demaund which he had in 40 acres of Towne land containing 2 oxgangs of lande abut on the west of the lands of Ann Garnett widdow, of the south of John Bygott late Anne Ramshaw and lying on the west side of the River Skyrne and the way extending itself to the south which the said John Middleton has of the graunt of Leonard Emerson for the term of divers years to come.

Fine 4s. od. Rent for both copies in all £2. 14. 7.

THOMAS DOBSON, younger son of Robert Dobson.

10 October 14 Car. The moytie of one cottage.

By surrender of Blesens Taylor. Rent 10d. Fine 6d.

ALICE DOBSON, daughter of Henry Dobson deceased and heir of her brother Christopher.

5 May 17 Car. One messuage and a garth on the backside adjoining betweene the tenements of Henry Dobson on the west and the tenement of Robert Dobson on the east which her said brother Christopher had in right.

Rent 6d. Fine 1s. od.

JOHN LANGSTAFFE

20 May 10 Car. One cottage with a garth.

By surrender of Robert Thorpe. Rent charged on Elizabeth Lang-staffe. Fine 1s. 8d.

MARY KING
4 May 23 Car. One cottage in Blackwell demised to John Dobson without paying any rent.

By surrender of John Dobson. Rent 1s. 8d. Fine 10d.

ROBERT SIMPSON
10 October 14 Car. One cottage and 12 acres of land in Blackwell nooke as they are now divided.

As heire of William Simpson deceased. Rent 1s. 3d. Fine 2s. 4d.

JOHN MIDDLETON, Gent.
21 January 7 Jac. Two oxgangs of lands and a fourth part of an oxgang of townland in which John Middleton his father had right.

Rent £1. 2. 9. Fine 11d.

17 November 18 Car. One messuage 4 oxgang of land and one cottage to the said messuage belonging.

Rent £1. 15. 9. Fine 13s. 4d.

17 November 8 Car. A fourth part of an oxgang of townland which was the land of John his late father.

Rent 2s. 0d. Fine 1s. 8d.

17 November 18 Car. Six acres of land lying in the moore of Black-well late George Garnett's land.

Rent 2s. 6d. Fine 2s. 0d.

MARGARET WARD, widdow.
16 September 21 Car. The moytie of one cottage.

Fine 3d.

Dat ut supra. One oxgang of townland.

Fine 1s. 8d.

Dat ut supra. The moytie of one cottage with a gardeine in Black-well (once Stephen Griffyd's).

Fine 4d.

Dat ut supra. A moytie of one cottage in Blackwell.

Fine 3d.

Dat ut supra. A moytie of one oxgang of towneland in Blackwell.

Fine 1s. 8d.

Dat ut supra. One oxgang of towneland in Blackwell.

Fine 2s. 0d.

Dat ut supra. A moytie of a messuage and of one oxgang and a half of land and parcell of a messuage and three oxgang and a half of land in Blackwell.

Fine 3s. 4d.

8 January—Car. One cottage and gardeine and 4 acres of lands lying in Blackwell Moore.

Rent in toto £1. 18. 7½.

ELIZABETH LANGSTAFFE

5 May 8 Car. One close and a cottage right late Bernard Langstaffe's her father.

Rent 3d. Fine 10d.

Dat ut supra. One close and one cottage right called coatright late John Longstaffe.

Rent 3d. Fine 10d.

ELIZABETH WILKINSON

22 October 3 Jac. One house and parcell of a gardeine, parcell of a messuage and gardeine lately Robert Tomlinsons.

Rent 6d. Fine 10d.

WILLIAM ROBINSON

21 June 7 Jac. One cottage formerly Stephen Virtue's.

Rent 1s. 8d. Fine 1s. 0d.

ANNE WETHERELL

23 April 11 Car. One messuage with a garden part of one messuage and of one third part of one oxgang of Board land.

As daughter and heir of William Wetherell deceased. Rent 1s. 0d. Fine 1s. 0d.

JOHN DOBSON

7 October 18 Car. One cottage and half an acre of land called Guest.

Rent 1s. 6d. Fine 2s. 0d.

ROBERT DOBSON

25 May 38 Eliz. One messuage and two oxgangs and a half of land and one cottage in Blackwell.

Rent £1. 4. 2. Fine 16s. 8d.

Dat ut supra. One messuage and the third part of four oxgangs of land and a half in Blackwell.

Rent 3s. 3d. Fine 5s. od.

29 October 4 Jac. The halfe of one oxgang of land in Blackwell.

Rent 4s. 0½d. Fine 3s. 4d.

29 October 14 Jac. One moytie of a cottage in Blackwell.

Rent 6d. Fine 1s. 4d.

Dat ut supra. One oxgang of land in Blackwell as it lyeth divided in the several fields there late John Dobson his father.

Rent 8s. 1d. Fine 6s. od.

PEETER GOLDSBOROUGH

11 July 5 Car. The halfe of one cottage with a gardeine.

Rent 9d. Fine 6d.

THOMAS GOLDSBOROUGH

25 August 7 Car. One croft and one gardeine called Pinkney Garth in Blackwell.

Rent charged upon William Middleton, George Harrison, and William Cornforth. Fine 2d.

9 October 18 Jac. One cottage and a gardeine And pasture for one cow and five sheepe upon the moore called Braken Moore.

Rent charged upon Robert Simpson. Fine 10d.

THOMAS MORLEY

By several dates. Three oxgangs and three parts of a foot of land in Blackwell. *Mem* a foot of land is the 4th part of an Oxgang.

Rent £1. 6. 8. Fine £2. 5. 0.

WILLIAM MIDDLETON

28 November 22 Car. The halfe of one oxgang of land conteyning 14 acres in Blackwell.

Rent 4s. 0½d. Fine 3s. od.

TOBY COOKER

10 December 8 Car. One halfe of a messuage and the one halfe of a gardeine in which John Richardson hath right.

Rent charged upon William Middleton. Fine 8d.

THOMAS BLEAMEIR

12 April 14 Car. One house and parcell of a garden and six roodes of

land being parcell of a messuage in which one Peeter Busby has right.

Rent 6d. Fine 2d.

MARY KING

26 February 22 Car. One cottage in Blackwell.

Rent 2s. od. Fine 10d.

WILLIAM ALLAN

The half of one parcell of land lately upon the waste with a house.

As son and heire of William Allan. Rent 1s. od. Fine 4d.

EDMUND HODGSON

By severall dates. A fourth part of one oxgang of land in Blackwell And a fourth part of a messuage and a fourth part of foure oxgang of land and a fourth part of a fourth part of an oxgang of land called Boordland and a fourth part of a cottage in Blackwell.

Rent 8s. 10½d.

WILLIAM BOORE

By severall dates. One cottage and also one cottage with the halfe of a cottage and two crofts and five acres of land lying upon Blackwell Moor.

Rent 1s. 11½d. Fine 4s. od.

ROBERT PLACE gent.

19 October 7 Car. One oxgang of land and one half oxgang of land called Linham parcell of messuage and one oxgang of Husband land and a half a land of Maylands And the halfe of one oxgang of townland and one husband land in Blackwell.

Rent 12s. 1½d. Fine 6s. od.

GEORGE GARNETT

By severall dates. One messuage and two oxgangs of Board landes and halfe an acre of lands and one cottage and the halfe of one oxgang of land and also two other oxgang of land and the halfe of an oxgange of lands and also one cottage and the half of a cottage and two crofts lately parcell of two messuages.

Rent £2. 10. 0. Fine £1. 4. 3.

RICHARD WHEATLEY

10 March 33 Eliz. One half of one half of one cottage in Blackwell.
Mem that Robt. Dockley is the immediate tenat.
Rent 1s. 6d. Fine 3d.

JOHN HARRISON and JOHN HARRISON

22 April 16 Car. One croft called Timbley Croft containing nine acres of land in Blackwell.
Rent 3s. 8d. Fine 3s. 0d.

THOMAS CORNEFORTH

By severall dates. One close called Starkitch Nooke parcell of one oxgang of Boordland and also one messuage and a gardene lying in Blackwell. (Mr. Thomas Corneforth hath several other copies of several other lands, but the rent in all is paid together).
Rent £1. 4. 7. Fine 6s. 7d.

PEETER BOWBANKE

By several dates. Three acres of land lying in Oxnett Flatt and also the one half of a halfe of husband land and one cottage and the half of half of an oxgang and a half of land, parcell of one messuage one cottage and three oxgangs and a half of land.
Rent £1. 2. 7½. Fine 6s. 8d.
Mem There is halfe an oxgange of Freelands comprehended within the above rent and payeth 2s. 8d.

WILLIAM CORNIFORTH

By severall dates. One messuage with a garden and a garth called Stanley Garth containing 1 acre and 1 rood of land and one acre of land parcell of six acres of land in which William Ward has right. and also two oxgang of land also one messuage and pasture for five sheep upon the common moor called Brakin Moore and also one messuage and one oxgang of land in Blackwell and one cottage with two acres and also one oxgang and a halfe of land and two messuages and foure oxganges of land and the half of an oxgang of land called Board land and also one other messuage and half one close called Stirkitch and also two parts of one cottage and two parts of one oxgang of lands containing one acre and also two parts of one Messuage and a garden and also one messuage and one cottage with a garden and parcell of lands called Stirkitch.

Rent £4. 14. 2½. Fine £3. 1. 4. *Mem* There are other copies to come in containing other lands but the Rent is charged in all as abovesaid.

WILLIAM MIDDLETON

By severall dates. One close containing the Garth containing nine acres and late John Bringhurst's and also one messuage with two gardenes lying on the east part of the tenement of William Corneforth.

Rent 7s. 8½d. Fine 4s. 4d. *Mem* That the rent for the messuage is paid by Mr. Swinburne who holds the lands formerly therewith occupied.

Cockerton Township Freeholds

ANTHONY GILPIN

11 August 4 Car. Ten acres of meadow in Cockerton holdeth of the Bishop in capite.

Rent 2s. 6d.

ROBERT SHEPHERD

4 July 16 Car. Parcell of freehold land formerlie bought by Arthur Shepherd his father of Sir Ralphe Conyers, Knt., within the township of Cockerton.

Rent 13s. 9d.

Cockerton Township Leaseholds

Sir PAULE NEALD

4 December 16 Car. who assigned to Richard Morley, yeoman, George Lodge, John Staynesby, Thomas Robinson, John Sober, and John Clement, on 4 December 16 Car. Pasture gates within the Grange Close neere Cockerton situated within the townshipps of Haughton and Darlington in the tenure of Edward Lively or his assigns by indenture 13 October 3 Car.

For 21 years, the immediate tenants to pay Sir Paul Neald 40s. per annum.

Rent £2. 0. 1. Improvement £6. 14. 4. (the Jury say £4. 0. 0.)

Cockerton Township Copyholds

ANTHONY GILPIN

22 September 10 Car. One close containing one acre of land parcell of one oxgang and a half.

By surrender of Anthony Gilpin his father. Fine 6d.

26 April 13 Car. One messuage with a garth.

By surrender of Elizabeth Hodgson. Fine 6d. The rent included in Wm. Hodgson's rent.

THOMAS NEWBY

16 October 9 Car. One close called Capse Close containing 22 acres of land and also one other close called Botham Hill containing 4 acres of lands with the house therupon built and also one other close containing 20 acres of lands and also 14 acres of lands and a half now called Cockerton Moor.

By surrender of Francis Newby his father. Rent 17s. 1d. Fine 16s. 4d.

PETER BOWBANCK

By severall dates. Pasture for 5 beasts upon Cockerton Moore, parcell of the half of one oxgang of land and the half of a half of an oxgang of land into 4 parts divided. And whole pasture in the pasture and Grange Close and Cockerton Moor and the halfe of an oxgange of lands.

Rent 15s. 1d. Fine 9s. 4d.

JOHN MORLEY, in right of Thomazin his wife, daughter of Robert Hutton.

4 May 7 Car. One messuage and garth parcell of the moyte of one oxgang of land.

By surrender of Robert Hutton. Rent 6d. Fine 6d.

WILLIAM BLAKEY

29 October 21 Jac. The halfe of one oxgang of land of Towneland and the moytie of one oxgang of Halland.

As heir of John Blakey. Rent 11s. 8d. Fine 6s. 8d.

GEORGE HEDDON

4 May 23 Jac. The west end of one house and parcell of one garth

lying on the backside of the same house conteining one rood, and the fourth part of one rood of lands and boundeing the half abutting on the house and garth of Peter Bowbank on the west of the lands of John Maunders and Alice his wyfe on the east, parcell of one house and of one garth in Cockerton.

By surrender of John Maunders and Alice his wife. Rent one wood henn. Fine 1d.

ALICE MAUNDERS, wife of John Maunders.

Dat ut supra. One house with a garth on the backside adjoining in Cockerton.

Paying rent with the other. Fine 2d.

THOMAS PIBUS
27 September 13 Car. One cottage.

By surrender of Francis Marshall. Rent 6d. Fine 6d.

ANTHONY ROBINSON
25 April 21 Car. One close called Westerhall Flatt containing 17 acres.

Rent 12s. 10d. Fine 6s. 8d.

THOMAS STAYNSBY
4 May 13 Jac. One messuage with a garden lying on the backside and extending itself to a certeyne water called Skyrne into the south with pasture for one beast in one close called Grange close used with the aforesaid messuage.

By surrender of Anthony Staynsby. Rent 4d. Fine 4d.

ROBERT SOBER
20 May 12 Car. One messuage and two oxgangs and a half of husbandland.

Fine 13s. 4d.

Dat ut supra. One oxgang and a half of land called Halland and one cottage.

Fine 9s. 8d.

Both held as son and heir of Dorothy Sober deceased. Rent £2. 2. 0. Mr. Thomas Pibus pays 6d. of this rent.

FRANCIS PARKINSON, gent. THOMAS ROBINSON JOHN STAINSBY EDMOND HODGSON.

4 May 13 Jac. By the severall commands of the Bishop take one close

called Grange Close to their use and to the use of the tenants of the said town of Cockerton under this form following, *vizt*

That when one of the fower dieth that then the heire of him and of every tennant of the said towne shall fine for the forth part of the said close called Graunge Close, and if two of them shall die then the moytie of the said close shall fine, and if three of them shall die, then the heires of them and all the tenants of the said town shall fine of new for 3 parts of the said close called the Graunge Close and if all of them shall dye then again they shall be fined for the whole close aforesaid.

Rent £7. 6. 8.

ANNE SQUIRE
13 October 22 Jac. One house or messuage.

As daughter and heir of Richard Atkinson deceased. Rent 2s. 8d. Fine 6d.

JOHN DENNIS
By severall dates. A fourth part of one messuage and a fourth part of two oxgangs of townland and a fourth part of a messuage with a gardeine and a fourth part of a parcell of land conteining half an acre and a fourth part of one other messuage with a gardeine and one fourth part of an Oxgang of Halland and a fourth part of one oxgang of Towneland and also a forth part of one oxgang of Husband-land and a fourth part of a cottage and pasture for five sheep.

Rent 13s. 4d. Fine 11s. 10d.

THOMAS MORLEY
26 April 13 Car. 4th part of an oxgang of land and a house and a 4th part of two oxgangs of land in the precincts of Cockerton.

Rent 13s. 4d. Fine £1. 5. 2.

WILLIAM THOMPSON
By severall dates. Three oxgangs of land within the town of Cockerton.

Rent £1. 7. 10. Fine £1. 8. 8.

WILLIAM HODGSON
24 April 10 Car. Two oxgangs and a foot of land in Cockerton.

Rent £1. 1. 8. Fine £1. 0. 11.

GEORGE LODGE
By severall dates. Four oxgangs of land in Cockerton.
   Rent £1. 18. 0. Fine £1. 13. 8.

THOMAS ROBINSON
By severall dates. Four oxgangs and three feet of land in Cockerton.
   Rent 16s. 4d. Fine £1. 18. 0.

MARMADUKE WILLIAMSON
27 September 13 Car. One oxgang and two foot of husband land.
   Rent 4s. 4d. Fine 5s. 6d.

THOMAS HEDDON
22 October 7 Car. Two oxgangs of land.
   Rent 13s. 4d. Fine 9s. 2d.

ROBERT STAINSBY
By severall dates. The half of all those lands which were lately John Thompson's. And the half of one oxgang of land and one cottage with a fourth part of an oxgang of land.
   Rent 19s. 4d. Fine 18s. 8d.

LEONARD PILKINGTON
11 October 14 Car. One messuage and one garden.
   (The same property as Anne Squires.) Fine 6d.

ANN HEVID
By severall dates. 2 oxgang and a foot of land.
   Rent £1. 2. 2. Fine 6s. 2d.

LAURENCE STAINSBY
By severall dates. One oxgang and a half of land and one close called Farr close also Rosterley Ley and one messuage and one oxgang of land lying in the Grange Close and pasture for two horses and two sheep and the third part of pasture for one beaste in fower parts divided in the aforesaid Graunge Close and also two acres of lands lying in Stowperdale and parcell of one messuage and two oxgangs of land called Dallingland in Cockerton and also one close containing one acre being part of a fourth part of an oxgang of land lying in Cockerton.

Rent £1. 6. 11. Fine 13. 4d.

EDMUND HODGSHON

By severall dates. A fourth part of a cottage and a fourth part of a pasture for five sheep and also a fourth part of a messuage and a fourth part of two oxgang of Husbandland and also a fourth part of a messuage and a fourth part of a garden and a fourth part of a parcell of land lying att the end of the garden containing half an acre and also the fourth part of one other messuage with a gardeine and a fourth part of one oxgang of Halland and a forth part of one oxgang of Towneland and also one close containing fourteen acres.

Rent 16s. 7d. Fine 13s. 9½d.

JANE THOMPSON

23 April 20 Car. One messuage and one close called Stainshawe being parcell of one half of an oxgang of Husband land.

Rent 2s. 4d. Fine 5s. 4d.

ANTONY GILPIN

17 July 13 Car. One close containing one acre of land parcell of one oxgang and a half of land.

Rent 2s. 6d. Fine 6d.

ROBERT BOWES

4 June 22 Car. One cottage and a garden in Cockerton.

Rent 2s. od. Fine 6d.

ANNE CONNE

13 October 20 Jac. One cottage.

Rent 2s. 4d. Fine 1s. od. *Mem* That this is comprehended within William Hodgson's rent.

JOHN MARSHALL

13 October 22 Car. One cottage in Cockerton.

Rent 2d. Fine 8d.

Whessay Township Copyholds

THOMAS SWINBURNE

23 June 18 Car. One parcell of land called Grassin Moore one parcell

of land called Kilngarth, one close called The Close, 2 closes called Newton Garth late in the tenure of Thomas Heddon, one other parcell of land called Cheseley one other parcell of land called East and West Myers one parcell of land called West Leazes, one other parcell of land called Annatt Thorne, one other parcell of land called Annott Well, one other parcell of land called Huntershields.

Rent £2. 6. 8. Fine 13s. 4d.

ROBERT SHEPHERD

3 June 4 Car. Messuages houses and edifices and lands lying on the south side of Cole land and one little close on the north side of the said Cole land adjoyning to Beamond Hill lands and 2 other closes late in the tenure or occupation of Richard Horner also Hornsby, parcell of 8 messuages one cottage one croft and 13 ox-gangs of land in Whessay.

By surrender of William Shepherd. Rent £2. 0. 0. Fine 5s. 0d.

Cottam Mundavill Township Freeholds

THOMAS KEY demised to Ralph Tunstall.

3 May 26 Eliz. Messuages tenements lands meadowes woods lying in the township and territories of Cottam Mundavill and Brafferton, and all that his messuage and tenement and two cottages in Cottam Mundavill.

Rent 11s. 3d. and a peppercorn.

Mem That Fetham Farm charged in the rentall is paid in by the several Greeves of Blackwell, Bondgate and Cockerton, the which inhabitants thereof payeth the rent of 6s. 6d. joyntly together every year.

Cottam Mundavill Township Leaseholds

THOMAS TUNSTALL

26 March 16 Car. All that farmland tenements closes meadows pasture comons commons of pasture in Cottam Mundavill called the Demeasne lands of Cottam Mundavill.

For the lives of Ralph Tunstall, son of Thomas Tunstall, and Ralph and Thomas Tunstall sons of the said Ralph.

Rent £6. o. o. Improvement £73. 6. 8. (Jury say £66. 6. 8.)

WILLIAM JACKSON

20 February 14 Car. Parcell of land meadow or pasture conteyning 18 acres lying within the township aforesaid commonlie called or known by the name of Waste land.

For the lives of Thomas Denham, now deceased, John Denham (40 years) and Cuthbert Denham (35 years).

Rent 10s. od. Improvement £4. o. o. (Jury say £5. o. o.)

THOMAS TUNSTALL

30 September 6 Car. Parcell of waste in Cottam called the Balle adjoyning upon the River of Skerne conteyning 2 roods. And all that river or water course of Skerne from the ground belonging to Ackley Dame to the low end or south end of the demesnes belonging to the said Bishop with libertie to cleans and scower the said channel and to plant and erect a water corne mill upon any part of it within the lymitt and extent aforesaid and to make and preserve a mill damme and millrace.

For 21 years.

Rent £1. o. o. Fine £1. o. o.

Cottam Mundavill Township Copyholds

JOHN GILL

11 April 3 Car. One parcell of lands called Redghille containing 4 acres.

By surrender of Francis Cattericke. Rent £2. 5. o. Fine 2s. od.

WILLIAM TUNSTALL

10 April 3 Car. One cottage and croft and toft.

Rent 4s. 6d. Fine 2s. od.

Haughton Township Freehold

CHRISTOPHER DICKON

24 April 14 Car. In consideration of the sum of £160 holdeth all that

messuage, tenement or farmehold and 2 oxgangs of land meadow and pasture and the little paddock in Haughton.

Rent 6s. 2d.

Mem That Thomas Harrison is to pay the remaynder of 13s. rent which is due by them both and the inheritance belongeth to John Robinson.

Haughton Township Leaseholds

KING JAMES

14 January 1 Jac. who assigned to Dudley Carleton of London, Esq. 10 March 1 Jac. assigned to Toby Mathew of London Esq. 26 April 2 Jac., assigned to Edward Easton of Crayke 24 January 5 Jac. assigned to Thomas Blakeston 3 September 5 Jac. assigned to Hugo Simpson for £95 on 17 December 11 Jac., granted to Robert Hixon, of Ferryhill, senior and Robert Hixon of the same junior.

30 April 3 Car.

Leased to King James for 80 years.

All that water corn mill nere Haughton together with all water and watercourses, fishings.

Rent £4. 0. 0. Improvement £16. 0. 0. (Jury say £20. 0. 0.)

KING JAMES

14 January 1 Jac. who assigned to Dudley Carleton of London, 10 March 1 Jac. assigned to Toby Mathew of London 26 April 2 Jac., assigned to Edward Easton of Craike firm in Middlesex 22 June 1 Jac., assigned to Thomas Blakeston of Newton in Co. Durham 30 September 5 Jac. assigned to John Gill of the City of Durham 16 April 8 Jac. for £160.

One close or parcell of ground called Halykeld near to Haughton, late in the occupation of Timothie Barnes gent.

Leased to King James for 80 years. Rent £4. 0. 0. Improvement £20. 0. 0. (Jury say £16. 0. 0.)

Haughton Township Copyholds

THOMAS SIMPSON

18 June 15 Jac. 4 Messuages and 4 oxgangs and one cottage.

Rent £2. 5. 0. Fine 3s. 4d.

JOHN GILL
14 April 10 Car. One cottage.
   Rent 2s. 4d. Fine 6s. 4d.
6 October 10 Car. Nyne acres of meadow called Leed Nyne Acres between the field of West Field and the water of Skerne. And also one close called West field with one parcell of land called Calfe Greene.

MARY NEWTON
17 October 18 Car. One cottage with a garden and three acres of meadow in Haughton.
   Rent 4s. 8d. Fine 5s. od.

VALENTINE BROWNE
4 May 12 Car. One cottage with a garden.
   Rent 2s. 4d. Fine 1s. 8d.

ROBERT WHEELEHOUSE
20 May 12 Car. One cottage with a garden.
   Rent 2s. od. Fine 1s. od.

CHRISTOPHER DICKON
20 April 17 Jac. One cottage.
   Rent 2s. od. Fine 6s. 8d.

ADAM HARRISON
19 October 6 Jac. Two messuages and three oxgangs of land.
   Rent £2. 2. 8. Fine 13s. 4d.

THOMAS RIPPON and Frances his wife.
27 September 13 Car. Demised to Philip Rippon all there whole right state title claim terme of year and demaund in one cottage with a garth after the death of the said Thomas and Frances for a thousand years then next following without paying any rent besides the fine to the Lord and the service therefore due and accustomed and giving to the Lord for admittance 2s. 4d.
   Rent 2s. 4d. Fine 2s. od.

ROBERT SYMPSON
19 October 7 Car. One messuage and one oxgang of land lying in the towne of Haughton.
   Rent 10s. od. Fine 2s. 8d.

Sadberge Township Freeholds

JOHN BUCK son of Miles Buck.
20 September 13 Jac. In capite by inquisition of escheat holdeth one messuage with a garden and 4 oxgangs of land and also one messuage and a garden and ten oxgangs of land and also 12 messuages or burgages.
Rent 18s. 4d.

FRANCIS HARRISON sone of Thomas Harrison.
7 October 2 Car. By inquisition of escheat in capite one messuage and 4 oxgang of land.
Rent 2s. 8d.

RICHARD COWLMAND by deed of sale from Richard Middleton.
21 March 20 Car. In capite all that messuage burgage or tenement with a little garth thereunto in Sadberge now in the tenure and occupation of the said Richard Cowlman and abutting upon the King's Street on the east upon the land of John Harrison on the south on the well spring on the west and George Garry ground on the northe.
Rent 6d.

JOHN HARRISON by assignment from John Burke.
14 April 5 Car. In capite 2 closes of meadow and pasture ground commonlie called Newton Gates and Say lande containing by estimation 140 acres with a house thereon standing paying three peppercorns to John Burke.
Rent 6d.

IDEM from William Allen.
24 May 18 Car. In capite 2 messuages with two garths lying on the backside of the messuage one little close called the Low Close and another close called the five acre close which acre or close contains 7 acres.
Also from John Buck by assignment 14 November 12 Car., one close.
Rent 7s. 8d.

RICHARD GARMONDSWAY by deed poll.
7 September 22 Jac. 3 burgages in Sadberge, 7 oxgang of land meadow and pasture.
   Rent 13s. 6d.

JOHN CUSSEN son of John Cussen.
5 October 19 Jac. By deed poll five messuages, 5 crofts, and 5 tofts and two oxgang and a half of land.
   Rent 5s. od.

BARTHOLOMEW RAE by deed of sale from John Buck.
20 May 18 Car. All that house and garth in Sadberge upon the north side of the said town being held in fee simple.
   Rent 6d.

RICHARD MIDDLETON by bargain of sale from John Buck.
20 September 8 Car. In fee simple one burgage or frontstede in Sadberge.
   Rent 6d.

ROBERT HOBLOCK
10 March 17 Jac. The moyte of one halfe of the wast containing foure burgage fronts and garth in Sadberge in fee simple.
   Rent 6d.

RICHARD PEACOCK by bargain of sale from John Casson.
12 March 14 Car. One tenement or house with a garth on the backside.
   Rent 6d.

HENRY WILKINSON
20 March 14 Car. In fee simple from John Allenson of Newbiggen in the parish of Bishopton yeoman all that cottage house and garth in Sadberge on the west row of the said town betwene a tenement of George Garry's on the south and upon a house of Richard Peacock late George Peacock on the north and on the garth of the said George Peacock on the west and upon the King's street on the east.
   Rent 6d.

MARMADUKE GARRY
28 July 5 Jac. One house with one garth in Sadberge which his son William Garry now holdeth.

Rent 6d.

WILLIAM ALLAN by assignment.
1 March 11 Jac. One burgage or tenement and one garth which George Peacock late held.
Rent 6d.

ROBERT STAYNSBY son and heir of Mathew Staynsby.
31 March 4 Car. One new erected messuage, tenement, or burgage with a garth or toft behind which his said father held from Richard Colman.
Rent 6d.

WILLIAM GARNETT son and heir of Cuthbert Garnett.
26 March 19 Jac. A messuage or seathouse in Sadberge wherein Cuthbert Garnett late dwelleth.
Rent 6s. 10d.

ANN GARNETT widdow by assignment.
26 March 19 Jac. One tenement and three yards in Sadberge wherein Bryan Garmondsway dwelt.
Rent 1s. 0d.

GEORGE GARRY
10 April 22 Jac. In fee simple as heire to his father Marmaducke Garry All that tenement or burgage lately wasted with one little garth thereto belonging in Sadberge bounding on the south side to a burgage or tenement belonging to one Richard Middleton of Sadberge aforesaid and wherein the said Richard now dwelleth on the north to a tenement belonging to one John Cussen of Sadberge and wherein one William Bulman now dwelleth, on the east to the King's Street and on the west the Well spring.
Rent £6. 0. 0.

Sadberge Township Copyholds

THOMAS WELFORD
11 March 22 Car. One acre of land in Sadberge.
Rent 13s. 4d. Fine 1s. 8d.

JOHN BUCK

4 June 5 Car. The whole demeasne lands of Sadberge with all lands meadow pasture pasture of mores and marishes.

By surrender of Thomas Buck, gent. Rent £8. o. o. Fine £2. 6. 8.

SURVEY OF THE MANOR OF EVENWOOD

Samuel Leigh   Tho Saunders   Edw Colston   Geo Dailes

Manerium de Evenwood
cum membris
6 April Anno Domini 1647
Jury

George Burne gentleman
Robert Ridlington gentleman
Ambrose Johnson gentleman
John Bell yeoman
John Sympson yeoman
George Lax yeoman
Robert Darlington yeoman
Robert Addamson yeoman
William Shippardson yeoman
Christopher Dobson yeoman
Robert Blake yeoman
John Dowson yeoman

Robert Vincent yeoman
Thomas Trotter yeoman
John Wood yeoman
Myles White yeoman
James Dunne yeoman
John Mayne yeoman
Thomas Hixon yeoman
Richard Hobson yeoman
Robert Adamson yeoman
William Adamson yeoman
John Slayter yeoman
Robert Laxe yeoman

1. Imprimis we present that the town of Evenwood has been and is part of the Barony of Evenwood in which there has been a goodly house but the same is utterly decayed and has so been many years since but there is no tymber about the same that they know of nor any sea roads or market town nerer it than Bishop Auckland which is between three and four miles, nor is there any orchards gardens or other outhouse belonging to the same mansion house called the Barony.

2. To the second article they present and say that there is a park belonging to the foresaid ruined house which park as they are informed conteyneth 300 acres and is letten for £120 per annum besides the rent paid to the late Bishop of Durham which is £20 per annum as they are informed but for the more certeity herein they refer themselves to the deed itself showed to the foresaid Surveyors. And they say that there is belonging to the said Barony or Manor of Even-

wood those townships following vzt. Killerby West Auckland and Evenwood but what acres the said towns conteyne or what rent they pay other than such as are mentioned in ther Leases and Coppies produced to the said Surveyors to which they referre themselves they know not nor do they know of any graung belonging to the foresaid Mannor or other answer make to this article other than this that the lands in the foresaid township are moorish.

3. To the third article they present that there is belonging to the foresaid Barony a great common or waste ground called Raley fell on which they put cattle without stint but there is no wood on the same nor any in the Barony. And other answer than they have made to the present Article they cannot make Saveing that there is no deer or cunnyes in the foresaid park.

4. To the fourth article they say that the Lord of the said Barony vizt the Bishop of Durham or some of his agents have gone about to improve some part of the said waste or common but they have from time to time been prevented or hindered by the tennants of the said towns when they have attempted any such thing.

5. 6. To the 5th and 6th articles they say that the Lord hath the waifes and strayes on the said moore but they do not know of any particular fishing within the said mannor and if any such be they do belong to the Bishop but the valew or worth per annum they know not.

7. To the 7th article they say that there is five watermill and no more that they know of belonging to the said mannor but what lands belong to the said mills or what rent the same pay or the valewes thereof they know not but refer themselves to the leases or writings by which the several tenants hould the same and the Survey of the Surveyors.

8. To the 8th article that they believe that the several tennants within the Soke of this mannor do grind at the foresaid milnes which is all the answer they can give to this article.

9. To the 9th article they present and say that there is a great colleyerie within this manor called Carter's Thorne which is in lease from the Bishop for lives at the rent of £70 per annum and letten by one Mr. Drake who is said to be a feoffee or trustee for some children who pretend to have right in the said lease now let for three years to Mr. Charles Vane and Mr. Thomas Bowes for £350 per annum, Mr. Drake payeing the Bishop's rent but it appears not how many of the said lives are yet in being nor do it appear unto

them or can anyways find out that there is any other mynes or quarryes (save only one other collyery at Butterknowle of very little worth) other than before expressed and the value of that they know not nor who holds the same.

10. 11. To the 10th and 11th articles we say that they do not know whether there be any freeholders within the foresaid mannor, and if there be it will appear to the Surveyors who have the perusall and right of their writings by which they hould the same and to which they refer themselves.

12. 13. To the 12th and 13th they say that most if not all the tennants within the said mannor are coppie holders and do all of them suit and service to the Lord's Court and do pay upon death or alienation such cesse or fine as are mentioned in their severall & particular fines which are certein in themselves the certainty thereof will appeare by their severall copies produced to the said Surveyors to which they refer themselves and other answer they cannot make to the said Articles or either of them.

14. 15. 16. 17. 18. To the 14th 15th 16th 17th 18th articles they say with relation to ther answers to some of the precedent interrogatories that they cannot make any but negative answers to the said several and respective articles.

19. To the 19th article they say that they know not what profit the Lord makes by his courts or of his waifes and strayes, fellons goods within the said Mannor.

20. To the 20th article the late Bishop as Lord of the foresaid mannor in the right of Jura Regal hath all manner of privileges, royalties, franchises and immunities but upon profit he made of them they know not.

21. To the 21st article they say that they do not know of any right of presentation the Bishop hath within the said mannor or several townships belonging to the same.

22. 23. To the 22nd and 23rd articles they say for the reasons aforesaid they cannot make any answer to the said articles.

24. To the 24th article they say they do not know by what mensuration the lands in this county are measured it being seldom used there.

25. To the 25th article they do not know what reprises pensions duties or fees are issuable and to be paid out of this mannor.

Further presented

1. That it appeareth by the testimony upon oath of William Gar-

grave that Mr. Raphe Eden of Hesley father to Mrs. Black wife of John Blackston had a lease of an parcell of land called Copeland in in West Auckland for one and twenty years from Dr. James late Bishop of Durham which land was afterwards let by Bishop Neale to Mr. Edward Lively his secretary upon a promise that the lease was forfeited for nonpayment of rent at the day which day of payment by no possibility they could observe by reason that the waters were so overflown at that time that none could pass without danger of life, not withstanding they do averr that the next day the rent was tendered but would not be accepted, the heir being then an infant and under age.

2. They present that by the oath of Mr. Robert Eden that there was a concurrent lease of certeine lands called Copelands and Hole-meadowe graunted from Dr. William James late Bishop of Durham for one and twenty years by the Bishop of Durham to Mr. John Eden Bishop but when the same was to commence it appeareth not but that Mr. Eden beleved the foresaid lease was to begin after the determination of a lease of the same land graunted to Mr. John Eden and other freeholders and copiholders of West Auckland, and further that it appeareth by the said testamony that the said former lease was apprised amongst the chattels of the said Raphe Eden after the death of the said Raphe Eden. And further it appeareth by the said testimony that the said Robert Eden did afterwards speak with Bishop Neale in the behalf of Mrs. Blackston then an infant, concerning the same lease and that the Bishop tould him that there was such a lease but that it was forfeited by reason of the forfeiture of the auld lease graunted to Mr. John Eden and others and further that the said Mr. Eden testified that he desired Bishop Neale that he would not take the advantage of an infant but the Bishop answered he had an infant of his own for whom he must provide.

3. They present that it appeareth by the testamony upon oath of Thomas Pearson that upon search of the Bishop's records at Durham he found that a lease of Copeland and Hole meadowes was graunted for one and twenty years by the Bishop of Durham to Mr. John Eden and others freeholders and copyholders of West Auckland which lease did bear date the Eleventh day of May in the year of 1606 but could find no lease graunted to Mr. Raphe Eden, but hath heard that there was a concurrent lease of the said land graunted to the said Raphe Eden to commence after the determination of the former lease graunted to Dr. John Eden and others.

4. They present that it appeareth by the testamony upon oath of William Gainford that about nineteen or twenty yeares since Richard Gargrave was made Collector of the Bishop's rent in West Auckland and had received the rent of Mr. John Eden and others for Copeland and Hole meadows and there falling a great flood of rain about the time that the Bishop's rents were to be paid into the Chequer at Durham which raised the waters so high that the collector could not go to Durham to pay in the said rents at the day of payment and that the said Collector did go to pay in the said rents upon the Munday following which was as soon as he could get to Durham by reason of the floodes but then the rents of Copeland and Hole meadow would not be received the Receiver pretending the lease of the said land graunted to Mr. John Eden and others was forfeited and further it appeareth by the said testimony that the said William Gainford and others went afterwards to Bishop Neale to treat with him about renewing the said lease which the Bishop was content to do: but upon a motion that the Bishop would secure them against the lease made to Mr. Raphe Eden Bishop Neale made answer that the forfeiters of the lease graunted to Mr. John Eden and others did forfeit the concurrent lease graunted to Mr. Raphe Eden by Bishop James and that he would not give the daughter of Mr. Raphe Eden then an infant to whom the concurrent lease was left a penny more than upon good will.

5. They present that it appeareth by the testimony upon oath of William Richardson that the time of the year at which the rent for Copeland and Hole meadowes should have bein paid in to the Chequer at Durham was about Martinmas in Winter at which time there fell so much rains that raised the waters so high that Richard Gargrave then Collector of the Bishop's rents in West Auckland who had received the rents for the said lands called Copeland and Hole meadowes could not go to Durham but that about two or three days after the said Collector did go to Durham but the rent for Copeland and Hole meadows would not be received.

Evenwood Township Copyholds

JANE SINGLETON

17 September 21 Car. Four gardens and two other gardens and 12 acres of lands in Evenwood.

As relict of Raphe Singleton. Rent 13s. od. Fine 6s. 8d.

EDWARD CORNY
22 October 17 Car. One parcell of land called Gorden containing 80 acres of lands and three acres of land late the lord's waste lyeing on the north of Gordon att Arkins Banke within Evenwood.

By surrender of Cozen and heir of Samuell Sands defunct.
Rent £1. 4s. 6d. Fine £1. 1s. od.

JOHN HODSHON
13 April 14 Car. One cottage wth a garden.

As heir to his father John Hodshon. Rent 8s. od. Fine 6s. 8d.

JOHN GARGRAVE & WILLIAM GARGRAVE
13 April 3 Car. One close called Eastburne close and half an acre of land parcell of half a messuage and the half of 80 acres of land att Toft Hill late John Darnton's.

By surrender of John Allison. Rent 3s. 4d. Fine 2s. od.

MARY GARGRAVE
13 April 3 Car. One close called Pitt close with free ingress and egress.

By surrender in widdowright of William Gargrave. Rent 2s. 6d. Fine 2s. 6d.

CHRISTOPHER STEVENSON
22 October 21 Jac. One house.

By surrender of Elisabeth Stevenson. Rent 4d. Fine 6d.

JOHN THOMPSON
20 June 15 Jac. One parcell of land of the Lord's waste containing two acres lying upon Brocken Hill nigh Morley.

By surrender of John Hodgshon. Fine 8d.

Ut supra. One acre of land lyeing at Brocken hill nigh Morley.

By surrender of John Hodgshon. Rent for both 1s. 2d. Fine 4d.

JOHN THOMSON & JAMES his son.
5 April 10 Car. One close and foure acres butting upon the Lambe close on the east and south and containing 6 acres.

By surrender of Christopher Tower. Rent 3s. od. Fine 1s. 4d.

JOHN THOMSON & ROBERT THOMSON
6 May 22 Jac. the half of the west of a close called Cowe close.
   By surrender of Wm. Gibbon. Rent 8d. Fine 2s. 6d.

JOHN THOMSON
11 May 1 Car. The half of the east of Cow close.
   By surrender of John Hodgshon. Rent 2s. 6d. Fine 2s. 6d.

JOHN THOMSON & JOHN his son.
11 October 18 Car. The west part of a messuage called the Eastmoore
vizt from the east end of a stable late in the tenure of Richard
Baddley as far as it is now divided.
   By surrender of Robert Thomson. Rent 5s. 6d. Fine 2s. od.

JOHN ROBSON
4 April 10 Car. The east part of a messuage called Eastmoore Place
vizt from the east end of a stable late Mr. Badleye's.
   By surrender of Richard Baddily. Rent 5s. 6d. Fine 2s. od.

GERRARD ALLINSON
27 October 16 Jac. One messuage and 80 acres of land late John
Darnton's.
   By surrender of Thomas Friend. Rent 4s. 2d. Fine 7s. 4d.

THOMAS HODGSHON & JOHN his son.
20 June 21 Jac. One close of meadow called Low field containing 6
acres of land in the north of Calfe Close.
   By surrender of John Hodghon. Rent 3s. 4d. Fine 4s. od.
11 May 1 Car. The northe part of a close called Cowe close now
inclosed in the possession of the said Thomas.
   By surrender of John Thomson & Robert Thomson. Rent 1s. 1od.
Fine 1s. 1od.

LANCELLOT WILDE & THOMAS WILDE his son.
2 October 11 Car. 30 acres of land.
   By surrender of Thomas Wilde senior and Thomas Wilde. Fine
5s. od.
   Ut supra. Three roods of land in Morley.
   By surrender of Thomas Wilde senior and Thomas Wilde. Rent
1os. 5d. Fine 3d.

LANCELLOTT WILDE younger sonne of Robert Wild.

8 May 16 Jac. Half of the north half of one acre of land late lyeing upon the lord's waste neere Mooreside wth a house built thereon and in his occupation.

By surrender of the aforesaid Robert Wilde. Rent 2d. Fine 1d.

LANCELLOT WILD

By special command of the lord 9 May 19 Jac. Two acres of land in the north part of a close at Morley.

Rent 8d. Fine 8d.

JOHN THOMSON

29 October 10 Car. One tenement and 10 acres of land at Morley.

By surrender of John Holmerawe. Rent 5s. 11d. Fine 5s. 11d.

JOHN ROBINSON

24 April 13 Car. Five ridges of land containing 4 acres in a close called Crowne feild.

By surrender of Raphe Hodgshon. Rent 1s. 4d. Fine 2s. 0d.

ALICE HODGSHON nowe wife of John.

the halfe of the whole tenure of 22 acres of land and a half att Dagill in Evenwood as it is now divided and in ther possession also one close called Birkeclose also Les close and a close called Highfield adjoyning to Wales moore a close called Pease lands a close called West Pasture adjoyning to Butterknowle and half a garden called Lyme Garth wth half a messuage.

By surrender of John Seddgkirk & Anne his wife. Rent 7s. 8d. Fine 6s. 7d.

JOHN HODGSON

12 October 14 Car. One close of meadow called the Smith field containing 10 acres of land lying on the east part of a close called Shawe hole & Wales Moore on the other parte.

By demise of Elizabeth Hodgshon for tenure of the life of the sd. Elizabeth. Rent 5s. 0d. Fine 5s. 0d.

EDWARD WRIGHT

11 October 12 Car. by several commands of the Bishop. Parcell of lands covered with water called Bolam Laugh and the fishing and

fowling in and upon the same as the said water extending itself at any time and sufficient land about the same for making of the dam and foure about the premises.

Rent 6s. od. Fine 6s. od.

JOHN ROBINSON

10 May 15 Car. One house and a frontstedd called the Faught Tree House with two parts of a garden called Stack Garthes parcell of two tenements or houses now built.

As heir to his brother Henry Robinson defunct. Rent 6d. Fine 6d.

THOMAS SAUNDERSON

13 April 14 Car. One messuage called Westerplace late in the tenure of Thomas Hodgshon with 6 acres of land lyeing in three several fields near the said messuage.

As heir to his father Francis. Rent 6s. od. Fine 5s. od.

GERARD ALLENSON

28 April 18 Car. One parcell of land lying at Cunderwell containing 6 acres of land.

As heir to his grandfather. Rent 2s. od. Fine 2s. od.

RICHARD HEVISIDE

28 April 41 Eliz. One tenement and 12 acres of land in the tenure of Thomas Holmeraw lying in Morley in the Barony of Evenwood.

By surrender of John Heviside. Rent 10s. od. Fine 10s. od.

WILLIAM GIBBON

6 April 22 Car. One close called Cornefield containing 12 acres of land in Evenwood.

By surrender of Margaret Hodgson. Rent 2s. 8d. Fine 2s. 8d.

10 April 8 Car. One parcell of land now in one close called Morley close containing 15 acres of land within Evenwood and one house lately built thereon.

Rent 8s. od. Fine 7s. 2d.

ANTHONIE DOBINSON

11 May 19 Car. One parcell of land containing 2½ acres of land late the Lord's waste and another parcell of land containing one acre late the lord's waste.

As heir to his mother Isabell Dobinson. Rent 1s. 4d. Fine 1s. 4d.

WILLIAM HODSON

6 April 22 Car. 10½ acres of land in Wakfield in Evenwood.
As heir to his father Christopher. Rent 3s. 4d. Fine 3s. 6d.

JANE SINGLETON

6 April 22 Car. The half of one tenement late in the tenure of William Watt containing 10 acres of land and one other half of another tenement late in the tenure of William Mawe containing 26 acres.
In widdowright of Raphe Singleton. Rent 8s. 8d. Fine 6s. 0d.

ELIZABETH WALKER & ANNE MARTIN

16 April 6 Car. One acre of land adjoyning on the west part of old acre late waste lands one messuage and one parcell of land at Roantree pitts containing 1 acre and one other acre of late the lord's waste adjoyning to the foresaid house.
As sisters as coheirs of Christopher Gibbon defunct. Rent 1s. 2d. Fine 1s. 2d.

JOHN WALKER

6 April 22 Car. 8 ridges of land containing 4 acres now divided with hedges adjoyning to the close called the Riggs Close on the north parcell of a close called the Cornefield containing 12 acres of land in Evenwood.
By surrender of William Gibbon. Rent 1s. 4d. Fine 1s. 4d.

MARGARET TOWER ELIANOR & GRATIA TOWER

12 October 12 Car. One close called High field late in the tenure of George Dixon.
By surrender of Christopher Tower and Elizabeth his wife. Rent 6s. 8d. Fine 4s. 4d.

CHRISTOPHER TOWER and Elizabeth his wife.

30 October 20 Jac. One close called Law field containing 6 acres.
By surrender of John Hodgshon. Rent 3s. 4d. Fine 10s. 8d.

CHRISTOPHER HOPPER

17 September 21 Car. One tenement late in the tenure of the widdow

Vicars containing 36 acres of land with a cottage and garden adjoyning.

As heir to his father John. Fine 7s. 8d.

dat ut supra. One close called Farthing Knoll containing 11 acres of land.

As heir to his father. Rent 14s. 4d. Fine 4s. 4d.

ANN MORGAN, MARY and MATTHEW

25 April 10 Car. One parcell of land in Evenwood lyeing on the east part of Bromehaugh containing 6 acres of land.

As heirs to their grandfather Robert Morgan. Rent 2s. od. Fine 6d.

JOHN SEDGWICK cozen & heir of Agnes Sedgwick defunct.

6 April 22 Car. One half of the whole tenure vizt of 22½ acres of land at Deggill in Evenwood as it is now divided and late in the tenure of John Sedgwick and Agnes aforesaid vizt the west of the mansion house and half the west part of a garden as it is now divided also a close called kilne flatt a garden called Stack garth also the shaw and a close called the Lamb close and half a garden called Lines Garth with half a messuage.

As heirs to Agnes. Rent 10s. od. Fine 6s. 8d.

WILLIAM DIXON and Anne his wife.

3 May 12 Car. 4½ acres of land and ½ rode of land in the tenure of the said William Dixon called Ramshaw and the third part of the knight field lying on the west part of the same as it lyeth and extendeth itself from the west of knight field to the water there.

By surrender of Thomas Dixon and Anthony Watson. Rent 11s. 4d. Fine 11s. 8d.

GEORGE DIXON

23 October 38 Eliz. by special command of the Bishop. One parcell of his waste containing one acre lying on the north part of the new house of the said George.

Rent 4d. Fine 4d.

DOROTHIE CRADDOCK

20 June 15 Jac. One peece of land lying on the west parte of Ramshaw field containing 10 acres of land and one close called knight field divided into two partes and another close lyeing at the

north end of knightsfield cont 4 acres of land.

By demise of Anthony Craddock. Rent 3s. 8d. Fine 5s. od.

HENRY DOUGHTIE
10 October 19 Car. One messuage and thirty acres of land called Ramshaw.

By surrender of John Briteman. Rent £1. 6s. 4d. Fine 13s. 4d.

LANCELLOT THIRKELD
13 April 3 Car. One peece of land lyeing on the south parte of Round Hill within Evenwood containing 24 feet in length with a house built thereon.

As heir to his father Lancellot Thirkeld. Rent 2d. Fine 4d.

WILLIAM GARTH
17 September 21 Car. One parcell of the moore or waste called West Thickley lyeing and abutting on the King's highway called Wattling Street on the east and on the north of the tenements of George Tonge Esquire called West Thickley containing 100 acres of land as it is now divided by meetes and boundes.

By surrender of George Tonge Esq. Rent £1. 13s. 4d. Fine £1. 13s. 4d.

GEORGE TONGE
11 October 12 Car. Mannor and town of West Thickley vizt arable land, meadow, feedings and pastures.

By surrender of Henry Blackston Gent. Rent £12. os. od. Fine £6. os. od.

THOMAS STEVENSON & HENRY STEVENSON
20 February 16 Car. One close of meadow called Bracken Close containing 2 acres of land.

By surrender of Thomas Hodgshon. Rent 4d. Fine 9d.

Evenwood Township Leaseholds

ROBERT DIXON as heir to William Dixon defunct.
14 May 10 Car. Water corne milne situate on the water or river of Gaunless called Evenwoode mill.

For the natural lives of Robert Dixon then aged 5, Wm. Bowser 10, and Joseph Egleston 10. All in being.

Rent £1. 6s. 8d. Improvement £6. 13s. 8d.

HENRIE FAIRFAX Esq & ROBERT HEIGHINTON & THOMAS HUTCHINSON

22 July 16 Car. Parcell of lands called the Old Parke and also one other parcell of ground called Northwood now or sometymes parcell of a park called Evenwood Park together with all the closes and parcell of lands being parcell of the Old Parke and Northwood formerly demised unto Sir George Bowes.

For the natural lives of Thomas Fairfax sonne and heir of said Henry, Thomas Dixon and Robert Dixon sonne of the said Thomas all in being.

Rent £20. os. od. Improvement £126. os. od.

Mem that the moytie of the next beforementioned lease is assigned by the abovementioned Robert Heighington by indentured dat 26 July 16 Car to George Henry Thomas Dixon and Richard Bowser in trust for the payment of the debts of William Dixon deceased and for the payment of £39 which is given for putting in a new life and further for payment of £20 a yeere for 7 yeeres to Susan Dixon Ann and Jane Dixon, daughters of the said William Dixon and also the debts so paid then they are to surrender the same to the said Robert Dixon.

Sir HENRIE GRIFFITHS BART, ALEXANDER DENTON and Sir JOHN MALLERY and FRANCIS DRAKE Esq feoffees in trust for the use of Mr. John Eure's children.

Colliery of Carter Thorne.

For the natural lives of William Eure uncle of the now Lord Eure William now Lord Eure and William Ireland son of Sir Francis Ireland.

Rent £70. os. od. Improvement £280. os. od.

WILLIAM MALLORY holder of Studley Co. Ebor.

11 October 14 Car. Collyery, cole myne, cole pitte & seames of coals as well as not opened in Evenwood Park containing all and singular the copyholds, copyhold lands of Evenwood Towne and towne fields and within all and singular the townes fields hamletts places and villages of Ramshaw Gordon, Morley and Toft Hill according to their ancient meetes and boundes within the Barony of Evenwood

together with full power and authority to breake the grounds and soyle and to dig and sink within the said park as many coal pitts as shall please the said lessee for the getting of colts as for drawing and carrying away of water etc.

For 21 yeares.

Rent £1. os. od. + £1. 13s. 4d. for every pit at which the said lessee or his assigns should winne worke and draw coles.

A covenant that the said lessee etc. shall de tempore in tempus during the tenure erect and make hovels and hedges over the pitts which the lessee should think most meet to work or to be wrought in the park [*This lease is not completed, and bears pg.no.20—a number which does not fit in with the existing arrangement of the folios*]

The persons hereafter named payeth these several rents hereafter expressed within the aforesaid township but whether the same be freeholds or copyholds or leaseholds it is not known to us they having produced no deed nor writings concerning the same.

Name	£	s	d
Apleby	1	10	0
Allenson Mathew			8
Darcy William Knt.		6	4
" " "	1	1	0
Downes	2	11	4
Eden Robert		2	0
Finch Hugh		12	6
Garth Wm		4	6
Howe Thomas		4	0
Hodgshan Katherine		7	8
Key William		10	0
Lambe John		9	6
Lambe Raiphe			6
Naxton et al	4	1	0
Ovington Robert			6
Sowerby Laurence			4
Smyth Henry			6
White George			4

Mem. that Edward Corney, a copyholder in Evenwood township hath wood now standeing upon his said copyhold which we have surveyed and conceive it worth to be sold £100.

Edward Colston   Geo. Daile   Saml. Leigh   Thomas Saunders

Killerby Township Leaseholds

ELIZABETH HILTON

10 October 16 Jac. A messuage and tenement in Killerby with the garths on the backside thereof.

Particulars: One dwelling house and a cottage. 3 closes called Horsewells, Newe Closes, and Intacke, the third bounded upon George Middleton's with a parcell of moore containing in all 33 acres.

For the lives of Francis Hilton, then 12, Launcellot Hilton, then 10, and Ann Hilton, then 8. All in being.

Rent £2. 5. 0., and one fat veal at Pentecost or 6s. 8d. Improvement £1. 5. 0.

JOHN HUTCHINSON

5 October 3 Car. One messuage or tenement formerlie demised to John Turton late in the tenure of the said John and now in the tenure of the said John the younger.

Particulars: One dwelling house with a barn, one cottage, 3 closes of arable lands lyeing together called the Banckes, parcell of moore bounded in, one other little close called the Meadowes containing together 60 acres.

For the lives of John Hutchinson, 23 years, Anne Hutchinson and Richard Pickering, both dead.

Rent £4. 11. 0. Improvement £15. 10. 0.

GEORGE CROSIER

20 October 1 Car. Water corne milne called Killerby Milne lyeing upon Killerby Green late in the tenure of Wm. Bayles then in the tenure of William Taylor.

For the lives of William Taylor, then 34, Margarett Taylor then 30, his wife, and Anne Taylor then 5 years. William dead.

Rent 11s. od. Improvement £5. 0. 0.

GEORGE MIDDLETON

12 January 13 Car. Tenement or farm in Killerby in the tenure of the said George.

Particulars: One dwelling house one barn and a cottage, five closes lyeing all together one parcell of meadow containing in all 45 acres.

For 21 years.
Rent £2. 16. 8. Improvement £15. 0. 0.

MATHEW SHAWTER by assignment from Thomas Birbeck.

12 January 13 Car. One messuage or tenement in Killerby sometime in the tenure of Martin Thompson.

Particulars: One dwelling house and a barn three closes of arable land and a parcell of meadow lyeing together containing in all about 33 acres.
For 21 years.
Rent £2. 0. 0. Improvement £11. 0. 0.

CUTHBERT SMITH

14 February 13 Car. Tenement messuage or farmhold lying in Killerby in the tenure of the sd. Cuthbert.

Particulars: A dwelling house and barn three closes and a small parcell of moore containing 45 acres.
For 21 years.
Rent £3. 0. 0. Improvement £14. 10. 0.

JOHN CLARKE

11 May 13 Car. Messuage or tenement in Killerby in the occupation of the said John and all that his messuage or tenement in Killerby late in the occupation of William Walton and now in the tenure of the said John.

Particulars: One dwelling house with 2 barns one cottage house one parcell of land called Ackworth one parcell of land called Milne Close one little parcell of meadow on the south of Darlington Road one parcell called Banck Close one parcell called Moorelands with the moores adjoining one other close lying on the west of Killerby loaning, 2 closes called Newcloses one other close called Newclose containing in all 46 acres.
For 21 years.
Rent £3. 5. 0. Improvement £13. 0. 0.

West Auckland Township Copyholds

WILLIAM SIMPSON and Meuriell his wife.

17 October 10 Car. One house with a garden lyeing betwene the

tenement of John Stevenson on the east part and Thomas Jackson on the west.

By surrender of Christopher Lawnesdale and Jane his wife, and Thomas Hodgson and Margery his wife. Rent 1s. 6d. Fine 3d.

WILLIAM GAINFORD

29 October 17 Car. One rood of land more or less on the west part of the back fines Wm. Smith and Wm. Key on the east Evenwood fields on the west and nine acres of lands lyeing in Backland and also six acres and one rood of moore more or less.

By surrender of William Williamson. Rent 15s. 11d. Fine 17s. 6d.

29 April 7 Car. One messuage with a garden on the backside with a house at the end of the said garden now used for a kilne.

By surrender of Anne Smith. Rent 2s. 8d. Fine 1s. 8d.

14 October 22 Jac. The west half of a messuage in the tenure of Nicholas Whitfield.

Rent 6d. Fine 6d.

RICHARD CORNEFORTH

8 May 9 Car. One close in W. Auckland late John Burke's and late in the tenure of Robert Wrenne lying nigh the close of Robert Dalton.

Fine 3s. 6d.

The 4th part of a parcell of land lyeing upon Raley Moor containing 60 acres of land vizt. the north and east part of the same from the ould hedge assending to Ramshawe hughe.

As heir to William his father. Rent 10s. 8d. Fine 5s. 0d.

CHRISTOPHER RICHARDSON

25 April 10 Car. One cottage and half an acre of land and one parcell of land containing 40 feet in breadth and in length 30 and another peece of land containing 20 feet in length and in breadth 10.

By surrender of Thomas Kitchen. Rent 1s. 6d. Fine 6d.

WILLIAM RICHARDSON

13 April 14 Car. A cottage.

As heir to his father Michael. Rent 1s. 6d. Fine 1s. 0d.

THOMAS HAWE and Jane his wife.

8 May 9 Car. East part of a house and east part of a close called

Quarryholes as it is divided with meetes and boundes and one rood of land late in the tenure of Anthony Thirkeld.

By surrender of George Garth. Rent 2½d. Fine 5d.

JOHN RAYNE

29 May 5 Car. The half of one cottage late in the tenure of John Highe.

By surrender of John Stevenson and Isabell his wife. Rent 2d. Fine 2s. 6d.

ANN DIXON

8 May 9 Car. One close lying in the north end of Knight field containing 4 acres of land with free ingress and egress from Knightfield to the Common moore called Rameshawe haugh.

In widdow right of George Dixon. Rent 1s. 4d. Fine 1s. 4d.

WILLIAM MALLORIE

12 October 14 Car. One parcell of land called North Lease containing 52 acres.

By surrender of Raiphe Eden. Rent 13s. 8d. Fine 6s. 8d.

MARGARETT ACKROYD

11 May 19 Car. One close called Calfe Close in West Auckland.
In widdowright of William Ackroyd. Rent 9s. od. Fine 2s. od.

GEORGE WHITE and THOMAS DIXON

17 October 2 Car. One parcell of land lying on Raley Moor containing 60 acres, one fourth part of the premises vizt the east and north parts from the ould Ramshaw haugh parcell of the premises.

By surrender of Anthony Watson. Rent 15s. od. Fine 15s. od.

This surrender was in trust for the use of Margaret Watson now wife of Anthony Wake.

ELIZABETH TISDALE

29 October 17 Car. 3 acres of land in the north part of the Shawes.
By demise of William Williamson. Rent 2s. od. Fine 1s. od.

CHARLES ANDERSON

29 October 17 Car. 20 acres of land and one rood in the Middle field abutting upon the Long Dike the land of William Richardson on

the east also 9 acres of land and three roods abutting upon the moor of Robert Eden on the south.

By surrender of William Williamson. Rent 12s. 9d. Fine 10s. 0d.

WILLIAM WALL

31 October 17 Car. 16 acres and 2 roods of land in Eastfield abutting on the lands of Brian Wright and 6 acres and a rood of moor abutting on the moor of Robert Eden on the south.

By surrender of William Williamson. Rent 10s. 0d. Fine 7s. 7d.

RICHARD GARGRAVE

12 October 12 Car. One parcell of land called Chequor Place containing 6 acre and one parcell of land called Fielding Loaning.

As heir to his brother John. Rent 2s. 6d. Fine 4s. 0d.

29 October 17 Car. 19 acres and one rood of land in the middle field abutting upon the lands of Charles Anderson on the east and also 9 acres of land abutting on his own lands in Middlefield.

By surrender of William Williamson. Rent 12s. 9d. Fine 10s. 0d.

CUTHBERT ROBINSON

29 October 17 Car. 9 acres of land in East field adjoining upon the land of William Richardson.

By surrender of William Williamson. Rent 3s. 2d. Fine 3s. 0d.

CHRISTOPHER STODDERT

29 October 17 Car. 20 acres of land in the middle field abutting on the lands of Anne Tower.

By surrender of William Williamson. Rent 6s. 4½d. Fine 6s. 8d.

WILLIAM RICHARDSON and Mary his wife.

29 October 17 Car. 19 acres of moor abutting on the lands of the said William in the East Field.

Fine 6s. 8d.

41 acres 2 roods of land in Eastfield abutting upon Middle field in the west.

Fine 13s. 4d. Both copies by surrender of William Williamson. Rent £1. 8. 6½.

WILLIAM GARFOOT

21 November 22 Car. The half of 23 acres of land in the Middle

Field abutting on the land of Raphe Eden on the east and 6 acres of moore abutting on the lands of Robert Eden on the south.

By surrender of Robert Johnson. Rent 12s. 9d. Fine 4s. 6d.

HENRY STODDERT
4 May 22 Jac. 2 messuages and 22 acres of land in West Auckland.

By surrender of George Martin and John Calvert. Rent 12s. 9d. Fine 4s. 6d.

JOHN LISTER
29 October 17 Car. 4½ acres of land in East field abutting on the way leading from West Auckland to Billershaw.

By surrender of William Williamson. Rent 3s. 2½d. Fine 1s. 6d.

MARY HUGILL
8 September 22 Car. The half of a cottage and one toft in West Auckland.

As relict of John Hugill. Rent 2s. 6d. Fine 2d.

WILLIAM MOUNCER
11 October 15 Car. The half of the east part of one messuage or tenement late in the tenure of Michael Whitfield one chamber called a parlour adjoining to one tenement of Elizabeth Teesdale.

Rent 6d. Fine 4s. od.

RAPHE WALKER
19 April 42 Eliz. The half of two closes called Chappell Garth and Chappelside acre.

By surrender of George and Mathew Coltman. Rent 4s. 3d. Fine 2s. od.

CHRISTOPHER HERON and Frances his wife.
6 November 14 Car. 6 acres of land called the Leaming lyeing between 27 acres of Gerard Wilson's on the east.

By surrender of William Williamson. Rent 2s. od. Fine 1s. od.

ROBERT STODDERT
29 October 17 Car. 20 acres of land lying on the west of Staindrop fields butting on the land of William Gainford on the west.

By surrender of William Williamson. Rent 12s. 9d. Fine 10s. od.

JOHN GARRIE

16 September 21 Car. One messuage in West Auckland.
As heir to his brother Anthony. Rent 4d. Fine 6d.

WILLIAM THOMPSON

9 October 4 Car. The half of one parcell of land called Brockenbury
Leaze.
By surrender of Christopher Byerley and Edward Hutton. Rent
13s. 7d. Fine 5s. od.

CUTHBERT WRANGHAM

9 October 4 Car. The half of one piece of land called Brockenbury
Leaze.
By surrender of Christopher Byerley and Edward Hutton. Rent
13s. 7d. Fine 5s. od.

MARIE JOHNSON, RAPHE EDEN alias DANIELL, JOHN EDEN alias DANIELL

29 October 17 Car. 16 acres 2 roods of land in the Eastfield adjoining upon the lands of William Wall on the north and also 15 acres
and 3 roods of land on the west of Robert Stobart.
Rent 12s. 9d. Fine 6s. 8d.

MARGRET MIDDLETON

One close called Nether Leyer lying on the east parte of the lands
called the Coalway containing 8 acres being parcell of Brockenbury
Leaze.

WILLIAM KEY

29 October 17 Car. 34 acres of land lying on the west of the Chequor
Leezes on the north of the way leading to the town of Evenwood, the
land of Robert Eden Esq. on the east and on the south of his free-
hold tenement and one other parcell of moore containing 29 acres
lying on the west part of the east moore on the north of the land of
William Gainford and Robert Stoddert the land of Robert Eden
Esq. on the south the new moors on the west the lands of William
Wall and Robert Johnson.
By surrender of William Williamson. Rent 12s. 9d. Fine 14s. 4d.

MICHAEL BUCK

24 March 11 Car. One messuage or tenement with an orchard or

garden lyeing behind it containing ½ acre land arable lyeing between the tenement sometime in the tenure of Ann Hynde on the west and the house sometime Peter Wilson's on the east lying on the north of Middlefield.

Rent 2d. Fine 2d.

One messuage with a cottage and one parcell of land in the Middle field containing 12 acres adjoining on the land of Richard Gargrave on the east the land of Ann Teward on the west also one parcell of the moore containing 19 acres lying on the land of Henry Stoddert on the west the land of Richard Gargrave on the east the land of Martin Watson on the south, the Middlefield on the north.

Rent 12s. 9d. Fine 6s. 8d.

Both copies by surrender of Simon Burbeck clarke.

WILLIAM BULMER

29 October 17 Car. A field or close called Wheatsyde except 4 acres of land in the same field allowed for the lord's waste containing 57 acres of land and 2 roods.

By surrender of William Williamson gent. Rent £1. 6. 6. Fine 13s. 4d.

RAIPHE EDEN

13 January 2 Car. One parcell of land called Billershaw containing 45 acres.

By surrender of Christopher Byerly Esq. Rent 3s. 4d. Fine 3s. 4d

West Auckland Township Leaseholds

RAPHE GARGRAVE

8 June 18 Car. Corn water mill in the parish or chappelrie of St Ellen Auckland and also one parcell of ground wherein the mill stands containing 6 acres of land adjoyning upon Copiland on the south late in the tenure of Barnaby Bell and Robert Stephenson.

For the lives of Raphe Gargrave 48 years William Dixon then years and William Anderson 6 years. All in being.

Rent £1. 0. 0. and 2 fatt capons or 5s. in lieu. Improvement £5. 15. 0.

WILLIAM GARGRAVE holds from Thomas Dixon who holds of the Bishop.

14 May 10 Car. Water corne milne called West Auckland Milne.
  For the lives of William Dixon then 5 years William Bowser 10
and Joseph Eggleston 10 years. All in being.
  Rent £3. 6. 8. Fine £8. 0. 0.

Sir PAULE NEALE

4 December 16 Car. Lands called Copelands and Hole meadow in
West Auckland.
  For the lives of Sir Paul Neale Dame Elizabeth his wife and
William Neale their son.
  Rent £2. 2. 0. Fine £10. 0. 0.

WILLIAM THOMPSON and FRANCIS JOLLIE

20 January 13 Car. Water corn mill called Bolam Mill late demised
unto William Thompson and Cuthbert Vaughan.
  For 21 years.
  Rent £2. 0. 0. Fine £5. 0. 0.

WILLIAM LEAVER

9 August 15 Car. Parcell of ground in a close called Wealeside in
West Auckland containing 4 acres adjoining upon the King's High-
way leading towards Darlington on the east.
  For 21 years.
  Rent 2s. 6d. Fine £1. 0s. 0d.

The persons hereafter named pay several rents hereafter expressed
within the foresaid township, but whether the same be freeholders,
copyholders or leaseholders it is not known to us they having produced no deeds or writings concerning the same.

Carr William		6	
Clifton John	3	0½	
Downes Lambton	3	4	—4 acres in the Ridding
Eden Robert	1	4	
,,	12	9	—copy
,,		10	—freehold
,,		6	—bull meadowes
,,		4	
,,		6	—mower's housestead
,,	1	7	—Freehold gates

Garrey John		1	0½
Hodgshon Raiphe		15	0
Hodgshon Peter		4	4
„ Anthony		2	0½
„ John	1	2	0
Key William		1	1
Lancellot		5	8
Longstaffe William			2
„		1	6
Moor George		1	0
Mason—vid	0	0	4
Pattinson			6
Robinson Christopher		1	0
Rumforth William		2	0
Robinson vid		3	2
Redmyre house		4	0
Sanders		1	10
Sanderson Thomas		4	8
Stephenson Christopher		11	0
Thorneberry vid		9	6½
Taylor Raphe		6	0
Thornberry Christopher			6
Wright Edward		1	0
Wells			9
Walker Raiphe		3	2
Younger		13	8
Summa	7	0	0½

Here followeth the full and perfect accompt of the rents entered and charged in this Survey.

Evenwood and West Thickley	128	14	1
Whereof paid into the Exchequer at Durham	90	0	0
To the Bailiff of Evenwood	14	19	9
To be gathered by the collector of West Thickley	13	13	4
Killerby	18	15	10
West Auckland	30	10	2

Whereof paid into the Exchequer at Durham	2	2	0
So there remains to be gathered by the collector	28	8	2
Sum Total	178	0	1
Improvements above the rent per annum	520	18	4
To the Bailiff of Eavenwood	2	0	0

Mem. that Edward Corney a coppyholder in Evenwood township being entered in 1st page hath wood now standeing upon his said coppyhold which we hath surveyed and conceive it worth to be sold £100.

Edward Colston
Geo Daile
Saml. Leigh
Thomas Saunders

SURVEY OF THE MANOR OF WOLSINGHAM

Imprimis we say that the town of Wolsingham is a large county town seated in a valley upon the River Wear, where the Bishops many years ago had a mansion house or dwelling (now totally disused) but the said river is not navigable by many miles nor is the said town neere the sea by 14 or 15 miles, and the market townes nearest thereunto are Barnard Castle and Bishop's Auckland equally distant seaven miles from the same. And we say that the donation gift and presentation of the rectory parsonage and tythes of the parish of Wolsingham did formerly belong to the Bishop of Durham and are worth per annum with the gleabe lands £250. And we find that one Mr. Johnathon Deverex, clarke, is the present incumbent there by virtue of an order or ordinance of the Lords and Comons dated the 22nd March 1647, which is also further confirmed by the patent under Greate Seale of England bearing date 28 March 24 Car. which we have seen. There is no viccar or viccaridge indowed in this place, but the tithes predial personal or mixed are paid to the rector thereof.

Item we say that the town of Stanhope also is a large county (but no markett towne) seated fower myles higher upon the river of Wear and further from the sea than the other the nearest Market Towne thereto (that we know of) the before mentioned but there are now remaining the Ruines and bare walls onely, not valiewable, of a castle or dwelling house the Bishops long since had at the place called the Westgate in Stanhope Parke. And we say that the donation guift and presentation to the rectory parsonage and tythes of the parish of Stanhope did formerly belong to the Bishop of Durham And are worth (together with the gleabe lands) per annum £300. And we find that John Bewicke clerke (by ordinance of the Lords and comons which we have seen) bearing date veneris November 1644 is present incumbent. There is no vicar or viccaridge endowed in the place but the tythes of all sorts are due and payable to the rector only.

Item we say that the mannor of Wolsingham is a very large mannor consisting of the several townships following (vizt) Wolsingham Greenewestside Wigside North Bedburne South Bedburne Linesack Stanhope Bishopley and Forest of Weardale. And there belongeth to the said mannor very large and spatous commons called the South and North field of Wolsingham and boundeth as follows (vizt) the bounder betwixt the late Bishop of Durham his mannor of Wolsingham and Sir William Darcye his mannor of Witton on the south side of Wear begineth at Dowsyke in the Blackbanke which said Syke runneth down to the east side of the said parish of Wolsingham and from the said Dowsyke to the west of Ballestead and from thence to Hartfowlings and from thence to the meeting of the burn at Northgraine foot on the Rapeshield and from thence up to South Graineburn and out at the loope of the said Southgraine to the westerend of the Browne Currocke and from thence to Shanebury burn at which said burn endes the bounders betwixt the late Bishop of Durham and Sir William Darcye as aforesaid. And then all the said Shanebury burne beginneth the bounder betweixt the said late Bishop of Durham and Sir Henry Vane, General, or Mr. Tobye Ewbanke, Lordship of the Manor of Egglestone which ascendeth up the said burn to the Shaftwell Head at which said Shaftwell head endeth the bounder between the said Sir Henry or the said manor of Egglestone and the said Bishop of Durham. And then at the said Shaftwell head beginneth the bounder betwixt the said parish of Wolsingham and the parish of Stanhope, both which parishes belong to the Bishop of Durham, from which Shaftwell Head the said bounder goeth to a place called the Longman and from thence to Hawkwood Head as water runneth from thence to the Easter Pawlawe and from thence to Westerharope head and soe downe the said burn to the river of Weare and from thence straight over the water and soe upp the north side of the water to the willowegate and from thence to the Deane and up the said deane to the West of Ireland and from thence to Bradley Carrock and from thence as heaven water headeth to Cloyer Lawe and from thence to the west end of West Rawe Parke where endeth the bounders betweene the aforesaid parishes, and where beginneth the bounder betweene the parish of Wolsingham and Muggleswick which goeth down the said Westrawe Parkeside to Westrawe burne and from Westrawe Parke Burne up Northwood to the top of the Edge as the heaven water leadeth to Drieishill where endeth the bounder between the said parish of Wolsingham and Muggleswick and where beginneth the bounder between the said parish of Wolsingham and the parish of Lanchester which goeth from the said Drieishill to Jordans Cross and from thence to Lambes Cross and from thence to the head of Adderley Clugh, from thence to the north Towlawe Carrock where endeth the bounder between the aforesaid parish of Wolsingham and Lanchester, And where also beginneth the bounder between the Bishop and the Chapter of Brancepeth which goeth from the said Towlawe Carrock over Dearens Head from thence to the Carrock over the top of the hill on the north side of Carrock Hill and so goeth downe to an old watergate and so down Haddesly Hugh burn to Houselopp where endeth the bounder between the said Bishop and Brancepeth Lordship. And for wast grounds commons heathes and moores we cannot further say but as by us is formerly set down. As also that there is no devision of bounders to our knowlidge amongst the freeholders, coppyholders, and lessees but their cattle go horn by horn and eate by byte of mouth without stinting and that one parish hath day rake and wynd rake of comon one with another without the aforesaid bounders without impounding or doeing any service or paying for the same but as hath been accustomed for their tenements, save onely by the tenants of Thornley and Helme Parke do pay to the said Bishop of Durham for outer comon (vizt) the tenants of Thornley 28s. od per annum at the feasts of Martinmas and Pentecost and the tenants of Helme Parke 33s. 4d. per annum at the Feasts of Martinmas and Pentecost which said summes art paid to the Coronor and are charged upon him in this survey. And the inhabitants of South Bedburn and Lynesack Township within the manor of Wolsingham do say that they have used to ryde the bounders and do clayme comon of pasture within the townships of Bishop Auckland, Escomb, and Witton within the bounders following, which begin at the west end of Blackebancke and so along to the wester bayle of Knitchley from thence to the three thornes under Knitchley from there to a standing stone in Heavy Hughe from thence to Stonefield thence to Pikestone and from thence to Craggstackgarth in North grayne from thence to Shieldmore Carrock from thence to Little Pawly thence to Longman thence to Steakbridge in Weardale from thence to Islestone upon Millstone rigg and over at Spurlwood Head from thence to fine close head and down Throw loaning and so to Gaunles Beck so along the bank to Butterknowle and from Butterknowle to Ramshawe from thence to Long Loaning head from thence to Etherley Moor and so down Tunstall green to Newton Bridge along all which places aforesaid tenants of the late Bishop within the manor of Bishop Auckland and the tenants of Escomb and the tenants of Witton aforesaid did ryde the same bounders together and had and hold intercommon of pasture in the said moores and waste and belonging to their severall townshipps and places within the said bounders. And we say that the Lord of this mannor hath right of common without stint within all the said comonfield and waste but that the lord may by inclosure improve any part of the said waste without the consent of the tenants. This the said tenants utterly deny.

Item we say the forest or ground called the High Forest of Weardale conteynes severall demesne lands letten by lease for lives or years. And also divers customary lands wherein the inhabitants occupyers or owners thereof do challenge to hold by yearly rents certain and by doeing and performing certeyne personal services in Wark upon the Borders of Scotland, at their own charge for and during the continuance of 14 dayes when occasion is, and that they are thereunto lawfully required or summoned. Within the said forest there is conteyned a very large ground fenced with a wall of stone (though much decayed) and severed thereby from the forest called Stanhope Park formerly well replenished with fallow deer but now utterly destroyed since the last warres. In the said ground or park are conteyned divers messuages and farmhouses and severall lands consisting of pasture meadow and arable therewith occupied which are holden of the late Bishop of Durham by severall leases for lives or years (all which are retorned in the present survey) as also in the said parke are conteyned divers other messuages tenements and farm houses and severall lands, pastures meadows and arrable therewith occupied. All which later premises the several tenants owners or occupiers thereof do challenge to be customary land holden by the like rents and personal services in war upon the Borders, as are those others in the High Forest of Weardale before mentioned. The said park with the aforementioned messuages of ground therein conteyned is about 7 miles in compass. Timber there is none in the said parke nor underwood, only a little brushwood at the Eastgate. The high forest of Weardale above mentioned cont. therein the said Park is in compass 21 miles or thereabouts and was formerly well stored with roed deere which are utterly destroyed. There is no tymber growing or remaining in the said Forest or coppices or underwood at all saveing a little brushwood or shrubs about the ground called Warehead of noe valewe And the said forest is thus bounded (vizt) Teesdale on the south by Alston Moor in the County of Cumberland in the west by Allendale on the north And by the Bayliwick of Stanhope in the East.

Item we say that there is a Court Baron or Halmott Court keept twice in everey yeare at Wolsingham, To which Court all the coppy-holders and freehold tenants within the said manor and bayliwick of Stanhope in Waredale with their severall appendices do repaire and do their suit and service accustomed and we say that the copyhold lands within the manor are held by custom and sesse certeyne and also that every freeholder upon death doth pay for and in the name of a relief one yeare's quitt rent. The perquisites of which courts were communibus annis valued at £8. 13. 4.

Item we say that the lord of this mannor hath free hauking hunt-ing fishing (although there be no free fishing or other royaltie leased out to any) fouling waifes and strayes, felons' goods etc which we value at £3. 6. 8.

Item we say that the lord hath free warren within the said forest or park and that there are no roed deere or fallowe deere (though formerly well stored with both) which have been destroyed since these warres.

Item we say that within these few yeares there hath been usually kept a court twice a year (vizt) at St. Ellenmas and Michaelmas called a Forrester or Foster Court in the parke of Stanhope about Westgate at the castle (now demolished) at which said Court the freehold coppyhold Leasehold and customary tenants and all other inhabitants within the said High Forest of Weardale and Park of Stanhope did usually appeare and doe their service and the said customary tenants did every one of them pay unto the lord at every St. Ellen court one penny called a Tack penny and no more. And also to the clerk of the said court for the time being at every alienation or death of them tenants one groat and no more as his due fee.

Item in the said courts usually were tryed all actions of trespass or debt under the value of 40s. also all afrayes bloodshed breach of the peace and misdemeanors. And the said courts did lay paynes and impose penalties for overstints or surcharging the pasture in their several stinted pastures called the Hopes and Fells and for all other misdemeanors of the like nature, Whereby did yearly accrue to the lord fines and amerciaments. And the said court did make inqurie of the fellons and goods of fellons fugatives wayfes strayes etc, which seised by the pinder brought alsoe profit to the lord. And the sub foresters or keepers of the said parke and forest did execute all warrants and Breach of the peace and misdemeanors and did (ex officio) supply the place of constable (the custom of the said place so requiring) And the pinder was by his place cryer of the courts and to take up all waifs and strayes etc. And the said keepers by there places were bound to distrayne for the said amerciaments and fines and to pay them in to the Bishop's Auditor or Receiver Generall All which profits and perquisites of the said courts we value at £6. 13. 4.

Item we say that there are certeyne mines or grooves of mettle or lead ore belonging to the Bishop of Durham lying and being in the High Forest of Weardale within the lordships mannors and parishes of Wolsingham and Stanhope. And the said Bishop by his moor master did order and supervise the working thereof at his pleasure. And the said Bishop hath the ninth part of the lead ore or mettle gained in any the said works for his share or lott, and the Rector of Stanhope the 10th part for his tythes, the other eight parts of the ore or mettle gotten of auncient custom is claymed by the moor master as belonging to his patent or place, and the remainder thereof which is much the greater part the workmen or groovers challenge to themselves for there labour in winning and waining the whole, for which they have noe other wages or allowances.

Item the names of the said severall grooves or places where they lye, and of the parties who now work the same as followeth (vizt)
Imprimis Allerclugh Groove wrought by Mr. Aisley and Raphe Fetherson.
Item Beconside wrought by Godfrey Disbury.
Item White wake wrought by Ralph Harrison of the Hill and Francis Peart of Hatheryclugh.
Item Barker Groove wrought by William Emerson of Ishoppburn and John Harrison of Wester Black Deane.

Item Sautishead Groove wrought by William Nattres of Wear-head and William Harrison of Blackclugh.

Item Peytree Groove wrought by Cuthbert Morgaine and his pastures in Bishop Groove.

Item Bishop Groove wrought by the said Cuthbert and his pastures.

Item another groove in Bolihope called Harringshawe wrought by Mr. Arthur Rawlinson.

Item we have with the advice and assistance of severall groovers and other men (the most skillfull in all those parts which love or reward could procure) carefully viewed the said lead works. Also we have conferred with the late Bishop's officers and servants and have obtained and had the view of the accompts of all the profits arising and made by the said Bishop of the said lead workes yearley from the year 1635 to the year 1644. And we find upon our view of the said several grooves and places (some of which are now almost quite worn out and wasted) the advice and assistance of the said men skillfull and the perusall of the said yearly accompts, that the bishop his lott parts and profitts arising from the said lead works were in and about the year 1640 as alsoe for some years both before and since worth communibus annis £15. o. o. And therefore we value the same accordingly at £15. o. o.

Item we find and say that there are within the said mannor matter of allom, ironstone and steele within the severall lands have been formerly wrought and some small quantityes made and granted which were experimented (especially the steele) to be good but in respect the said materialls lye so far of from the sea port and the River of Wear in this place for many myles not navigable thereto and the great charge in winning and workeing them over ballancing the profits thereof to be made the said works have been forelet and left for these many yeares last past and therefore we thought fitt onely to mention them, but to value the same at nil.

Wolsingham Township Leaseholds

Sir PAUL NEALE of Bishopthorpe Co. Ebor.
4 December 16 Car. All that his parcell of ground called the de-mesnes in Wolsingham.

For the lives of the said Sir Paule Neale, Dame Elizabeth Neale and William Neale their son.

Rent £1. 11. 4. Improvement £20. 0. 0.

JOHN VESSEY

4 June 16 Car. One meadow close containing 9 acres 9 acres of ground and 8 pasture gates in and upon the grounds called Bishop Oake quarter. 3 pasture gates in the Bale Hill field and 3 pasture gates in Crookeford ground lately demised to William Dixon yeoman and heretofore in the occupation of William Crooke or his assigns.

For the lives of John Harrison, Nicholas his son, and William Wren son of William Wren of Wolsingham. All in being.

Rent 13s. 4d. and one fat veal at Pentecost or 3s. 8d. in lieu. Improvement £6. 0. 0.

ANN COLSON assignee of John Colson.

10 December 10 Car. One close or parcell of meadow ground called the Greate Right with a coate house or a calfe house standing in the said close. One little meadow close standing at the nether end of the said close, one close called the Little Right adjoining on the west side of the Greate Right and 4 pasture gates in the Hollinghall pasture. All which premises are lying and being in Wolsingham Park. And also the moytie of a tenement called the Lodge which was lately demised to one Henry Aire and the said John Colson.

For the lives of Ann, Alice and Isabell Colson. Ann is dead.

Rent 10s. od. Improvement £5. 0. 0.

HENRY AYRE and JOHN BELL the younger.

10 December 11 Car. All that messuage or house called the Lodge standing in Wolsingham Park and also all that close or parcell of ground called the Hilies and also all that parcell of ground lyeing between the foot of the Hiles and Townstead Burne all the moytie of the tenement called the Lodge lately demised unto Henry Ayre and John Colson.

For the lives of Launcellot Ayre, 14 years, Michael Ayre, 18, sons of the said Henry, and of William Bell, 7 years, son of the said John Bell.

Rent 10s. od. Improvement £5. 0. 0.

Mem These three foregoing leases for lives are parcell of the ground called Wolsingham Park, and when (amongst other things) the said park was demised to Queen Elizabeth for many years to come (as by the entry of the said leases in due place is to be found) these forementioned premises were then held and enjoyed by the then Keeper of the said park as the reward peculiar to their patents and places, which being taken from them by Bishop Neale have been by him and his successors demised ut supra. And therefore being a part of the same and inclosed within the walls of the said parke Wee think it convenient that they should be sould together.

WILLIAM CROOKE (but made to Thomas Crooke his father).
7 September 6 Car. Certeine land meadow and pasture lyinge in the hall fields of Wolsingham parcell of the demesnes there and certain lands meadows and pasture being parcell of the said demesnes commonly called the West Field or Hall Field then in the tenure or occupation of the said Thomas Crooke or his assigns.

For the lives of Thomas Crooke aforementioned deceased William Crooke son of that said Thomas then aged 10 years and John Crooke another son, then 5.

Rent £1. 1. 8. Improvement £10. 0. 0.

QUEEN ELIZABETH
24 October 24 Eliz. who assigned the lease to Roger Gifford, Doctor of Physick 7 March 25 Eliz. who assigned to Henry Bispham and Henry Barnes, 29 November 29 Eliz. Henry Bispham died, so Henry Barnes, Emanuel and John Barnes, sons of Richard Barnes, Bishop of Durham assigned the premises to Mrs. Carlton widdow 20 April 5 Eliz.
The Grand Lease of Wolsingham Park:— the park called Wolsingham Park, the water corn mill of Wolsingham and one parcel of ground called the Chapel Walls and all houses buildings etc. to the same belonging, (except always out of this present grant all wood and underwoods within the said park, and also excepted all manner of fees and dutyes belonging to the keeper thereof and all mines of coals and lead within the same.) That parcell of three parks called Tunstead House and parkhead.

Granted to Queen Elizabeth for 80 years.

Rent £6. 13. 4. Improvement £30. 0. 0.

CUTHBERT BURNHOPE, JOHN BELL, RICHARD JOPLIN, JOHN ATKINSON, and THOMAS HEALES.
Another parcell of the said park called Hallnighall.

Rent £3. 6. 0. Improvement £20. 0. 0.

ANN COLSON widow.
Another parcell of the said park called Barkston Bank.
    Rent £3. 0. 0. Improvement £9. 6. 8.

JOHN WARD gent.
Another parcell of the said park called Baile Hill House and the old spring.
    Rent £3. 13. 4. Improvement £13. 6. 8.

WILLIAM COLSON
Two parcells in the said park called Crookes Ford and Crooke lands.
    Rent £3. 6. 8. Improvement £16. 0. 0.

WILLIAM COLSON, JOHN TROTTER, WILLIAM DIXON, JOHN HARRISON, JOHN COLSON, and JOHN TAYLOR.
Another parcell of the said park called Bishop Oake Quarter.
    Rent £6. 13. 4. Improvement £35. 0. 0.
    Old rent reserved upon the said park in toto per annum is £26. 13. 4. plus the improvement £123. 13. 4.

JOHN WARD
Another parcell of the Grand Lease called the Chappel Walls.
    Rent 13s. 4d. Improvement £6. 13. 4.

TIMOTHY DRAPER gent.
The water corn mill in Wolsingham.
    Rent £6. 13. 4. Improvement £16. 6. 8.

Wood and timber in the said park worth to be sold is £100.

Sum of these last mentioned parcells is £30. 6. 8. so that the whole Grand Lease before writed with the rent reserved and improved rent per annum will be in toto £180. 13. 4.

THOMAS TROTTER
29 11 Car. Certaine grounds arable meadow and pasture lying in the fields and precincts of Wolsingham, parcell of the demesnes there called Causey Meadow.

For 21 years.

Rent 14s. 2d. Improvement £7. 10. 0.

ROWLAND THOMPSON

18 September 6 Car. One fourth of certain land meadow and pasture in the West Field there.

For 21 years.

Rent 3. 0½. Improvement £1. 13. 4.

CUTHBERT SNOW

18 September 6 Car. One fourth part of certain land meadow and pasture in the Hallfields also West field.

For 21 years.

Rent 3s. ½d. Improvement £1. 13. 4.

JOHN COLSON

13 February 15 Car. Certain land meadow and pasture in the Hallfields or Westfields parcell of the Demesnes there now in the tenure or occupation of the said John Colson.

For 21 years.

Rent 3s. 4½d. Improvement £1. 13. 4.

JOHN ATKINSON

2 February 12 Car. A close or parcell of grounds called Hencrofte in the fields and precincts of Wolsingham now in the occupation of John Atkinson and one certain land meadow or pasture in the Hallfields or Westfields of Wolsingham parcell of the demesnes.

For 21 years.

Rent 5s. 5d. Improvement £11. 10. 0.

(Improvement for Henry Crofte £8. 0. 0., West Field £3. 10. 0.)

ELIZABETH AYER

29 October 11 Car. Certain land meadow or pasture lying in the Hallfield or Westfield of Wolsingham parcell of the demesnes there now in the occupation of the said Elizabeth or her assigns.

For 21 years.

Rent 5s. 5d. Improvement £3. 6. 8.

JOHN HARRISON

29 October 19 Car. Certain land meadow or pasture lying in the Hall-

field or Westfield of Wolsingham parcell of the demesnes there now in the tenure of George Harrison and also certain other lands meadow and pasture lying in the Hallfield or West Field of Wolsingham parcell of the said demesnes late in the tenure of George Harrison.

For 21 years.

Rent for the first 5s. 5d., for the second 5s. 1d. Improvement for both £6. 13. 4.

PETER FINCH and TOBY FINCH

28 October 10 Car. 4½ acres and 32 perches of Chatterly Greene.

For 21 years.

Rent 3s. 4d. Improvement £1. 6. 8.

JOHN RICHARDSON senior and JOHN RICHARDSON junior.

All that sheale called Peates Carr without the park of Wolsingham.

For 21 years.

Rent £2. 0. 0. Improvement £2. 0. 0.

Mem There is a lead or smelt mill in Wolsingham town which formerly was a walk or fullers' mill formerly granted to one John Parsons gent. at the yearly rent of £10. 8. 0. but now is in the possession of one Mr. Wharton, moor master.

Rent £6. 13. 4. Improvement £6. 13. 4.

JOHN WHELDON

29 September 6 Car. Certain lands meadow and pasture containing 7½ acres in Westfield also Hallfield. These premises assigned to George Harrison for 21 years on 30 May 18 Car.

For the lives of the said John Wheldon, Christopher and George Wheldon, his sons.

Rent 5s. 5d. Improvement £3. 6. 8.

THOMAS DAILE of Gilfield in co. Durham, assignee of Francis Appleby of Lartington Co. Ebor.

10 December 7 Car. Certain land meadow and pasture lying in Hallfield or Westfield of Wolsingham parcell of the demesnes there.

For 21 years.

Rent 12s. 2d. Improvement £6. 13. 4.

ELIZABETH AYER

18 September 6 Car. One half or moytie of certain land meadow and

pasture lying in Hallfield or Westfield parcell of the demesnes there lately in the tenure of John Grange or his assigns and were in the occupacon of Elizabeth Ayer or her assigns.

For 21 years.

Rent 6s. 1d. Improvement £3. 6. 8.

Collieries

EDWARD WANLES ROBERT SUERTIES WILLIAM HALL THOMAS PEARSON and EDWARD TAYLOR

21 June 4 Jac. All those colepitts called Hargill and Grewburne.

For the lives of Thomas Harbecke son of John Harbeck lately deceased, George Weight son of Richard Weight and William Walton son of Hugh Walton.

Rent for Grewburn £20. 0. 0., for Hargill £18. 0. 0.

JOHN RICHARDSON the elder, and JOHN RICHARDSON the younger.

15 January 10 Car. All those coal mines and coal pits as well opened as not opened, found or to be found, commonly called Tollow Pits in the lordship and parish of Wolsingham also all those mines, quarries and heapes of free rough flagg slat lyme stones or any other stones in the lordship and parish of Wolsingham.

Rent for the Coal mines 14s. 4d., for the limestones 14s. 4d.

WILLIAM HALL and JOHN HEIGHINGTON

30 October 7 Car. All that parcell of waste ground in the township of Lynesack in the parish of Hamsterley with all mines of coals.

For 21 years.

Rent £1. 0. 0.

Mem That the collieries expressed in these 3 last wryted leases are returned in the Survey of Chester (with their several values, tenures and improvements, amongst other collieries there to which we refer. But the 14s. 4d. for the slate quarry is a decayed rent not to be improved.

There are within the mannor and parish of Wolsingham very many freeholders and copyholders who pay small rents into the lords of the said mannor.

Free Rents in the parish of Wolsingham paid to the coronor	9.	2.	6.
Copyhold rents in Wolsingham town	12.	17.	1.
Greenwellside (a village in the said parish)	8.	1.	1.
Wigside (another village or scattered houses)	6.	14.	3½.

	Summa total	£36. 18. 11½.

Bedburn Township Leaseholds

WILLIAM HOWSON, the eldest son of him the said Bishop of Durham.

3 September 7 Car. The mansion or dwelling house in Bedburne Park and all houses and buildings together with the herbage and grazing of all meadowes closes and grounds inclosures within the walls ditches and bounds of the said park. Sometymes in the occupation of William Barnes, Barbara Barnes and Christopher Barnes.

For the lives of the said William Howson, John and Nicholas Howson, (two other younger sons of the said Bishop). William is dead.

Rent £2. 0. 0. Improvement £40. 0. 0.

And further grant unto him the said William Howson, the office of the Keepership of Bedburne Park and wood together with all topps and barke of such wood as is or shall be felled there.

For the lives of the same.

A covenant on the Bishop's part for him and his successors with the said William Howson, his heirs and assigns and every one of them shall and may have and take necessary and sufficient house boot, hedge boot, plough boot, fence boot, and carte boot to be spent and occupied on the demised premises, provided always that the said William Howson, his heirs and assigns for and during the tenure aforesaid shall sufficiently maintain and uphold the premises.

Wood and timber upon the grounde to be sold worth £600. 0. 0.

And one John Hester is the present tenant in possession and occupies the premises and hath been for many years last past.

Mem We have seen a deede or indenture of assignment made sealed and delivered by the above mentioned John Howson by the names and stile of John Howson of Toft juxta Newton in Co. Lincoln, clerke to the said John Hester of the park and premises bearing date 28 June 18 Car. A.D. 1642 reciting a new lease or graunt of the premises (upon resignation of the old) to be made and sealed by Thomas late bishop of Durham unto the said John Howson, for the lives of the said John Frances his wife and John Howson their son. Which latter lease, if any such be, was not produced to us nor can we find it recorded in the book of entry, is by the said indenture of assignment thereof made to John Hester.

Mem That the park of Bedburn lyeth in the Chappelrie of Witton upon Weare, but it is a part and belongeth to the mannor of Wolsingham as do other villages within the said chapelry which are freeholders and coppyholders of the said mannor of Wolsingham, and pay small rents unto the lord thereof. The entries of which rents are : —

Free rents in North Bedburn	15. 15. 0.
Coppyhold rents within Lynesack	10. 15. 10.
Coppyhold rents in North Bedburne	6. 7. 10.
Coppyhold rents in South Bedburne	15. 6. 8.
Total	£48. 5. 0.

Weardale Leaseholds

Sir PAULE NEALE

4 December 16 Car. Lands and meadows called Burnhope in Weardale.

For the lives of the said Sir Paul and Elizabeth his wife and of William Neale their son. All in being.

Rent £4. 0. 0. Improvement £13. 6. 8.

JOHN EMERSON

31 October 7 Car. The moiety of a tenement with 7 acres of pasture in Burtreeford in Weardale.

For 21 years.

Rent 8s. od. and one fatt lam at Pentecost (or 3s. 4d.) and one fat goose at Michaelmas (or 1s. od.) Improvement £3. 13. 4.

RAPHE FETHERSTONHAUGH
29 September 6 Car. All those pasture grounds called Killhope and Wellhope and one parcell of ground called Sparkefields in Weardale.

For the lives of John, Raphe and Mary Fetherstonhaugh. All in being.

Rent £1. 17. 4. Improvement £15. 0. 0.

The premises are in the possession of one Mr. Elstobb an infant.

JOHN WHITFIELD of Lintzgarth gent.
29 October 11 Car. Messuage or tenement called Horsley Head also Over Horsley within Stanhope Park.

For the lives of George the son of the said John Whitfield then 12 years, Elizabeth wife of Thomas Emerson of Lintzgarth and Ann Whitfield, daughter of John Whitfield then aged 15. Only George living.

Rent £3. 10. 0. Improvement £22. 10. 0.

During the said term the lessee at his own proper costs and charges shall maintain an able horseman with an able horse and good furniture when he shall be lawfully called. And the lessee is to be and continue of good demeanour within the Forest of Weardale And shall not hunt or hurt any kind of deer or game within the said forest except by lawfull warrant.

GEORGE STOBBS of the Springhouse in Weardale.
15 February 12 Car. The moyety of one parcell of ground commonly called the Parrock situate at Westgate.

For the lives of Raphe Stobbs of Westgate John Emerson junior son of Rowland Emerson of Winleside and Ann Stobbs daughter of the said George.

Rent 10s. od. and one fat capon at Martinmass (or 2s. od.) Improvement £4. 10. 0.

JOHN WHITFIELD of Linsgarth, yeoman.
20 October 11 Car. The moyety or one half of a messuage or tenement called Linsgarth.

For the lives of George Whitfield aged 12 and son of the said John Elizabeth wife of Thomas Emerson of Linsgarth and Ann Whitfield daughter of the said John.

Rent 6s. 8d. and one fat hen (or 1s. od.) Improvement £3. o. o.

GEORGE STOBBS of Springhouse in Weardale.

15 February 12 Car. Messuage called Springhouse within Stanhope Park.

For the lives of John aged 6 Jane aged 12 and Elizabeth Stobbs then aged 10 years. Jane is dead.

Rent £1. 4. o. Improvement £12. o. o.

GEORGE EMERSON

4 July 14 Jac. Messuage or tenement called the Eastgate in Weardale and all that part of ground called the High of the Park.

For the lives of George, John and Henry Emerson sons of Raphe Emerson. George is dead, being slain at Edge Hill. Henry is living in Wolsingham, John in Ireland.

Rent for the tenement £7. 6. 8., for the High £3. 6. 8. Improvement for both £60.

Mem This is in the possession of John Emerson of Newcastle, merchant.

LAUNCELLOT TROTTER of Langley in Weardale.

13 February 15 Car. The messuage or tenement called Langley in Weardale.

For 21 years.

Rent £2. 13. 4. Improvement £18.

This lessee to exhibit within 3 years into the office of the Auditor a survey or terrier of the true quantity of the ground belonging to the demised premises with the abutting and abounding of every part thereof.

FRANCIS LEE of Sunderland in Weardale, widdow.

24 September 7 Car. Moyety or one half of the messuage or tenement within the parish of Stanhope called Sunderland late in the tenure or occupation of John Lee or his assigns.

For 21 years.

Rent £1. 13. 4. Improvement £16. 10. o.

Mem This by assignment is come to Thomas Emerson who married one of the daughters of John Lee.

JOHN EMERSON

2 September 6 Car. Moyety of a messuage called Sunderland.

For 21 years.
Rent £1. 13. 4. Improvement £16. 10. 0.

Mem JOHN EMERSON

14 October 2 Car. A messuage or tenement called Winside upon the tearmes expressed in the foregoing lease, the lease expired yet the lessee holds the premises without any demise from the retainors or others.
Formerly for 21 years.
Rent 8s. 4d. Improvement £4. 0. 0.

Mem MARGARET BAINBRIGG widow.

14 October 2 Car. Another messuage or tenement in Weardale for the tearm aforesaid, which lease is also expired yet held as aforesaid.
For 21 years.
Rent 8s. 4d. Improvement £4. 0. 0.

WILLIAM STOBBS

20 October 7 Car. The moyety of one parcell of ground called the Parrock.
For 21 years.
Rent 10s. 0d. Improvement £4. 10. 0.

Here followeth the names of such severall places and respective persons who hold by lease several parcells of land within the said mannor belonging to the late Bishop but have produced no leases notwithstanding we gave them several summonses, yet for your better satisfaction we have returned you the several rents thereof, yearly pay and the improvements we upon our view have set upon them severally and respectively and ould rents of leases which we now retorne but more we cannot.

ELIZABETH FETHERSTONE

16 March 11 Jac. Messuage or tenement called New Park.
For the lives of the said Elizabeth, Phillipe her daughter and Samuell her son. All in being.
Rent £5. Improvement £43. 6. 8.

GEORGE PHILIPSON

The moyety of a tenement called Linsgarth.

For the lives of George Phillipson the elder, George Phillipson the younger and William Phillipson.

Rent 6s. 8d., and 1s. od. for a fat hen. Improvement £3. 6. 8.

Mem Whether any of the lives are in being or no we know not, nor can be informed though we have made all the enquiry possibly.

Sir JOHN ZOUCH, knt.

20 April 6 Car. *Faylers*. All the mines, quarries delfes and veynes of steele and ironstone in the wastes moores fells commons or common ground within the parish of Stanhope and on the north side of the river of Bedburn within the parish of West Auckland as also liberty to digg for stone or ironstone in any of the said fields and to erect forges furnaces bloom smithies windless dammes poolls weares or to build cottages or dwellinghouses upon any the fells wastes, etc.

For 21 years from Lady Day then last past.

Rent £5. Improvement nil.

Mem The reason why we set no Improvement is because there hath been no profit thereof made and no rent paid for the same for many years last past. Nor will any profit ensue without vaste change and expense. And the premises are by assignment said to be in the possession of Mr. Wharton.

EDWARD LIVELY

29 November 3 Car. Lead ore in Weardale.

For 21 years.

Rent £5.

Mem This lease is expired nor was there any rent paid or profitt thereof whilst the said lease was in being.

ARTHUR EMERSON

5 October 18 Jac. Messuage or tenement in Burtreeford.

For the lives of William, John and Margarett Emerson children of the said Arthur.

Rent 8s. od. and 1s. od. for one fat hen. Improvement £3. 13. 4.

Mem This we have extracted from the old leger book.

William and Margarett are dead, the other alive for ought we knowe or can by any means learn, although we have made diligent enquirye of their neighbours, the party himself standing in contempt and producing no lease to us.

JOHN RICHARDSON, junior.

21 September 18 Jac. All that messuage or tenement called Wearhead.
For 21 years.

Rent £1. Improvement £5. 0. 0.

Mem That this lease is now expired we find entered (inter al) in the old leger book aforesaid and is now said to be in the possession of one George Watson but by what right or title he holds the same we do not know, and for him (though often summoned over) not appearing before us.

JOHN FEATHERSTONHAUGH the younger
RALPH FEATHERSTONHAUGH the younger and
ALEXANDER FEATHERSTONHAUGH.

27 June 4 Jac. All that water corn mill in Stanhope.
For their own lives.

Rent £5. 0. 0.

Mem That this mill is long since decayed as also the rent but in liewe thereof there is a mill set up at Westgate in the ground of one Raphe Stobbs upon the Bishop's land and payes rent. One Mr. Elstobb, an infant (by his gardian Mr. Ridley) pretends a title in the same, though in truth there hath been no lease produced to us.

Rent £5. Improvement £7. 0. 0.

Stanhope Park

QUEEN ELIZABETH

17 January 27 Eliz. All those 13 messuages or tenements lying in Stanhope Park late in the tenure of William Stobbs Nicholas Featherston Ralph Emerson of the Springhouse William Emerson Widdow Bainbrigg George Meir John Emerson William Harrison George Robinson Thomas Young John Fryer Nich Stobbs Ralph Stobbs and each paying for their messuages: —

William Stobbs	£1.	6.	8.
Nicholas Featherston	1.	6.	8.
William Emerson	1.	8.	4.
Widdow Bainbrigg	1.	8.	4.
George Meir	1.	8.	4.
John Emerson	1.	8.	4.
William Harrison	1.	8.	4.

George Robinson	1.	8.	4.
Thomas Young		14.	2.
John Fryers		14.	2.
Nicholas Stobbs		14.	2.
Ralph Stobbs		14.	2.

And it is also covenanted that such person or persons as shall hereafter be assignee or assignees of the same shall during the said demise well and truly preserve and cherish the deer in the said park and shall suffer them quietly to rest and feed without baiting slaying hunting or chasing or anie other incumbrance. And shall also find and have in readynesse for every of the said severall tenants one horse and horseman with arms and weapons furnished to serve the Queen's Majestie and her successors and shall do all other dutyes and services accustomed to the said Reverend Father.

Mem A concurrent lease under the Episcopal seal was made by Thomas late Bishop of Durham of the before mentioned premises to Thomas Eayton gent. bearing date 16 May 1636 for 21 years, reserving the ancient rents and services in the precedent lease to be found. Which concurrent lease though we find it entered in the ledger books of records belonging to the Dean and Chapter of Durham yet was never confirmed under the common seal of the said Dean and Chapter, and therefore as we conceive of no validitie.

Mem The present tenants of the premises do disclayme to hold any estate by virtue of the said lease for 70 years by the Bishop made as forsaid but do acknowledge to hold the premisses by the very service upon the borders and under the severall rents in and upon the said lease reserved, intitling themselves customary tenants. And to strengthen theyre clayme and supposed title thereunto did produce the coppie of the dimission of a suit then defending in the Queen's Court of Exchequer at London touching upon the premises between John Stanhope, Esq, her Majesties assignee by letters patent complainent and William Stobbs and others pretending themselves customary tenants defendants The said dismission bears date Thursday 14th December 36 Eliz And was granted upon hearing council both sides. And the said tenants did also produce a Leiger Book in parchment fairlie written conteyning, (inter alia) the copie of a commission of enquiry bearing date 19th September 37 Eliz. directed by Toby then Bishop of Durham to certeyn officers and servants of him the said Bishop to enquire into the tenancies, rights and privileges be-

longing to the See of Durham within the said parke of Stanhope and
Forest Weardale who therupon summoned and empanelled a jury
of 16 men of the neighbourhood and produced and examined divers
witnesses upon oath to inform the said jury, which jury (upon the
whole matter) did present that the then several tenants of the premisses did hold the same as customary tenants indeed under payment of the severall and respective rents upon each particular messuage and land in the said lease reserved and by the same border
service therin mentioned, but not as by virtue of the said lease. All
which considered we thought it our duty as surveyors nakedly to
present the whole matter unto you to be advised on by Counsell
learned. And we estimate the premises (except the messuage called
the Spring House which since came to the Bishop by attaynder and
you will find particularly returned and valued by ittselfe in the
present survey) worth over and above the rent reserved at £140 per
annum.

Marmaduke Trotter and Thomas Marshall by lease made and
graunted by Gilbert Marshall and Anthony Smyth your Receivor
hold one parcell of Stanhope Park called the Frith or Shrubbs heretofore in the possession of the Bishop by him kept for the mowing
of hay and repasturing of his deer then being within the said park
for which they pay £15 per annum. Worth upon improvement £15.

Mem That the severall forest keepers and their officers within the
said forest and park had their severall and particular allotments of
meadow for hay and pasturage of cattle out of or upon the said Frith
or Shrubbs as is expressed or implyed in their severall particular
patents by us returned and valued in this survey. And the Bishop's
deer had also the libertie of the whole ground, the tenants being
tyed by their leases not to slatr hunt or hinder them from depastur-
ing there.

Mem There were within the parish of Stanhope and mannor of
Wolsingham very many freeholds coppyholds customary tenants who
pay severall small rents into the lords of this mannor, the entreys of
which coppies and deeds would have spent much labour and time
to the great charge of the state and have been of very little use and
therefore we have left the same undone and return the rents in grosse,
ut sequit.

Free Rents in Stanhope	11.	16.	6.
Coppiehold rents there	22.	0.	7.
Coppyhold rents at Bishopley	3.	17.	4.
Customary rents in the same	47.	3.	10.
Customary rents in the Forest of Weardale	35.	5.	0.

Summa totalis £118.	3.	3.	

A Supplementary Survey or Certificate of Thomas Saunders, Edward Colston Esquire two of the Surveyors of the lands belonging to the Bishop of Durham. Made 19th June 1649

We say that in the valuation of the mannor house park and appurtenances of Bedburn we had respect unto the boats allowable by covenant of the late Bishop to the present tenant as his due and they are valued in improvement set upon the same and returned in our former survey without any respect at all unto the top and bark.

We say that the valuation of the wood and timber standing and growing in Bedburn Park we did make no reprisal for or upon the value of the top and bark granted by the late Bishop to the keeper of the said wood in express terms in respect we did not find in former leases of the premises expired any other than general woods, vizt— all profits emoluments advantages etc belonging to the same but we say that if the said lease or grant now in being wherein top or bark are granted in particular woods be good in law, which we take not upon us to judge, then we conceive that the full half value of the said wood (being returned at £600) ought to be defaulted out of the same. And if the same shall be judged to extend to warrant trees only or timber granted to be felled by the late Bishop for his tenants or used by himself for reparation then we think fit to have a defaulcation made in liew thereof out of the said £600 one hundred pounds.

We say that the £5 per annum set as a valew in reversion upon the Moore Master's patent or lease, the £5 decayed rent now in the Moore Master's hand and the £5 upon the expired lease of the lead ore to Mr. Lively are set as improvements upon the revertions of the said estates to be sold, and are not part of the £15 per annum in reversion set upon the mines.

We say that the 20 dayes moweing upon the Frith or Shrubbs belonging to Mr. Blackstone the forester, the 4 days belonging to Mr. Emmerson, the 3 dayes moweing belonging to the pinder, the 20 dayes moweing belonging to Mr. Trotter as keeper of Stanhope Park, the 20 days moweing belonging to Christopher Emerson as keeper of the same park and any of them are to be taken and had upon part of the land called the Frith or shrubbs, every man knowing his particular division. And we say further that that part of the Frith or shrubbs now let by the Trustees Receivers for £15 per annum is worth £15 per annum over and besides the foresaid severall dayes' works. And we likewise say that the several pasture gates returned by us belong to the severall officers are distinct from that part of Stanhope Park (as we conceive) which the 13 tenants hold and are not to be taken upon any other part of Stanhope parke or the manor of Wolsingham otherwise than we have already returned and valued them that we know of or could learn.

We say that the officers cannot as we conceive distreyne for their fees since by patent if the same be not paid within the parkes or upon their other part of the mannor of Wolsingham for it doth and may appear by their severall patents by us already returned how and where the said several and respective fees are to be paid.

And as to the tenants' estate of the 13 tenements in Stanhope Park valud at £140 per annum in revertion, we have in our former survey returned with the rents of what we find in fact but take not upon us to judge their validity or of the pretended lease in being which are formerly returned, or of the value of their customary estates but leave the same to the greater judgement of the committee of trustees and their Councell learned in the law consider the same to be included in the sume of £47. 3. 10. returned as customary rent in that parish.

And as for certifying what part of Mr. Cressett's estate is for lives what for years or for your approving your improved rent of £32 per annum set upon the same disburst to eyther part we cannot do it unless we were upon the places again and could see the writings which yet we have not done nor conceive it we may be benefittiall to your state the doing or not doing of it being onely for the use of private men.

And lastly as to Mr. Wharton's estate in the lead mill or melt mill, Mr. Elstobb's estate in his mill sett up in Westgate in Weardale or Philipson's estate in the moytie of your messuages called Lynes Garth we cannot ascertaine the same as is desired unless we could see their severall deeds by which they hold your farm or were upon the place again we having upon sure evidence as we could then get and upon our owne veiwe made our former returne of the said particular least the premisses should have beene utterly lost or concealed to the prejudice of the state.

11th June 1652.
*By the Commissioners for removing obstructions in the sale of Bishops lands**
Upon consideration had of the desire of Sir Arthur Hesilrig in his petition to the late committee for removing obstructions in the sale of the said lands concerning his purchase made of the manor of Wolsingham parcell of the Bishopric of Durham *Ordered* that the surveyors who surveyed the said manor do certify unto us forthwith whether there be any court leets within the manor, and if there be then to put a value upon it. And also to certify whether the £15. 15s. od. free rent certified by them to be payable out of lands lying within the township of North Bedburn in the manor of Wolsingham be returned in the manor of Auckland, and whether they have returned a lease of a farm in Middridge in the possession of one Butler, true or not.

Will. Roberts
France Missenden
John Berner
Robt. Aldworth

The humble Certificate of Edward Colston, John Duncalfe and John Horsell gents, surveyors for the lands of the Bishop of Durham. By Commission dated the 24th September 1652 A.D.

We certify as followeth, vizt.
First we have examined and viewed divers records remaining in the

---

* This document is to be found in the Weardale Chest Collection, Number 39, University of Durham, Department of Paleography and Diplomatic. I am grateful to Mrs. Drury for pointing it out to me.

Registry at Durham and also examined several gents of good ability and sometimes officers to the late Bishop but do not find nor cannot be informed that there hath ever been any court kept by name or stile of a court leet within the manor of Wolsingham. Nor needed the Bishop, as we conceive, to hold any such court within the mannor of Wolsingham having Jura Regalia within his diocese and having a sherriffe of his own within the Countye Palatine which was an officer by patent for life, who twice in the year did (betweixt the Rivers Tyne and Tees) hold his Sherriffe hurne where all things inquirable in court leet were enquired of and presented but in mannors further remote as Bedlington in Northumberland and Crake and Howden and Northallerton in Yorkshire court leets were kept by stewards commissioner by the Bishop for that purpose.

To the Second queere we certify that the £15. 15s free rents as certified to be payable out of the lands lying within the township of North Bedburne in the manor of Wolsingham is returned also in the manor of Auckland so as the same in truth is twice returned and therefore a defalcation, as we conceive, ought to be paid out of the purchase money paid or to be paid for the manor of Wolsingham.

To the third queere we certify that a lease of a farm in Midridge in the possession of Elizabeth Lydall late Butler is twice retorned as one lease in the name of the said Elizabeth and the other in the name of Rowland Butler.

10th February 1652.
By the Commissioners for removing obstructions in the sale of Bishop's lands*

Whereas it being alledged by Sir Arthur Hesilrigg that the words court leets are not inserted in the conveyance, which is to be passed unto him of the manor of Wolsingham, parcell of the possessions of the late Bishoprick of Durham, and that for want of such words the said conveyance cannot be made perfect and that thereby he is hindered from paying in of the second moiety of his purchase money for the said manor, and desired by the said Sir Arthur that the said words courts leets are inserted in the conveyance of the manors of Auckland and Evenwood and for other manors in the county and bishoprick of Durham it is thought meet by us *Ordered* that the said words courts leets be put into the conveyance for the said manor of

Wolsingham and in case the said Sir Arthur shall receive no benefit by the inserting of the said words into the said conveyance, that then the said Sir Arthur be reprised for the same, and the Register for the sale of the said lands or his deputy is hereby required to enter this order upon the survey of the said manor, and mende the particular thereof accordingly.

Will. Roberts
Henry Pytt
Jo. Parker
Jo. Berners
Robt. Aldworth

We being informed that you are in the northern parts near Durham, desire for our better satisfaction in some matters now depending before us concerning the collieries of Grewburn, the collieries of Hargill and the colliery of Linesack farmed for the use of the poor of Durham. That you will with what convenience may be certify unto us what the covenants are in the said leases of the said collieries and whether the said collieries be worked out or not and what else you shall find to account therein.

25th November, 1652   Your loving friends
                           Wm. Roberts
                           Hen. Pitt
                           Jo. Berners
                           Mat. Valentine

For our loving friends Mr. Colston, Mr. Duncalfe our surveyors at Durham or elsewhere in the county there.*

A Certificate or Supplement to a former survey of the said manor made in the month of December in the yeare of our Lord God 1652

Hargill, Grewburn and Lynsack Collieries Leaseholds

ROBERT SUERTYES mercer EDWARD LES dyer WILLIAM HALL draper THOMAS PEARSON mercer and EDWARD TAYLOR cordwainer all of the City of Durham.

* Weardale Chest op cit.

21 June 4 Jac. Collieries and Pitts called Hargill lying and adjoyning
near unto Bitchburn on the east, the Holme Park on the west, the
Earl of Westmoreland's lands on the north and the Lord Eure's lands
on the south. And above all colemines and pitts called Grewburn
adjoyning to the river of Gaunless in the south, the Lordship of
Softley in the north, the Fro Loaning on the west, the Rock or
Stones called Butterknowle and the New Cross on the east part.

For the lives of Thomas Fairbeck son of John Fairbeck lately
deceased, Jarrard Wright son of Richard Wright, mercer and William Walton draper. Gerrard Wright is dead.

Rent for Hargill £18. 0. 0. for Grewburn £20.

The lessees shall during their terme serve the Bishop and his successors for his and their houses wherever he or they shall lye or be
with good coale to be gotten at the charge of the said Robert Suertyes
Edward Les William Hall Thomas Pearson and Edward Taylor,
the said Bishop and his successors payeing for every horse load a ½d.
and for every waine load 4d. And it is further covenanted that the
said Robert Suertyes or the said other persons or their assigns shall
not dureing their term work above two pitts at one time without
the speciall license of the said Bishop or his successors. Provided
always that if at the end of the said term there shall be any coals
remayning above the ground within the limits aforesaid the same
shall be left to and for the benefit of the said Bishop and his successors.
and that the said lessees at the end of their term shall leave all manner
of ropes rundles barrows shovels toolls picks and all other necessary
utensils and implements belonging to the said collieries and pitts in
such good sort and manner as the same are and remayne. And if it
happen that the said colemines and pits do decay within the said
term that then upon the surrender of the said lease of that part of
ground wherein the said lessees cannot win or get coals to the said
Bishop or his successors the rent to cease and not to be payable to
the said grounds according to the true meaning of this indenture.

[The profts of the Collieries (if any were) belong to the poor of
Durham]

Hargill Colliery is boundered according to the lease and did lye as
useless until of late one Mr. John Hodgson for the good of the poor of
Durham did undertake to try if he could make any profit of her but
neither he nor any other person (as he affirm to us) can do any good

or will give above £5 per annum for her so long as she is a going colliery. And gave us severall reasons for it, the truth of which reasons we have examined and believe.

First because the coles which the said colliery now cast are fetched away by the inhabitants of the chapelry of Witton upon Weare upon such considerable terms. vizt—for a groat or fother or waine load, claiming the same due at that rate by ancient custom, and one penny for one horse load. That it is impossible for such pits and work them at that rate. Besides the lordship of Brancepeth the township of Hunwick and Newton Cap pretend also an ancient custom to have all their coals from that pit at sixpence a wayne load and will give no more, and a penny for a horse load. Every wayne carryeth at least ten corves and a horse a corfe at least and every corfe holds at least ten pecks and costs for heaving, putting and drawing up the shaft above bank eightpence every twenty or score of corves, besides the charge of candles shovels trains corves hacks ropes man rolls and other charge incident to collieries. All which together with the great charge of sinking of pits and stapling out of her water courses, costs as much, if not more than, is or can be made of the coals.

Secondly the seam is but an ordinary coal and cannot last because no coals can be got on her eastward bounder being thrown out by a dike or rock of stone. Her westward course is a broken seam and not workable for her northern course which was her best is all wasted and wrought out. So as the pit and pitts now in in work or workable lyeth to her southern bounder and would cast a considerable quantity of coal before she were wrought forth if it would permit cost and charge. But that, we are credibly informed, she will not do for the reasons precedent, and hereafter expressed. And last of all, which is worst of all, that if any considerable quantity of coals should be wrought out of the said mines or seams gained or to be gained, there would be more rent for them there neighbouring towns being served, in regard there are several collieries about for of late won and wrought which work better coals and can and do afford them upon better terms than any farmer of this colliery can.

Grewburn Colliery by reason she is won and wrought at her eastern bounder called Butterknowle bears that name and is boundered according to the lease and eight pit rooms or thereabouts is wrought in her. But at the present and for a year or more past the same has been totally drowned and no coals can be wrought or got out of her without the expense of a great sum of money to set on and keep her ginns going to draw her water down which is several fathoms above her working or seam of coal which charge in regard Sir Henry Vane the elder hath won a colliery which is now going on the south-ward of the colliery where her best custom and market lay, and one pit in the lordship of Softley on the northwest of her, and Carter-thorne colliery in the north east, we are credibly informed and in-duced to believe the colliery is very inconsiderable and hardly worth the expense and time of gaining and working again.

WILLIAM HALL and JOHN HEIGHINGTON

13 October 7 Chas. All those seam or seams of coals as well opened as unopened lying and being in a parcell of waste ground in Lyn-sack, containing by estimation 48 acres, and is thus boundered: — On westwell and Froloaning on the east on Rabye Park on the west the river Gaunless on the south and the edge of the moor on the north.

For 21 years.

Rent £1. o. o.

This colliery is all wrought out unless it be one pit room which as we are credibly informed by judicious men in collieries will cost at least £20 the sinking, and then she may, as they conceive, cast coals two years or thereabouts, but will be of very small profit in regard there is of late another colliery now within the lordship and within twice twelve score of her which take away the customers from this, that they assure us she will not give above £10 or £12 a year at most.

SALES OF BISHOPRIC LANDS*

1647 October 18 Certain farms parcell of Houghton manor to Adam Sheppardson	352	0	0
February 2 Houses shops and waste on Tyne Bridge to Francis Alder	59	2	6
March 8 Bishop Auckland manor to Sir A. Hesilrigg	6102	88	11½
March 24 Stockton manor to William Underwood and James Nelthorpe	6165	1	2½
1648 April 19 Parcell of Gateside manor by Tyne-bridge to James Baylis	63	15	10

	£	s	d
June 9 ⅔ Tanfield Moor coal mines to Richard Marshall	91	16	0
⅓ Tanfield Moor coal mines to Archibald Lovett	17	6	8
March 7 Part of Wolsingham manor to John Emmerson	406	13	4
1649 May 2 Durham Castle to Thomas Andrews, Lord Mayor of London	1267	0	10
May 30 Parcell Wolsingham manor to Richard Marshall	158	11	8
September 21 Frankland Wood, park, colliery and meadows in Durham Moor, Borough of Gateside, Gateside tolls to Thomas Redge	2559	2	0
November 9 Bishop Middleham manor to Thomas Hesilrigg Esq.,	3306	6	6½
Sunderland Burrough and Houghton manor to George Fenwick	2851	9	6
1650 June 1 Parcell of land in Rivehopp to George Fenwick	2091	16	3
Wolsingham manor to Sir Arthur Hesilrigg	6764	14	4
March 24 Easington manor to Walter Boothby	8528	2	3
1651 April 18 Durham Burrough and Framwellgate to Durham Corporation	200	0	0
May 2 2 parcels of land near Durham to Richard Marshall	8	13	4
March 12 7 parcels of land on Tynebridge to Francis Alder	52	5	8

* Durham Cathedral Library, Allen MSS 22

INDEX OF PLACES

Ackworth, 136
Adamland, 99
Adderley Clough, 147
Akes Rawe, 36
Aikesraw, 76
Annatt Thorne, 113
Annott Well, 113
Arkins Bank, 126
Ashletts, 78
AUCKLAND CASTLE, 10-14, 87-8
Auckland Park, 37

Backhouse Garth, 52
Backland, 137
Bale Hill Field, 153
Baile Hill House, 155
Balle, 114
Ballestead, 147
Banckton Close, 68
Banks, 135
Barkers Land, 28
Barkston Bank, 155
Barrat Green, 17
Bayly Dubbs, 23
BEDBURN, 159-60
Bedburn Park, 159, 168
Bicotts Land, 22
Billershaw, 142
BINCHESTER, 16
Birkeclose, 128
Birtley Wood, 4, 36
Bishops Close, 45
Bishop Groove, 152
Bishops Meadow, 34
Bishop Oak Quarter, 155
Blackbank, 147
Blackclough, 152
Blakeley Hill, 36
BLACKWELL, 101-6
Blackwell Nook, 102
Bolam Lough, 128
Bolts Burne, 35
Bolts Fyne, 35
BONDGATE IN AUCKLAND, 15-33
Booker Land, 37
Booreland, 99
Boote Hill, 62
Botham Hill, 108
Boordland, 105

Bowbagg, 16
Bracken Close, 132
Bracken Hill, 76
Brackes Close, 17
Bradley Carrock, 147
Bracken Moor, 104
Brakes, 78
Braxes Close, 82
Broad Meadow, 76
Brockenbury Leaze, 141
Bromehaugh, 131
Bulmer Hey, 100
Burnhope, 160
Burtreeford, 160, 164
Butterknowle, 128
Bydale Bank, 97
BYERS GREEN, 41-6
Byers Moor, 4

Calfs Close, 98, 127, 138
Calfs Green, 116
Canongate, 18
Caper Close, 21, 22
Capse Close, 108
Carr, 55
Cathedral Free, 67
Carrock Hill, 148
Causey Meadow, 155
Chappell Garth, 140
Chappelside Acre, 140
Chapel Walls, 154
Charwell Rice, 42
Chatterly Green, 157
Chequor Leaze, 141
Chequor Place, 139
Cheseley, 113
Chowbank, 100
Church Lees, 19
Clagrand, 93
Clarkhouse, 42
Clover Lawe, 147
Clubhill, 58
Coalway, 141
COATHAM MUNDEVILLE, 113-4
COCKERTON, 107-12
Cole Land, 113
Coleswell, 59
Collieries, 6, 8, 25, 36, 122, 133, 158, 172-5
Comon Park, 33
Coniers Riding, 78

Copeland, 124, 143
COPELAW, 67
Cornefield, 129, 130
Cornehill, 45
COUNDON, 46-52
COUNDON GRANGE, 52-3
Coundon Oxe Close, 32
Cow Close, 21, 127
Cow Moor, 66
Craggstackgarth, 148
Cranley, 52
Crawley Bank, 50
Cronny Croft, 25
Crookeford, 153, 155
Crooke Lands, 155
Crosshope Carr, 50, 51
Crosshouse Field, 78
Crossetowngate, 17
Cunderwell, 129

Dagill, 128, 131
Dallingland, 111
DARLINGTON, 89-100
Dearens Head, 148
Dell Bank, 21
Delves Bank, 28, 31
Divil Ridway, 56
Dobsons Close, 89
Doddridge, 66
Dowsyke, 147
Drieishill, 147
Dunston Green, 20
Dyehouse, 8
Drydon, 48

Easell, 48
East Close, 48
East John Long, 49
Easter Pawlawe, 147
Eastmoor, 127
Edmonds Close, 60
Ellins Close, 100
ESCOMBE, 53-62
Escombe Hirst, 57
Etherley Moor, 5
Ettle, 48, 52
Ettle Meadow, 34
EVENWOOD, 125-34

Farr Close, 111
Farthing Knoll, 131
Faught Tree, 129

Fencings, 78
Fethams, 90
Fielden Bridge, 35
Fielding Loaning, 139
Flaver, 72
Four Acre Close, 77
Free Flatt, 50
Freelees, 46
Free Noke, 48
Frith, 167, 169
Fryers Flatt, 48

Galgarth Croft, 81
Garrends Close, 70
Garre Ends, 72
Gate Close, 43
Gibbs House, 22
Gibchare, 25
Glendhirst, 79
Gordon, 126
Grange Field, 94, 99
Grayes Bank, 35
Grayes House, 42
Greate Right, 153
Green Field, 18, 35
Greenes Close, 68
Grumwellside, 44

Haddesly Burn, 148
Hall Meadows, 20, 38
Hallnighall, 154
Halykeld, 115
Hartfowlings, 147
Hatheryclough, 151
HAUGHTON, 114-6
Haver Close, 34, 47
Hawkwood Head, 147
Haysett, 42
HEIGHINGTON, 62-70
Heilde, 60
Helme Park, 148
Hencroft, 156
HENKNOWLE, 16
Hermeth Hugh, 46
Highfield, 128, 130
High Park, 90
Highside Bank, 70
High Flawlyes, 46
High Side, 42
Hiles, 153
Hirst, 53, 54
Holdsworth, 29
Holemeadow, 124, 143
Hollinghall Pasture, 153
Holridge, 49, 51
Hooke Meadow, 17
Horsewells, 135
Horsley Head, 161
Howlefoot, 29
Howletch, 48
Huds Burn, 56

Hulberke, 34
Huntershields, 113
Hunwick, 174
Hunwick Moor, 5

Intack, 135
Ireland, 147
Ireshopeburn, 151
Ivefield, 46

Jackley Peece, 50

KILLERBY, 135-6
Killhope, 161
Kilngarth, 113
Kimbleburn, 72
Knightfield, 138

Lamb Close, 126, 131
Lambes Cross, 147
Lambeside, 53
Lamelands, 21
Langarth, 44
Lang Horne, 55
Langley, 162
Lawme Laine Haugh, 54
Laymeswell Head, 51
Law Crooke, 26
Leaming, 140
Leed Nyne Acres, 116
Lease, 48
Les Close, 128
Lines Garth, 131
Lingie Close, 78
Lintzgarth, 161
Little Right, 153
Little Thorne Close, 32
Lockies House, 42
Lodge, 153
Londonston Garthes, 50
Long Close, 78
Long Dike, 138
Long Flatt, 52
Long Lands Riding, 32
Longman, 147
Low Close, 117
Low Drithop, 49
Lowfields, 98, 127, 130
Low Park, 90
Lowsery Side, 75
Lyme Garth, 128
Lynes Garth, 170

Marleridge Dale, 52
Marleway, 28, 31
Martin Peece, 48
Maylands, 93, 105
Meadows, 135
Middle Field Close, 54
MIDDRIDGE, 71-4, 171
Middridge Moor, 5

Mill, Corn, 5, 6, 38, 68, 77,
    81, 132, 135, 142, 143,
    154, 155, 165, 170
Mill, Fulling, 37, 157
    Smelt, 167, 170
Mill Hill, 21
Mine, Iron, 6, 152
    Lead, 151, 152
Mires Chase, 22
Moore Close, 18
Mooreside, 128
Morebrow, 53
Myers, 113

Nabhill, 20, 22
Nether Leyer, 141
New Closes, 135, 136
NEWFIELD, 46
New Park, 163
New Pasture, 23
Newton Bridge, 148
NEWTON CAP, 74-80, 174
Newton Garth, 113
Newton Gates, 117
North Graine Foot, 147
North Leaze, 138
Northwood, 133
Nuttinghagge, 44

Old Hall, 46
Old Park, 133
Oremoor, 65
Over Horsley, 161
Over Small Lees, 77
Oxe Close, 24
Oxehouse, 22
Oxnett Flatt, 97, 106

Panmire, 21, 24
Parke Close, 36, 76, 79
Parkhead, 154
Park, Somer 15
    Winter, 15
Parke Land, 42, 43
Park Place, 45
Parrock, 161
Parsons Peece, 50
Peace Lands, 128
Pearebank, 49
Peates Carr, 157
Penny Batts, 17
Pikestone, 148
Pinkney Garth, 104
Pitt Close, 126
Pollard Brack, 50
Pollards, 25
Poppie Field, 25
Pounder Close, 93
Picksley Hills, 36

Quarryholes, 138

Raley Fell, 5
Ramshaw, 131
Rapeshield, 147
Rathingburne, 77
Rawe Crofte, 51
Redgill, 114
REDWORTH, 80-1
Redworth Fell, 5
Richmond Close, 23
RICKNELL GRANGE, 67
Ridding Gate, 35
Riggs Close, 130
Roantree Pitts, 130
Robsons Close, 20, 37
Roddingburn, 75
Rosterley Ley, 111
Rough Mires, 4, 15
Round Hill, 132
Rombaldy House, 77
Rumby Hill, 5
Rumby Loaning, 35
Rydeing Hill, 60

SADBERGE, 117-20
Savoy Close, 76
Say Land, 117
Serviside, 75, 76
Shaftwell, 147
Shawes, 138
Sheapethorne, 32
Sheriffe Tower, 9
Shieldmore Carrock, 148
Skinnergate, 96
Smallees, 79
Small Thorney Close, 33
Smiddy, 35
Smithside, 48, 50, 52
Smithy Close, 77
Snaylecroft, 20, 23, 24
South Dike, 43
Sparkefields, 161
Sponthaugh, 43, 44

Springhouse, 161, 162
Spurlwood House, 148
Stacc Gakthes, 129, 131
Stainshawe, 112
STANHOPE, 146-52
Stanhope Park, 165-7
Stanley Garth, 106
Starkitch Nook, 106
Steakbridge, 148
Stockgarth, 42
Stonefield, 148
Stowperdale, 111
Sunderland, 162
Sunny Croft, 21
Swinherd Field, 79

Tenters, 20
Tepper Mires, 130
Thickley Dike, 74
Thorney Close, 32
Three Acres Close, 89
Throw Loaning, 148
Tile Close, 4, 15, 32
Timbley Croft, 106
Tindall Morehouses, 23
Todhills, 44
Toft, 48
Toft Hill, 126
Tomb Close, 36
Toms Close, 74
Toopehome, 62
Topleggs, 50
Tothaugh, 51
Townstead Burn, 153
Tree Flatt, 52
Tressam, 101
Trotters, 78
Tunstall Green, 148
Tunstead House, 154
Two Loughs, 46

Upper Crooke, 53

Varringer, 79

Wakfield, 130
Wales Moor, 128
Wardoesend Close, 50
Wardsworth, 76
Warlehead Close, 51
Wealeside, 143
Wear Batts, 26
Weardale, 160-5
Wearhead, 152, 168
Wellestoft, 51
Wellhope, 161
WEST AUCKLAND, 136-44
West Close, 76
Wester Black Deane, 151
Westerhall Flatt, 109
Westerplace, 129
West Free, 55
Westgate, 161
Westhaugh, 54
West Leazes, 113
West Pasture, 128
West Rawe Park, 147
Wetherell Close, 98
Wheatefield, 46
Wheate Land, 49
Wheatesyde, 142
Whelad, 47
WHESSAY, 112-3
Whin Close, 77
Whinnes, 36
Whinny Close, 32, 50
WHITWORTH, 9
Wideopen, 5
Winside, 163
Witton Park, 35
Wigton Walls, 21
WOLSINGHAM, 146-159
Wolsingham Park, 153-4
Woodhouse Close, 38
Woodhouses, 5
Wrightes Fine, 35

INDEX OF PERSONS

Abrey, John, 91
Ackroyd, Margaret, 138
Adamson, Anthony, 19, 20
  John, 18, 19, 21, 23, 27,
    32, 33, 34
  Raphe, 25
  Robert, 2, 3
  Susannah, 21
  William, 2, 3, 25, 121
Addamson, Robert, 121
Addison, Raphe, 56
Addy, John, 92
Aire, Henry, 153
Allan, William, 105, 119
Allanson, Raphe, 52
  Thomas, 20
Allen, William, 92, 117
Allenson, Anne, 29
  Anthony, 28, 29, 77, 78,
    79
  Gerard, 126, 129
  John, 16, 37, 77, 78, 118
  Mathew, 134
Allison, John, 126
Anderson, Charles, 138, 139
Andrew, William, 92
Andwood, Francis, 81
  William, 81
Appleby, Jane, 96
  John, 62, 96
Applegarth, John, 95
Ariam, Anthony, 65
Armstrong, James, 97
Askew, Thomas, 25
Atkinson, Anthony, 64
  Brian, 55, 57
  Henry, 66, 70
  John, 64, 66, 76, 77, 154,
    156
  Margaret, 76
  Richard, 110
  Thomas, 57
Aude, William, 74
Ayer, Elizabeth, 156

Baddeley, Richard, 48
Baddley, Richard, 127
Badley, Richard, 32
Bailes, Miles, 97
Bainbridge, Henry, 71

John, 71
  Raphe, 71
Bainbrigg, Margaret, 163
Baker, Robert, 2, 3, 16
Barnes, Thomas, 82
  Timothy, 115
  William, 90, 159
Bateman, Mary, 77
Bayles, Ann, 23, 59, 74
  Henry, 37
  James, 74, 75
  Raphe, 23, 26, 58, 59
Baxter, Whitwirth, 16
  William, 98
Bell, Anthony, 22
  Barnaby, 142
  Brian, 56
  Carill, 20
  Christopher, 20
  John, 2, 3, 18, 95, 98, 121,
    153, 154
Bellamy, George, 97
Bellasis, Henry, 17
  Sir Thomas, 17
  Sir William, 38
Bellingham, James, 92
Bennett, John, 78
  William, 78
Beswicke, Hugh, 27, 34
Bewicke, John, 146
Biers, Christopher, 46
Bigland, Edward, 18
Binchester, Thomas, 60, 61
Birbeck, Simon, 59
  Thomas, 136
Blackston, Henry, 4, 132
Blake, Robert, 121
Blakeston, Barbary, 75
  Henry, 26, 36
  Sir William, 75
Blakey, William, 108
Blackwell, Ralph, 92
Bleameir, Thomas, 104
Bolt, Brian, 55, 57, 59, 60
Boore, William, 105
Bowbanke, George, 91
  Peter, 106, 108
Bowes, Robert, 116
  Thomas, 122
Bowser, Mathew, 17
  Richard, 17, 36, 71

Boyle, Henry, 33
Brabant, George, 67, 70
  Hercules, 67
  John, 81
Brabint, William, 21
Bradforth, John, 92, 96
Bradley, George, 23
Browne, William, 49
Brass, Thomas, 39
Brasse, Cuthbert, 34
  Thomas, 16
  William, 34, 45, 75
Briggs, Robert, 30
Bringhurst, John, 107
Briteman, John, 132
Browne, Christopher, 91
  Katherine, 48
  Margaret, 54
  Thomas, 48, 50
  Valentine, 116
  William, 91
Bucke, Gregory, 24
  John, 117, 120
  Michael, 141
  Mile, 117
  Thomas, 120
Bullock, Thomas, 53
Bulmer, William, 142
Burbeck, Simon, 142
  Thomas, 92
Burke, John, 117, 137
Burne, George, 2, 3, 121
Burnett, William, 96
Burnhope, Cuthbert, 154
Butler, George, 74
  Gregory, 37
  Rowland, 74
Byerley, Anthony, 73
  Christopher, 71, 72, 141
    142
Byland, Edward, 33

Cairesley, Brian, 43
  Robert, 43
Calverley, John, 23, 42
Calvert, John, 140
Carleton, Sir Dudley, 38
Carr, James, 18
  William, 143
Carre, Robert, 18
Carrington, Cecillia, 30

Cuthbert, 30
Catterick, Francis, 114
Lawrence, 100
Thomas, 94
Charlesworth, William, 97
Cholmley, Adelyne, 67
James, 67
Church, William, 82
Clarke, John, 136
Claxton, James, 67
Cleaton, Robert, 72
Clement, John, 107
Clifton, John, 143
Clover, Oswald, 30
Coaforth, John, 48
Coatesworth, John, 52
Cockerell, Richard, 92
Coleman, Thomas, 19
Coleson, John, 18
Colling, Ralph, 93
Colman, John, 54
Richard, 119
Colson, Ann, 153, 155
John, 153, 156
Mariola, 30
Thomas, 30, 50
William, 30, 32, 155
Colston, Edward, 1, 2
Colt, Christian, 54
Mathew, 140
Conne, Anne, 112
Cooke, Agnes, 59
Elizabeth, 54, 58
William, 53, 54, 59, 65
Cooker, Toby, 104
George, 47
Corneforth, John, 91, 100
Richard, 76, 79, 101, 137
Thomas, 106
William, 44, 79
Corney, Edward, 134, 145
Cornforth, William, 86
Corniforth, Cuthbert, 99
Jane, 99
William, 106
Corny, Edward, 126
Coultman, Cuthbert, 51
Elizabeth, 51
Courtpenny, George, 16, 46
Cowlman, Richard, 117
Coxon, Jane, 18
Coxon William, 18, 31
Craddock, Dorothy, 13
John, 18, 25, 27, 33, 34, 39
Margery, 20, 22, 39
Cragge, Richard, 72, 74
Craweshaw, Nicholas, 19
Crawforth, Robert, 66
Cresset, Francis, 65, 67
Crooke, William, 54, 153,

154
Crosier, George, 135
The Crown, 38, 45, 89, 115, 154
Curry, Christopher, 26
John, 18, 19, 26, 27
Raphe, 26
Cussen, John, 118

Daile, George, 82
Thomas, 157
Dalton, John, 56
Dalton, Robert, 137
Dame, George, 28
Henry, 26
William, 25
Damport, Elianor, 20
William, 21
Damson, John, 25
Darcy, Sir William, 33, 55, 62, 67, 80, 134
Darlington, John, 89
Robert, 89, 121
Darneton, Robert, 2, 3
Dark, John, 92
Dawson, John, 2, 3, 16, 121
Thomas, 80
Deanes, Anthony, 58
Denham, John, 114
Dennis, John, 97, 110
Deverex, Jonathon, 146
Dickon, Christopher, 116
Dickon, Hugo, 92
Dirkett, Gregory, 24
Robert, 22
Thomas, 28
Dixon, Ann, 138
George, 130, 131
Peter, 33
Robert, 132
Thomas, 131, 138, 142
William, 131, 133, 153, 155
Dobinson, Anthony, 129
Dobson, Alice, 91
Christopher, 2, 3, 121
Dorothy, 30
Elizabeth, 63
Henry, 107
James, 30
John, 68, 102, 103
Mary, 63
Mathew, 63, 64, 66
Robert, 103
Thomas, 63, 66, 68, 70, 81, 101
William, 81
Dossy, Robert, 100
Doughtie, Henry, 132
Downe, Raiphe, 16
Downes, George, 20, 76

Henry, 18
Lambton, 143
Doyle, Francis, 96
Draper, Timothy, 155
Duckett, Thomas, 31
Dunne, George, 73
James, 2, 3, 121
John, 73
Thomas, 98, 99

Easton, Edward, 38
Eden, John, 60, 141
Raiphe, 60, 61, 124, 134, 141, 142
Robert, 141, 143
Edmonson, William, 67
Elgye, John, 98
Elgye, Mary, 98
Ellington, Thomas, 22
Emerson, Arthur, 164
Christopher, 169
George, 162
John, 160, 162, 163, 165
Leonard, 101
Raphe, 162
Thomas, 42, 98, 161
William, 151, 164, 165
Eslington, Thomas, 21, 28, 29, 30
Ettringham, John, 42, 43
Ettis, Lancellot, 25
Eure, Raphe, 55
Samson, 52
Lord William, 35, 52, 55, 133

Fairfax, Henry, 133
Thomas, 133
Fawcett, Meriell, 93
Featherston, Nicholas, 165
Fetherson, Raphe, 151
Fetherstone, Elizabeth, 163
Fetherstonhaugh, Alexander, 165
John, 165
Raphe, 161, 165
Finch, Hugh, 134
Peter, 157
Toby, 157
Fleming, Nicholas, 8
Thomas, 8
Forrest, Nicholas, 49
Foster, George, 63
Hugh, 30
Richard, 91, 92
William, 92
Fowler, Edward, 63, 65
Leonard, 63, 65
Frevile, George, 45
Friend, Thomas, 127

Fryers, John, 166

Gainford, William, 125, 137, 140
Gainforth, Ellianor, 92
Garfoot, William, 139
Gargrave, John, 126
  Mary, 126
  Raphe, 142
  Richard, 139, 142
  William, 124, 126, 142
Garmondsway, Bryan, 119
  Edward, 92
  Richard, 118
Garnett, Ann, 101, 119
  George, 102, 105
  William, 119
Garrie, John, 141, 144
Garry, George, 119
  John, 75
  Marmaduke, 118
Garth George, 138
  William, 132, 134
Garthwaite, Thomas, 66
Garvie, John, 49
Gastony, William, 95
Gawthwaite, Giles, 80
Gibbon, Christopher, 130
  William, 129
  George, 81
Gill, John, 94, 114, 116
Gilpin, Anthony, 91, 107, 108, 112
  Nicholas, 17
Goldsborough, Peter, 104
  Thomas, 104
Grainger, John, 92
Graye, William, 44
Greaves, Thomas, 92
Green, Elizabeth, 77
Green, Raphe, 35, 77
Green, William, 38
Grice, Emanuell, 5, 21, 34, 38
  Henry, 21, 22
  John, 21, 38
  Oswald, 21
  William, 54, 56, 59
Griffyd, Stephen, 102
Grimdon, Anthony, 23
  Mary, 23
Grimstone, Martin, 16

Hall, Christopher, 91
  Henry, 42
  Isabell, 63
  Stephen, 73
  Thomas, 63
  William, 158, 172, 175
Harper, Henry, 51
  Martin, 54

Harperley, Anne, 31
  Nicholas, 32
Harrison, Adam, 116
  Cuthbert, 60, 61
  Francis, 117
  George, 157
  Isabell, 64
  John, 92, 106, 117, 151, 153, 155, 156
  Raphe, 151
  Thomas, 117
  William, 152, 165
Hastley, Robert, 46, 51
Haward, Leonard, 93
Hawe, Thomas, 137
Hawside, Richard, 32
Head, Isabell, 52
Heales, Thomas, 154
Hearne, Christopher, 18
Heddon, George, 108
  Thomas, 111, 113
Hedge, Stephen, 42
Hedworth, John, 93
Heighington, Frances, 50
  John, 63, 158, 175
  Robert, 133
Heron, Christopher, 140
Hesilrig, Sir Arthur, 170, 171
Hester, John, 159
Hevid, Ann, 111
Heviside, Richard, 129
Hevyside, Richard, 18
Hey, Christopher, 75
Highe, John, 138
Hilton, Elizabeth, 135
  William, 97
Hixon, Robert, 115
  Roger, 65
  Thomas, 2, 3, 121
Hoblock, Robert, 118
Hobson, Richard, 2, 3, 121
Hodgshon, Edmund, 112
  Henry, 16
  John, 52, 126, 128
  Katherine, 134
  Lance, 93
  Raphe, 128, 144
  Richard, 59
  Thomas, 24, 127, 129, 132
Hodgson, Edmund, 99, 105, 109
  Elizabeth, 30, 75
  George, 30
  Henry, 57
  Isabell, 24, 25
  John, 25, 26, 34, 75, 98, 173
  Margaret, 129
  Raphe, 39
  Richard, 54, 55, 56

  Robert, 57
  Thomas, 15, 31, 39
  William, 108, 110
Hodshon, Christopher, 62
  Henry, 36
  John, 126
Hodson, William, 130
Holbeck, Agnes, 65
Holmeraw, John, 128
  Thomas, 129
Hopper, Christopher, 130
Hopper, Cuthbert, 47
  John, 48
  Richard, 43, 47, 50
  Samuell, 50
  Thomas, 50
  William, 43
Horner, Richard, 113
Hornesby, Elizabeth, 81
Howe, Thomas, 134
Howson, John, 159, 160
  William, 159
Hugill, Mary, 140
Hull, Thomas, 44
Hunter, Robert, 71
Hurworthe, Lando, 92
Husband, Dorothy, 91
Hutchinson, John, 135
  Nicholas, 62
  Thomas, 78, 133
  William, 22, 93
Hutton, Edward, 141
  Robert, 108
  William, 27
Hynde, Ann, 142

Inglewoods, Nicholas, 19
Isle, Bulmer, 89
  James, 90

Jackson, Adalena, 42
  Ann, 42
  Cuthbert, 76
  Elizabeth, 42, 80
  George, 72
  Jane, 42
  John, 92, 93
  Margaret, 42
  Richard, 93
  Simon, 17
  William, 70, 72, 114
Jennyson, Thomas, 45
Jewett, Roger, 97
John, Brian, 6
Johnson, Ambrose, 2, 3, 121
  Ann, 44
  John, 9
  Mary, 44, 141
  Nicholas, 92
  Robert, 93, 139
  Thomas, 44, 93

Jollie, Francis, 143
Joplin, Richard, 154
Jowell, Margery, 63
Juslipp, Robert, 30, 31
Roger, 21, 22, 28, 29

Key, Thomas, 113
William, 39, 134, 141, 144
Killingworth, William, 92
King, Mary, 102, 105
Kirkby, George, 84
Kitchen, Thomas, 137
Knaggs, Margaret, 51

Laing, Francis, 95
Robert, 51
Lambe, John, 134
Raphe, 134
Lang, John, 47
Thomas, 48
Lange, John, 52
William, 51
Langhorne, Richard, 32
Langstaffe, Bernard, 103
Elizabeth, 103
Jane, 17
John, 101
Thomas, 34
William, 144
Lanze, Thomas, 52
Lawe, William, 34
Lawnesdale, Christopher, 137
Lax, George, 2, 3, 14
Laxe, Nathan, 31
Robert, 2, 3, 121
Thomas, 20
Layton, Dorothy, 95
Thomas, 67
Leaver, William, 143
Lee, John, 162
Leigh, Samuell, 1, 2
Les, Edward, 172
Liddell, Elizabeth, 73
Lisle, John, 94
Lister, John, 140
Lively, Edward, 107, 164
Lodge, George, 107, 111
Thomas, 96
Longstaffe, Thomas, 16, 17

Maddison, Anthony, 57
Maine, Robert, 28, 29
Maines, Roger, 30
Mallory, William, 133, 138
Manners, Robert, 21
Markindale, John, 53
Marshall, Francis, 109
Jane, 94
John, 92, 99, 112
Thomas, 167

Martin, Anne, 130
George, 140
Lancellot, 63
Martindale, Charles, 44, 47
George, 47
Martindell, John, 38
Maughen, Henry, 20
Maunders, John, 109
Mawe, William, 130
Mayne, John, 121
Robert, 22
Mayor, John, 2, 3
Meason, Edward, 65
Megson, Roger, 72
Meir, George, 165
Middleton, Edward, 19
George, 135
Jane, 23, 34
John, 97, 101, 102
Margaret, 141
Richard, 117, 118, 119
Susan, 30
Thomas, 95
William, 18, 33, 104, 107
Milbanke, Marke, 92
Miles, George, 92
Moor, George, 144
Moore, George, 23, 55, 59, 61
Thomas, 16, 19
Moorman, Anthony, 32
More, Thomas, 20
Morgaine, Cuthbert, 152
Morgan, Mathew, 131
Morland, Richard, 75
Morley, George, 69
John, 69, 98, 108
Richard, 107
Thomas, 104, 110
William, 68
Morly, Dear, 92
Mouncer, William, 140

Natteres, Elizabeth, 78
Nattres, William, 152
Neale, Sir, Paul, 35, 36, 38, 107, 143, 152, 160
Nelson, George, 16
Nertie, Thomas, 25
Newby, Francis, 108
Thomas, 108
Newton, Mary, 116
Thomas, 96
Nicholl, Robert, 53, 54, 55, 58, 59, 60
Nicholson, Cuthbert, 99
Nicholson, Grace, 94
North, John, 65
Nowe, William, 58

Oliver, Oswald, 16

Oswald, Elizabeth, 91
Francis, 94
Henry, 100
John, 95
Mary, 100
Richard, 99
Ovington, Robert, 134

Packton, Thomas, 32
Painter, John, 39
Pallacer, Richard, 72, 73
Robert, 72, 73
Parker, Agnes, 49
James, 50
Parkin, Elizabeth, 47
Jane, 48
John, 46
Richard, 27, 51
Thomas, 38, 47, 49, 50, 51, 52
William, 47, 48, 50, 51
Parking, Robert, 50
Parkinge, Thomas, 39
Parkinson, Edward, 62
Francis, 109
Parnabie, John, 65
Parsons, John, 157
Peacock, Richard, 118
Pearson, Anthony, 51
Pearson, Christopher, 56, 59
Richard, 52
Thomas, 52, 158, 172
William, 43, 46
Peart, Francis, 151
Pecton, Thomas, 39
Pemerton, Michael, 92
Ralph, 92
Phillipe, Robert, 22, 28
Phillips, Arthur, 36
Phillips, William, 76
Phillipson, George, 163
Pibus, Thomas, 109
Pickering, Cuthbert, 80
Hartley, 70
Hercules, 80
William, 70
Pilkington, Leonard, 79, 95, 111
Pinbury, Richard, 20
Pinkney, Leonard, 28, 31
Margery, 92
Richard, 16, 26, 31
Place, Robert, 105
Plaice, Christian, 89
Plard, Rowland, 92
Pollards, Leonard, 23
Raphe, 23, 28
Prierman, Mary, 64
Michael, 64
Priscott, William, 91
Pudsey, George, 92

Rae, Bartholomew, 118
Raine, Christopher, 67
Raine, John, 67
Ramshaw, Ann, 101
  George, 39
Rawlinson, Arthur, 152
Rayne, John, 138
Rea, Mary, 30
Rey, William, 19
Reynolds, Isabell, 96
Richardson, Christopher, 137
  Frances, 25
  Henry, 46
  John, 104, 157, 158, 165
  Martin, 49
  Richard, 17, 18, 25, 26,
    27, 33, 34, 39
  Thomas, 17, 74, 92
  William, 25, 37, 137, 138,
    139
Richmond, Christopher, 66,
  81
  James, 69
  John, 61, 69
  Martin, 64, 66, 69, 70, 71
  William, 69
Riddell, Sir Peter
Ridlington, Robert, 2, 3, 46,
  121
Roberts, John, 37
Robinson, Anthony, 109
  Christopher, 144
  Elizabeth, 33, 98
  George, 53, 55, 56, 166
  Henry, 67, 129
  Jane, 41
  John, 16, 21, 22, 32, 37,
    41, 62, 81, 97, 128, 129
  Nichols, 49
  Peter, 95
  Ralph, 92
  Richard, 69, 70, 81
  Robert, 91
  Thomas, 49, 70, 107, 109,
    111
  William, 91, 103
Robson, John, 9, 26, 127
  Margaret, 20
  Margery, 39
  Thomas, 38
  William, 20
Rowser, Richard, 16
Rudderforth, Eleanor, 16
Rumforth, William, 144
Runthwaite, William, 69, 70

Salvin, Gerard, 52
Saunders, Thomas, 1, 2
Saunderson, Thomas, 129,
  144

Saurkeld, Lance, 93
Sayer, Laurence, 57
Scurfield, William, 93
Seamer, Francis, 96
  John, 80
Seamor, Margarett, 80
  William, 80
Seddgkirk, John, 128
Sedgwick, John, 131
Shafto, Mark, 57, 80
Shauter, George, 68
Shawe, Seith, 44
  William, 42, 45
Shawter, Mathew, 136
  Thomas, 68
Sheatley, Simon, 32
Sheetly, Raphe, 32
Shepherd, Robert, 107, 113
  William, 2, 3
Sheraton, James, 47
Shippardson, William, 121
Shirfoote, Robert, 57
Shorte, Raphe, 51
Shortridge, Agnes, 19
Simpson, Jannet, 73
  John, 27, 74, 81
  Richard, 27
  Robert, 102, 104
  Thomas, 115
Simpson, William, 102, 136
Singleton, Jane, 125, 130
  Raphe, 126, 130
Skelton, John, 67
Skepper, Moses, 30, 89
Skipper, Christopher, 89
Slayter, John, 2, 3, 121
Slater, William, 34
Smethwayte, Thomas, 75
Smerthwaugh, Alice, 80
Smith, Cuthbert, 136
  Edward, 34
  Elizabeth, 95
  Henry, 92
  John, 91
  Richard, 16
  Robert, 20
Smithson, John, 2, 3
Smurthwayte, Roger, 78
Smurthwaite, Thomas, 26
Smyth, Henry, 134
Snow, Cuthbert, 156
Sober, Edmond, 93
  John, 93, 107
  Robert, 93, 109
Somer, Ann, 64
  Anthony, 21, 27, 28
  Elizabeth, 22
  Richard, 22
Somers, Mathew, 21
Sowerby, Laurence, 134
Squire, Anne, 110

Sampson, 95
Standforth, Richard, 93
Staniforth, John, 75
Stanley, John, 96
Starkie, William, 19
Stainsby, Laurence, 111
  Robert, 111
Staynsby, Anthony, 109
Staynesby, John, 107, 109
Staynsby Robert, 119
  Thomas, 109
Stephenson, Christopher, 144
  Ropert, 142
Stevenson, Anthony, 17, 26
  Christopher, 126
  John, 90, 137, 138
  Thomas, 132
Stobart, Hugh, 75
Stobb, Edward, 32
Stobbs, George, 161, 162
  Nicholas, 166
  Raphe, 165, 166
  William, 163, 165
Stockdale, William, 24
Stockton, Elizabeth, 32
Stoddart, Christopher, 60
Stoddert, Christopher, 139
  Henry, 140
  Robert, 140
Stokell, Frances, 64
Storey, 89
Studdick, John, 60
Strangewick, John, 34
Suddick, John, 55, 58, 59,
  78
Suddicke, Mary, 55
Suerties, Christopher, 80
  Robert, 158
Suertyes, Robert, 172
Suthwick, John, 56
Swarmeston, John, 20
Swinbank, Rayphe, 81
Swinburne, Thomas, 101,
  112
Sympson, Elizabeth, 60
  John, 121
  Robert, 116

Taylor, Edward, 158, 172
  Francis, 41, 77
  John, 155
  Mary, 42
  Raphe, 144
  Roger, 44
  Thomas, 62
  William, 63, 135
Teale, Percival, 62
Tewart, John, 68
  Robert, 68, 70
  William, 68
Tewer, Henry, 62

Thirkeld, Anthony, 138
    Lancellot, 132
Thirsbie, Simon, 63
    William, 63
Thompson, Ann, 92
    Elizabeth, 61
    Jane, 112
    John, 16, 18, 23, 27, 33, 34
    Martin, 136
    Nicholas, 69
    Richard, 32
    Robert, 24, 33, 99
    Rowland, 156
    William, 60, 110, 141, 143
Thomson, Elizabeth, 54, 55
    John, 25, 56, 57, 126, 127, 128
    William, 56, 57
Thornberry, Christopher, 144
Thorpe, Robert, 91, 93
Tisdale, Elizabeth, 138
Todd, Anthony, 58, 62, 75, 76
    Christopher, 81
    Cuthbert, 58
    John, 55, 57, 58, 60, 61
    Richard, 23, 53, 56, 81
    Thomas, 54, 58
    William, 57
Tomlinson, Robert, 103
Tonge, Sir George, 35, 36, 38, 132
Tower, Christopher, 126, 130
    Lamerick, 64
    Margaret, 130
    William, 63, 64
Towndrye, Francis, 97
Trotter, Anthony, 79
    Christopher, 67
    Elizabeth, 44
    George, 45
    Gertrude, 79
    Henry, 77
    James, 81
    John, 33, 77, 155
    Lancellot, 162
    Marmaduke, 167
    Mary, 56
    Thomas, 121, 155
    Raphe, 58, 77
    Robert, 54
    Thomas, 2, 3, 42, 67
    William, 56, 57, 59, 61
Tunstall, Ralph, 113
    Thomas, 93, 113, 114
    William, 114
Turner, John, 100
    Thomas, 100

Vane, Charles, 122
    Sir Henry, 175
Vaughan, Cuthbert, 143
Vasey, Cuthbert, 54, 56
Venham, William, 64
Vessey, John, 153
Vincent, Robert, 2, 3, 121
Virtue, Stephen, 103

Waiscell, John, 24
Waitering, William, 93
Wake, Barnard, 66
Walby, Anthony, 27
    John, 21
Walker, Bryan, 22, 30, 35, 39, 43
    Elizabeth, 130
    John, 20, 26, 27, 35, 41, 43, 45, 71, 130
    Margery, 41
    Raphe, 6, 27, 30, 39, 43, 47, 140, 147
    Robert, 71, 72
    Thomas, 42
    William, 93
Wall, Bryan, 60, 61
    James, 75
    Richard, 75
    William, 139
Walles, Robert, 46
Walton, John, 8
    Michael, 91
    Thomas, 37
    William, 39, 136
Wan, Robert, 92
Wanles, Edwards, 158
Ward, John, 155
    Thomas, 95
    William, 106
Warde, Elizabeth, 16
    George, 46
    John, 32
Warmouth, Henry, 90, 92
Wastell, Henry, 92
Watson, Anthony, 131, 138
    John, 37
    Thomas, 31
Watt, William, 130
Welford, Thomas, 92, 119
Wetherell, Anne, 103
    William, 93, 103
Wharton, James, 39
    Philip, 94
Wheatley, Anthony, 19
    Richard, 106
    Simon, 19
Wheelhouse, Robert, 116
Wheldon, John, 157
White, Agnes, 21
    Elizabeth, 43
    George, 59, 134, 138

Laurence, 43
Marie, 45
Miles, 2, 3
Robert, 42, 76, 78
Rowland, 42
Thomas, 78
William, 59, 78
Whitfield, Ann, 22
    Cuthbert, 19, 32
    James, 72
    John, 161
    Mary, 72
    Michael, 140
    Thomas, 93
Whitton, Giles, 97
    William, 95
Whitworth, Robert, 24
Whyte, Miles, 121
Wild, Simon, 19
    Thomas, 19
Wilde, Lancellot, 127, 128
    Thomas, 127
Wilkinson, Christopher, 95
    Elizabeth, 103
Wilkinson, Henry, 118
    John, 6, 35, 36, 38
    Robert, 93
    Thomas, 93
    William, 64
Williamson, Marmaduke, 111
    William, 19, 138, 139, 141, 142
Willis, Peter, 81
Willson, Roger, 28
    Thomas, 95
Wilson, Edward, 33
    Gerard, 140
    Jane, 25
    Jannett, 37
    Katherine, 33
    Lancellot, 37
    Peter, 28, 142
    Robert, 32
Winent, Robert, 19
Wivel, Marmaduke, 91
Wood, Dorothy, 91
    John, 91, 121
    Richard, 94
    Thomas, 94
    William, 95
Woods, John, 2, 3
Wormersley, Robert, 93
Wraine, Christopher, 66, 81
Wrangham, Cuthbert, 141
Wren, William, 153
Wrenn, Christopher, 60
    Col, Francis, 4, 15, 16, 17, 38
    Lindley, 9, 18, 23, 33, 34, 38, 46, 75, 79

Robert, 137
Wright, Agnes, 137
  Anthony, 79
  Bryan, 18, 33, 34
  Christopher, 78
  Edward, 83, 128, 144

Isabell, 33
Jane, 79
John, 42
Stephen, 39
Thomas, 93
Wrighte, Anne, 24

Elizabeth, 20
  Richard, 19

Young, Francis, 66
  Thomas, 166

Zouch, Sir John, 164